Poison
Heartbeats

A Novel

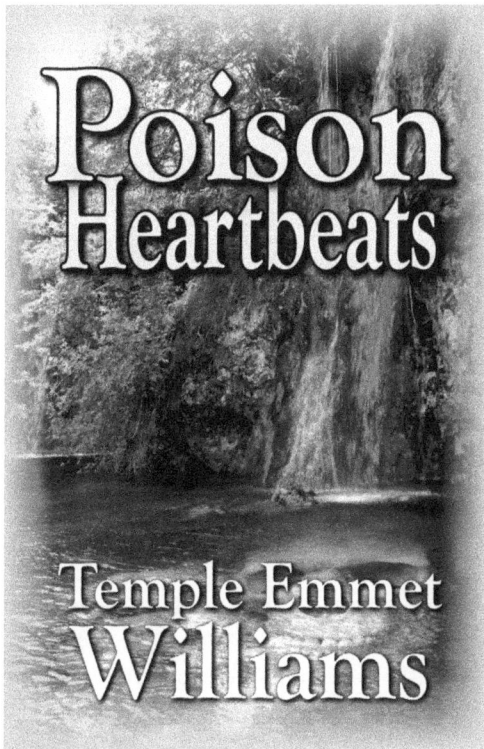

Templeworks

Properties, LLC

Published by Templeworks Properties LLC
3755 Mykonos Court, Boca Raton, Florida 33487
(561) 241-6323 Fax: (561) 241-6358 (office)
http://www.poisonheartbeats.com
http://www.templeworks.biz
mail to temple@templeworks.biz

Williams, Temple Emmet
Poison Heartbeats: A Novel
1. Thriller-Terrorism 2. Mystery-General 3.Action 4. Homeland Security

ISBN-13: 978-0-9908433-5-1

Library of Congress Control Number: 2016905002

Dedication

*To one of my favorite role models,
my older brother and very original artist,*
Philip Hone Williams

Books by Temple Emmet Williams

Fiction: Wrinkled Heartbeats
Poison Heartbeats
African Heartbeats
Non-Fiction: Warrior Patient
Warrior Patient Heartbeats

Table of Contents

Author's Notes

Three generations of George McKlanes appear in this book. The oldest is Captain George McKlane, a Korean War veteran who won the Medal of Honor, and who has a son, Brigadier General George McKlane, who works in the Pentagon. His grandson, George McKlane III, has the nickname of "Mac."

Homeland Security operates a special division with the acronym of CWMD. It stands for Countering Weapons of Mass Destruction, and. Mac McKlane is one of its's directors. It has a worldwide directive to protect America.

Poison Heartbeats is the second novel in the author's *Heartbeats* series, which will eventually include six books. The first novel was the award-winning *Wrinkled Heartbeats*.

The books share characters; they shake hands with one another, but you don't have to read one to understand the next or the previous one. It can help, of course.

The third novel, *African Heartbeats*, was published in the summer of 2020

Chapter 1

The Story of Holly Smolkes

A Child of War Born in Nuristan, Afghanistan

For centuries, the sounds of fighting sent women and children scrambling into the steep, rocky mountains surrounding the river that tumbled through their tiny village. Young warriors remained behind, moving up the laddered farming plateaus to the highest dwellings in the town, where they waited to fight.

The elders usually gathered in the public square, often unarmed. They wanted to see if they could negotiate peace rather than die for it.

The Nuristani village, in northeastern Afghanistan, did not have many older men.

In ancient times, the Nuristani tribe fought against the drumbeat of Alexander the Great's invincible army. Little remained afterward, other than blond, blue-eyed children.

In 1888, Rudyard Kipling's book, *The Man Who Would Be King,* celebrated the people of Nuristan, a name which translated into English as the "Land of Light." Eight years later, they were conquered, converted to Islam by Emir

Abdur Rahman Khan. A hundred years later, the villagers heard the voice of war in the air-splitting thuds of Russian helicopter blades. The sounds had reached them before the gray metal beasts swooped around the rocky outcroppings that concealed their approach. Three Mi-24 Soviet gunships, trailed by four Mi-8 transport helicopters, roared up the valley, following the course of the river through the jagged, evergreen-speckled mountains.

Major Gregor Chabachenko piloted the lead gunship. He had been in Afghanistan from the beginning of Russia's occupation, arriving a few days after Christmas in 1979.

The helicopter air assault that he now led would be his final battle before returning to Leningrad after nine years in a country he both disliked and dishonored.

Shortly after arriving in Afghanistan, he had taken as a surrogate wife, a young woman who lived in the village that he was about to destroy.

"The most beautiful woman in the entire country," he told his comrades over the intercom as he banked the gunship to the right. The Mi-24 was the most dreaded and effective Soviet weapon used against the *mujahideen,* Afghanistan's freedom fighters, who were backed by America.

The commander sighed into the intercom, an exaggerated sound. "She had eyes of blue steel," he said, using the past tense even though she was still alive. "Golden hair. The personality of a Persian leopard. I still wear the tattoos of her fingernails on my back."

The crew, confident, smiled quietly to themselves at their commander's oft-told story. Chabachenko banked the Mi-24 gunship back to the left and caught a glimpse of the village beyond the next rocky outcropping. He scanned the jagged edges of the landscape below, expecting small weapons' fire to come from the *mujahideen.*

"No mosquito bites," his machine gunner said as the pilot plunged lower towards the river.

"They have run away," another crew member said through the intercom. "They have lost their courage and are hiding once again."

Chabachenko pulled the nose of his gunship higher, a cobra ready to strike at the heart of the community, which suddenly filled his view. He pushed the controls and slanted the gunship at the village.

"Time for a quickie divorce," the Russian major said.

Laughter filled his earphones as the gunship shook with withering anger, emptying its cannons. Buildings disappeared in dust. Then he was beyond the village.

The gunship behind him extended the pattern of destruction, which was then repeated by the final gunship. The three Mi-24s scaled the side of a mountain and slowly circled for a second run that would let the transport helicopters drop into the plateaued fields around the town. They would establish their assault landing zone. Then the Russian troops would quickly spread out to destroy everything in their path.

Major Chabachenko glanced to his left, searching for the house where he had spent drunken nights abusing his surrogate Afghan wife.

She stood in the doorway, her face uncovered, defiant, holding a weapon he had never seen before.

Chabachenko hovered the helicopter and slowly turned towards her. She threw the weapon around the corner of the mud-brick house and started running down the footpath leading to the river. His gun site traced her retreat. She dissolved in red dust.

"Divorce granted," he said.

His crew was silent. He continued to hover the gunship, glancing back at the mud-brick home. His flight team did not like being stationary.

Chabachenko saw his eight-year-old daughter standing around the corner of the house, but he could see no sign of her twin brother.

A uniformed man with red hair stood next to the girl. The man was not *mujahideen*. Major Chabachenko slowly turned his gunship towards them. The weapon his daughter held on her shoulder seemed too large for the girl.

The stranger patted Chabachenko's daughter on the head. She fired the weapon balanced on her shoulder, falling to her knees as it released its missile. Suddenly alarms screeched through the Russian gunship's headphones. It was one of the last sounds that any of the crew ever heard as the attack helicopter exploded in a ball of fire.

Only four of the villagers died that day. The red-headed man had warned them 24 hours earlier of the Russian attack. Charles Smolkes worked for the CIA, but only a few of the village leaders knew him. Everyone had a difficult time understanding what the American said.

Agent Smolkes spoke some Pashto, a little Dari, but no Nuristani. None of the locals trusted him. The red-headed man showed them weapons that he called Stingers, and he told the warriors that using them was "child's play."

"Then we will let a child use it," the village leader said.

Charles "Red" Smolkes thought that was a good idea. It would show the Nuristani men how simple it was to destroy Russia's mighty gunships.

The *mujahideen* chose the daughter of the most disgraced woman in the village for Smolkes' "child's play." They also selected her twin brother.

Then they retreated into the rocky crags of the mountains surrounding the village and waited for the spectacle that the CIA agent promised.

They silently watched as the Russian gunships destroyed their mud-brick homes and stores along the river. Then the gunships rose and curved down the mountains north of the village, turning back towards their target.

A few of the *mujahideen* took shots at the helicopters, but most of the warriors remained hidden.

They were not afraid.

They simply did not believe what was about to happen.

The red-headed American from the CIA had lied to them. Nothing had stopped the awesome, destructive powers of the helicopters.

They watched the disgraced mother disappear in a cloud of dust as she ran towards the river from her home.

They would not mourn her.

Then the Stinger missile slammed into the first gunship and turned it into a ball of fire.

A second Russian helicopter exploded, struck by a missile fired by the daughter's twin brother, Ahmed Khan.

They watched as the eight-year-old girl, Abira Khan, launched another ground-to-air missile into the third gunship, destroying it as well.

Then one of the transport helicopters exploded, raining down bits and pieces of Russian machinery and troops.

Suddenly the mountain came alive with warriors shouting as the three remaining transport helicopters turned and fled back down the river.

A missile chased after them, but it failed to connect. The noise of the *mujahideen* slowly died down, fading into silence as men turned to their leader.

A reverent name escaped from the leader's mouth, almost a song.

"Malalai!" he shouted. "Malalai!" Soon the word was being chanted from every direction: "Malalai! Malalai!"

The mountains echoed the name.

"What is that?" the CIA man asked his Nuristani translator. "What is Malalai?" He had never heard it before.

"Malalai of Maiwand," the translator said. "A great folk hero. She was our, how do you say it, Joan of Arc. The daughter of a shepherd, who took off her veil and used it as a flag to lead our warriors to victory over a century ago against the British, and this on her wedding day!"

"Malalai," Charles Smolkes said quietly, feeling like a stranger in a strange land.

Suddenly the translator said something, a single sentence. It sounded almost like a song.

"If you don't fall in the Battle of Maiwand, by God, someone is saving you as a symbol of shame."

It was a proverb known throughout Afghanistan.

Then the translator put his hand on the head of the eight-year-old girl, Abira Khan.

"Malalai!" he shouted.

"Malalai!" a hundred voices roared back.

The eight-year-old girl became Holly Smolkes, the adopted daughter of Charles Smolkes. He was an unsung CIA legend in the removal of Russia from Afghanistan, after ten years of Soviet occupation.

"The spoils of war," he told his wife when he returned to America with the girl under his protective custody.

Betty Smolkes could not have children of her own, and she quickly fell in love with the beautiful child. Holly seemed unaffected by her war-torn years, although she promptly angered when her adoptive father told the story of "Malalai" to strangers.

"Stop it, Red," she would say, with a deep voice that possessed a maturity far beyond her years.

She never called him Dad, or Father, or Pop. He was always "Red," and he and his wife, whom she called Betty, accepted it from their legally adopted daughter.

Others sometimes found it strange.

The family finally abandoned the story of Malalai after Holly was sent home from school one day.

In her Fifth Grade English class, students wrote about their parents.

Holly was a very bright student, quick to learn English, poised, self-assured, but quiet.

After two years in America, she spoke English perfectly with no accent, no hint of her origins.

Her Fifth Grade English teacher called on the now-ten-year-old girl, her star pupil, to take what she had written, go to the head of the classroom, and read her "very first public speech." The teacher had not seen what she wrote.

"My father was a Russian helicopter pilot who murdered my mother when I was eight years old," she told the class. "He raped my mother, and she was his whore for nine years. I killed my father when his gunship destroyed —"

That was as far as she got.

It took her adoptive parents, her English teacher, and the Lower School principle two meetings and four hours to agree on how and when Holly Smolkes would be able to return to the school.

Holly was the only person in the discussions who did not get angry or use bad language.

She was briefly the focus of attention among her fellow students when she came back to the classroom. Their interest in Holly Smolkes quickly disappeared when she refused to discuss her past with anyone.

At the end of the school year, all of her teachers wrote about her intelligence and poise, but several of them suggested that she lacked leadership skills.

Her physical education instructor took exception to this characterization, noting that when the class bully had taunted her, she knocked him out with two quick punches without uttering a single word.

"She appears to have *some* leadership qualities," he wrote.

The fight was over before anyone could stop it. The bully outweighed Holly by 23 pounds.

She broke his nose.

In the end, the PhysEd instructor agreed with all her other teachers.

Holly Smolkes was a loner. She did not seem particularly interested in making friends.

She was also stunning.

Holly Smolkes' father died in Syria in October of 2008, four months after Holly graduated from The University of Miami with a degree in Political Science. She spent a year trying to make a living as a swimsuit model, but that career ended with a jagged five-inch slash across her left cheek in a barroom brawl in Key West.

Holly's mother, Betty, visited her in the hospital. It was the same hospital in which her mother would die two years later after a routine operation that crippled her with infection.

The assault and battery charges against Holly's barroom slasher were withdrawn by Holly when the defendant failed to show up at a hearing. Holly's lawyer wanted to sue for damages and record the judgment. She fired him.

The lawyer had not worked on her case for more than six hours, including less than an hour in court. He turned around and presented her with a carefully itemized bill for $10,485 in legal fees.

He later withdrew his inflated claim after an overnight trip with Holly to an oceanside townhome in Jamaica, at her request. Office gossip suggested that the lawyer received payment in kind, a claim he neither made nor denied.

What happened in Jamaica sealed his lips forever.

Holly had walked into the offices of Lewis, Herald, Smythe, and Fiddwick early on a Friday morning and given her lawyer, Sampson Fiddwick, a round-trip, first-class ticket to Montego Bay.

"I'll see you at the airport," she said. "We'll have fun. My treat." Sampson Fiddwick considered Holly Smolkes as his best-looking client, ever, even with the jagged scar on her left cheek. She was 23 years old; he was 46, plump, and divorced. He thought he had hit the jackpot.

He cleared his weekend schedule.

They arrived in Jamaica on Saturday evening in a heavy rainstorm. Fiddwick drank two small bottles of scotch in First Class after the pilot announced, thirty minutes before the plane began its descent, that the passengers might be in for a bumpy landing.

Holly did not drink. She never did.

A black limousine met them after a surprisingly smooth arrival. "Who owns the limo?" Sampson asked.

"Angelo Rossellini," Holly said. "He's a big developer up in Boca Raton and a good friend. He has loaned us his townhouse in Montego Bay for the weekend."

"I've heard his name," Sampson lied. He had no dealings with real estate people. That was the bailiwick of James Herald, one of his partners.

Fiddwick reached over and fumbled to hold Holly's hand, which she let him do.

"Angelo's townhouse is right on the water. It's extraordinary," Holly said. "You walk down steps into what would normally be a basement, and you're sort of in a bedroom aquarium. Well, I guess a glass-bottomed boat might be more accurate. The floor is all glass, and you can see the reef, the fish, the coral, everything underneath. It's a wonderful experience."

Briefly, Sampson Fiddwick wondered *Why me?* He was middle-aged and overweight and not particularly handsome. He knew that he was not a desirable man, even if he sucked in his stomach and threw out his chest. His first name was an oxymoron since he lacked the strength of his biblical forerunner, even if that great warrior had been shaved bald. Then the scotch dissolved such thoughts and replaced them with expectations that had become just a memory. He thought he was about to have a real adventure, although he worried a little about his ability to perform.

"I'll give you a tour of the bedroom first," Holly said. She had a beautiful smile, although it did not reach her eyes.

When they arrived at the townhome, the lights were on. The limo driver carried their luggage into the vestibule, placed it on the marble floor, and retired to the servant's quarters.

"He looks like a bodyguard, not a limo driver," Sampson said as the large Jamaican disappeared.

"He is," she said.

She took out her cell phone and put it on a small table. She turned it off, first.

"No live cell phones in Mister Rossellini's property," she said. She smiled and raised her eyebrows at Sampson Fiddwick. He quickly took out his cell phone, turned it off, and then placed it next to hers.

"Come," Holly said, leading him down marble steps to a candlelit bedroom. Shag throw rugs covered much of the glass floor. The nighttime ocean beneath was dark, revealing only shadows and the mystery of stormy seas. Occasional lightning flashes from above filtered brightly through the water, but they showed very little.

"Sit," Holly said, motioning to a series of chrome barstools lining the wall opposite a large bed. He sat, feeling some excitement that promised he would have no trouble performing. A long silence followed. He half expected Holly to start disrobing, but she just stared at him.

"How much money do I owe you, Mister Fiddwick?"

Suddenly he was *Mister* Fiddwick, after being Sampson throughout all their prior dealings.

He studied the beautiful woman with the five-inch scar, about whom he knew very little. He did not slur his words with the scotch he had been drinking.

"Ten thousand four hundred and eighty-five dollars, Miss Smolkes," Sampson Fiddwick said.

He had always called her Holly after their initial contact. *Miss* Smolkes. Two could play the same game.

After a long pause, Holly said: "I want you to forgive the debt, Sampson."

After a short pause, he said: "It's a lot of money."

"I want you to forget about it."

"I can't do that. My time and expertise are all that I have to sell. My partners would not let me dismiss such a large portion of the firm's valuable resources."

He glanced at the bed and added: "Not for any reason, Miss Smolkes."

Sampson Fiddwick prided himself on his shrewdness. He knew how to play hardball.

"I want you to forgive the debt," Holly repeated. She handed him an envelope. As he opened it, she walked over and closed the door to the aquarium bedroom.

Fiddwick watched the door as it shut, then he looked at the contents of the envelope, a single page. He read it carefully, folded it, and reinserted it.

"No," he said.

He thought of adding *this is extraordinarily strange foreplay*, but he did not.

In hardball negotiations, Fiddwick knew that silence was always sharper than words.

Holly clicked a button on the wall, an intercom, waited for an answer, presumably from the big Jamaican bodyguard, and then said: "Could you turn on the floodlights, Charles?"

The ocean below the bedroom suddenly came alive with coral, fish, the tapestry of an ocean floor in crystal water.

"That's quite beautiful," Sampson Fiddwick said.

"Not all of it," Holly answered. She leaned down and tossed a few of the throw rugs aside, revealing more of the ocean beneath. Sampson Fiddwick reacted slowly because, at first, he did not know what he was seeing. Then he scrambled off the barstool and threw himself against the wall.

"Jesus Christ!"

A bloated body tethered to a concrete anchor slipped back and forth below the bedroom floor. You could tell it was a naked woman, young and blonde, but colorful fish nibbled at her, starting with the softest parts. She had no eyes.

"What have you done!"

Holly stepped to the door and opened it. The bodyguard was standing there, expressionless. "I have asked you to forgive the debt," Holly said. "We can talk about it again in the morning. I hope you have sweet dreams, Sampson."

She closed the door. Several locks bolted it shut. Who built a bedroom door that could only shut from the outside, rather than from the inside?

Jail cells work that way, the lawyer thought.

Sampson Fiddwick patted his jacket, searching for his cell phone, quickly realizing that the no-phone policy of the townhome was part of the trap into which he had fallen.

He backed slowly along the wall, staying as far away as possible from the dead body floating below the glass. He fumbled on the intercom, finally making a connection.

"This is outrageous," he said, using his deepest possible voice. It was the rich, dramatic baritone he usually saved for jury summations. He also used it when answering the phone with a potential new client.

By the time the night was over, his voice had jumped several octaves. Nobody ever responded. The fish continued their work on the corpse. He managed to keep it out of view. He wanted to replace the throw rugs, but he could only reach them by walking over the area of the body. He left the shag mats where Holly Smolkes had tossed them.

He curled up in a fetal position at the top of the bed.

The lights remained on in his locked cell.

At some point, he fell asleep. He woke in darkness, startled by something.

Muffled noises filled the room. Sampson knew there was a bedside lamp he could turn on, but he could not move. He shouted several times.

Sitting up, he thought he saw the corpse move, swim away. He scrambled back to the top of the bed, moaning. Nothing happened, and everything went silent again.

He looked at his watch. Sunrise slowly brought light to the room. He crept to the edge of the bed.

The body had disappeared.

The cement anchor was gone.

Shafts of light revealed only the beauty of the ocean floor below, including a lot of pink coral.

Shortly after eight, the door opened, and Holly brought in a silver tray with freshly-squeezed orange juice, toast, poached eggs, and a coffee pot.

There was only one place setting.

"Did you sleep well, Sampson?"

"No, I did not," he said.

The bodyguard stood at the doorway.

"Perhaps tonight, you will sleep better," Holly said.

"I'd like to return to Miami," he said.

"Have you signed the debt forgiveness contract?"

"No," Fiddwick said.

She poured a cup of coffee and stared at him.

She walked over, picked up the envelope, produced a pen, and held it out to the lawyer.

He took it and signed the document, carefully placing a "U.D." after his signature, and handed it back.

Holly looked at it, ripped it up, and let the pieces flutter to the floor.

She turned and walked out of the room, bolting the door shut behind her.

She returned five hours later, with a new envelope containing an identical debt forgiveness contract.

"Please try hard not to add 'Under Duress' this time, Mister Fiddwick."

He took the envelope, signed it with his signature without adding "U.D." afterward, and then he returned it to Holly Smolkes.

"That's very kind of you," Holly said. "Charles will take you to the airport. He'll change your reservation to the next available flight."

She turned to go, pausing at the doorway.

She had a soft smile, but again it did not move to her eyes. "I hope that you never forget this weekend, Mister Fiddwick. Of course, you will never talk about it."

Holly Smolkes was living in Delray Beach, Florida, 13 years later. She was the owner and skipper of a charter boat named the *Wholly Mackerel.*

She remained good friends with Angelo Rossellini, for whom she had turned the Russian euphemism "wet work" into a lucrative business. Originally coined by the KGB as a synonym for spilling blood, Holly had expanded the "wet" part of the phrase to include swimming with the sharks. She offered this as a private service to Angelo Rossellini, a final voyage for any of his designated enemies.

Holly was married three times. She openly admitted that she had a hard time forming lasting relationships. She buried all three of her husbands far out to sea, one of them when he was still alive.

Chapter 2

The Story of Ahmed Khan

The Birth of a Radical Terrorist in Afghanistan

Ahmed Khan, like his twin sister, Abira, was reborn at the age of eight, in the smoking trails of American Stinger rockets. They called his sister, "Malalai." In the moment of her redemption, he also became a powerful and essential talisman of his Nuristani tribe. His mother's martyrdom cleansed his past, setting him on a course that would reveal his destiny as one of greatness among all of his Nuristani people.

Even before the Russians retreated from his village in the valley, Ahmed Khan showed terrific promise to the *mujahideen,* the freedom fighters backed by America.

Ahmed excelled in school.

He understood something that only a few of his fellow students could grasp.

Ahmed Khan understood and built computers.

He did not, however, understand what happened to his twin sister, Abira "Malalai" Khan. The red-headed man from the CIA had taken his sister away the day after the destruction of the Soviet helicopters. The elders told Ahmed that his sister Abira, who would forever be known as "Malalai," was in the great city of Kandahar.

Ahmed Khan did not know how the red-haired American would use his twin sister, but his imagination leaned towards the abominable acts of his Russian father. Ahmed Khan vowed vengeance on the man that they called "Red" Smolkes.

Ahmed's computer expertise lifted him out of the small valley in Nuristan. His life traced the raging river of terrorism, which gripped the Middle East. He traveled to Pakistan, to Yemen, to Iraq, to Ethiopia, to Syria.

The last Russian soldier left Afghanistan on February 15, 1989. Nine months later, on November 9, 1989, the Berlin Wall ceased operations in Europe. It had taken a few more years to knock it down finally.

These two events were milestones in the collapse of the Soviet Union.

In Afghanistan, Russia's withdrawal put a chokehold on the flow of funds from Washington to the *mujahideen*. Without money and political backing, the holy warriors could not unite to govern Afghanistan.

Time-honored bloodshed between warlords inevitably followed the lack of money.

It gave birth to the Taliban, whose view of the world remained parochial, not global: Afghanistan for the Afghans.

The leadership of al-Qaida by Osama bin Laden brought the entire world into the crosshairs of radical Islamic terror.

The Taliban initially greeted the warriors of Osama bin Laden as guests, joint followers of Islam in need of shelter. It was part of their Muslim creed, to aid any Muslims in need of help. Al-Qaida quickly shredded the Taliban's welcome mat with bullets, bombs, and the assumptions of power.

The Islamic State of Iraq and the Levant (ISIL) briefly joined with al-Qaida but broke away with the brutality of thugs and criminals turned loose on civilization. ISIL believed in a worldwide caliphate under the leadership of Abu Bakr al-Baghdadi, who declared himself the Caliph, the leader of all Muslims worldwide.

Ahmed Khan's journey and his loyalties as a Muslim warrior transformed itself from *mujahideen* in Nuristan to the Taliban in Afghanistan, then to Al-Qaeda in Pakistan, Yemen, and Syria, and finally to ISIS and ISIL in Ethiopia and Iraq.

On Sunday, October 26th, 2008, Ahmed Khan was in the town of Sukkariyeh in eastern Syria. Unable to sleep, he climbed to the top of a building from which he could see the faint shimmering of the Euphrates River in the distance. The sun would not rise for three more hours. He sat against the outer stairwell wall, cradling an AK-47 in his arms. He was a valued member of Al-Qaeda at the time.

He could feel the dark presence of four Black Hawk helicopters before he saw them. They made very little noise. He scrambled into the stairwell as they loomed over his headquarters, a building still under construction. From his hiding place, Ahmed watched ten men quickly slide down ropes thrown from two of the helicopters.

They did not land on the roof but in the construction site surrounding the new building. The other two helicopters remained on point, hunters protecting the operation. He could see no markings on the helicopters, but he knew that they were American, not Syrian.

In the stairwell, he could hear men shouting. The silenced weapons of the Americans made no discernable sound. The AK-47 assault rifles of Al-Qaeda echoed loudly up the stairs.

Ahmed Khan knew that the target of the Americans had to be the man to whom he reported, a senior logistics coordinator named Abu Ghadiya. Ahmed stepped out of the stairwell, closed the metal door, and braced a large piece of construction timber against it. Then he crept to the edge of the building, protected by a partially-built, mud-brick wall. Ahmed cradled his AK-47, waiting for the Americans to burst through the door. He watched the helicopters hovering to his left, below the edge of the building.

He saw a man pull off his headgear and throw it angrily on the deck of the helicopter. Everything occurred in slow motion, and all of Ahmed's senses sharpened with adrenaline. He could not believe his eyes. In the aircraft, he saw the red-haired man who had taken his twin sister twenty years earlier when they were children in Nuristan.

He was confident it was the same man.

Now Ahmed Khan would die. He stood and emptied his AK-47 at the helicopter. Khan saw men turn in surprise, and then the chopper veered off towards the Euphrates. He saw the other helicopters lift off the ground and follow after it. His gun empty, he shook it in the air.

He shouted: "Malalai! Malalai!"

He collapsed on the roof, shaking with anger and shame, wondering why he was still alive. Everything grew quiet for a while, and then women were wailing. He stood, walking very slowly to the wooden beam he had braced against the stairwell door. He kicked it aside.

Bullet holes riddled the door. Ahmed opened it and saw the carnage left in the stairwell. Abu Ghadiya fell backward from the top of a pile of men, onto the roof, dead.

The attack would become known as the Abu Kamal raid, carried out by CIA paramilitary officers of the Special Activities Division and the United States Special Ops Command. It was a successful operation, although they wanted to capture Abu Ghadiya alive.

One American lost his life: Charles "Red" Smolkes.

The Op file included a stairwell photo that showed the dead target, Abu Ghadiya, at the top of the stairs.

The Syrian government officially called the raid "terrorist aggression." They said that America violated its sovereignty. Before the invasion, however, Syrian Air Force Intelligence had promised the United States that it would not intervene in the strike.

Al-Qaeda presented universal problems.

At the CIA's headquarters in McLean, Virginia, over 100 colleagues gratefully and respectfully remembered Agent Charles "Red" Smolkes.

His wife, Betty, and his adopted daughter, Holly, were told that he died in a car accident in Syria.

Only Holly would ever know the truth.

⸱⫙⫙⫙⫙⫙⫙⸱

Abu Bakr al-Baghdadi met with Ahmed Khan in a safe house in Iraq six months before the leader of ISIL vanished following an airstrike in Syria in June of 2016, on the fifth day of Ramadan. Baghdadi supposedly was wounded in the raid, but he surfaced later. Then he disappeared again.

Other than bodyguards, Baghdadi was alone when he met Ahmed Khan.

"*As-salāmu-ʿalaykum,*" said the leader of the jihadist militant organization known as ISIL: *Peace be upon you.*

He said it softly, in a voice that was higher than Ahmed Khan had expected.

"*Waʿ alaykumu s-salām,*" Ahmed said, almost a whisper: *And upon you Peace.*

"Why are your hands shaking?"

"I am trembling in the shadow of your presence."

"Camel dung," Baghdadi said. He smiled. "Your leaders tell me you are intelligent. They tell me that you are very good with computers."

Ahmed said nothing.

"They say that you are unafraid."

Ahmed remained silent.

"Are we here to talk, or do I have to listen only to myself, Ahmed? Would I be a leader if I listened only to the words that spill from *my* mouth?"

"No," Ahmed said, but he jumped when Baghdadi clapped his hands together.

"You have a voice!"

Suddenly they both laughed.

"People tell me you also have a plan to which I should listen," Baghdadi said. "It does not involve Muslims."

"But we control it," Ahmed said. Baghdadi rolled his right hand impatiently, *go on, continue.*

"There are many people in America who are very unhappy, very angry. They do not have to be Muslims. They must be angry at their leadership. The Devils in America prey upon them."

Baghdadi simply rolled his finger this time. *More. Keep talking, Ahmed Khan.*

"They do not have to be followers of Islam to become the weapons of our Jihad."

An uncomfortable silence followed this statement. It ended with Baghdadi stroking his beard, nodding.

"But I do not know if we can do this with people who are not believers," Baghdadi said. "You must be able to chamber a round, pull the trigger, and know that your bullet will find its target and not your sandals."

"Yes," Ahmed said. "But my computers can find people that the Devil States consider trusted infidels, and yet their government has turned against them. The Devils have stolen their lives."

He told his leader that some of them had even been soldiers who have fought in Afghanistan, Ahmed's home. "They have killed us in Syria and Iraq, which is your home."

"The Caliph has no home," Abu Bakr al-Baghdadi said. But it was an empty statement, a castoff. He was listening to the words of Ahmed Kahn, tasting them. The great leader of ISIL leaned back, still doubting Ahmed Kahn.

"How can we control or influence the actions of such an infidel warrior? How can he become our weapon? Would it not be better if he were Muslim?"

"It would be better if he were NOT," Ahmed said.

Baghdadi looked at him, narrowing his eyes.

"In a forest of infidels," Ahmed said, "every tree looks the same. He will be invisible."

Baghdadi laughed.

They spoke for another half an hour. Abu Bakr al-Baghdadi felt that the approach had to be tested outside of America first, to make sure that it worked. America had proven itself a problematic target since the triumph of the World Trade Center. All of the other ISIL and ISIS successes since the great collapse of the Twin Towers possessed the seed of Islam: the roadside explosion at the Boston Marathon, the nightclub slaughter in Orlando, Florida. Yet none of the seeds had grown into the Tree of Terror Baghdadi demanded.

Ahmed Khan would receive whatever resources he needed from the Islamic State in Iraq and the Levant. ISIL needed proof that his theory would work.

Chapter 3

A Funeral and a Wedding in Virginia

An Angry Killer Digs a Grave in Appalachia.

Torbjorn Petersson buried his grandmother "Gammy" in the family graveyard behind their log cabin in the northwestern Appalachians of Virginia. When he started digging, anger filled every shovelful of dirt and rocks. His mind wandered to similar holes that he had dug as a Marine Corps sniper in the mountains and valleys of Afghanistan.

Those holes kept you alive. This hole honored the death of his 85-year-old grandmother, who called him "son" because her child, his father, had died in a minefield in Quang Binh province in Vietnam, and his mother passed away when she heard the news.

War had erased an entire generation of their family.

Exhausted by cutting through roots that had been there longer than he had lived, Torbjorn sat on the edge of his grandmother's grave and thought about how Gammy died.

"What's this?" she had asked, handing him an official-looking envelope. She had walked a mile and a half to the rusty postbox at the end of the dirt and gravel road winding through their 526-acre farm. They lived twenty miles from Hot Springs, Virginia.

She handed Torbjorn a brown envelope.

He opened it and read out loud the first five words that headlined the official document. "Virginia Landowner's Bill of Rights."

He sat down and started reading silently. Gammy wandered off.

The document was from the Tennessee Valley Authority. It took Torbjorn sometime before he finally realized that 486 acres of their farm were about to be taken away, condemned by the government.

His ancestors had cleared the acreage after they escaped from the poverty of Sweden in the 18th century.

Bureaucrats at the TVA had approved the Gathright Dam, named after old "Uncle" Tom, long dead, who had been the Petersson's next-door neighbor for years.

Uncle Tom's place was a few miles down the Jackson River. When he died, Tom Gathright had donated his land to the George Washington National Forest, initially approved by Congress in 1947. The authorization included a dam.

"They're gonna turn our farm into a lake," Torbjorn said to his grandmother.

"What're you talking about, son?"

"It looks like the government's gonna put our farm underwater, Gammy."

"Why would they do that?" She sat down hard.

"They're gonna build a dam on Uncle Tom's place and make something called Moomaw that'll flood the farm."

"What the hell is a 'Moomaw'?" she asked.

"Don't know. It's a lake. Lake Moomaw."

The Moomaws were a famous Virginia family, initially in the fruit canning business, prominent leaders in church affairs, and a driving force for business in the area. Benjamin Moomaw, who lived down in Covington, was the man who had pushed the project forward.

The plan to build a dam had been on the drawing boards since the end of World War II.

"They can't just put our farm underwater," Gammy said. "Can they do that, son?"

"Well, it looks like they can, and they will," Torbjorn said. "They're condemning everything but 40 acres up the top of the mountain. Says here we should consult a lawyer. But it doesn't look like it'll do any good."

"They can't just do that," Gammy said.

She banged her fist on the table.

"They can't just do that." Thud.

"They can't just do that."

She stopped after a few more thumps of diminishing strength, laying her head in her arms.

Torbjorn watched her shoulders shake. She calmed down slowly, breathing softly.

He went back to reading the notice. As landowners, they had rights, but any attempts to stop the government's exercise of eminent domain were pointless. The authorities would limit any legal action to defining "just compensation" for the Peterssons.

The lake that formed behind Gathright Dam would be for public use, a recreational area, as well as a safety zone for spring floods in the Jackson and James River Basins. Both facts made resisting the condemnation difficult.

No court in the land would hear the case. No lawyer would take up the Petersson's cause. The farm was going to drown beneath the shoreline of Lake Moomaw.

The government had outlined all the stages of the condemnation process carefully. It was a tight timetable.

When they completed the Gathright Dam, Lake Moomaw would cover 2,530 acres of the valley flatland and have a maximum depth of 152 feet.

"Gammy," Torbjorn said, "I've been all over the world, and this log cabin is the only place I've ever been willing to call my home. This farm will be our home until my last breath, I promise you." She never heard him.

He looked at Gammy. He reached over and touched her. He immediately knew that his grandmother was dead. A trickle of blood dripped from her nose.

He picked her up, surprised at how light she was, like a child. He put her in her bedroom adjacent to the kitchen, and then he searched her closet for a dress to bury her in. He finally settled on the blue housecoat she was already wearing.

He went out to dig her grave in the family cemetery overrun by foliage. He dug a deep hole next to the grandfather he never knew and parents that he only remembered from fading photographs.

Finally, with his legs draped over the hole, he realized he might be making a mistake.

He probably needed to call the Bath County Sheriff over in Warm Springs.

He knew that they had a medical examiner. He thought about the Sheriff and the Coroner coming out and confirming the death of his grandmother, walking around the centuries-old cabin.

They would notice things. That was their business. They would wonder about the industrial generator in the back of the cabin.

They might want to see inside.

If they looked into the main bedroom on the ground floor, which they might assume was his grandmother's space, they would discover a room filled with blinking computer equipment and blacked-out windows.

He did not need a death certificate to claim the land. Ernestine Petersson had already given the title to the 526-acre farm to Torbjorn, years earlier.

He stood up and looked at the rectangular, deep hole he had dug for his grandmother.

He decided to skip the bureaucracy of death.

He walked back into the cabin. As gently as possible, he wrapped his grandmother in Industrial Glad Bags, offended by the irony of the product's name.

Then he carried her out to her grave.

He returned to the cabin and took a Bronze Star off the wall outside her bedroom.

For over 65 years, Gammy brushed her fingers over it when she went to bed at night, and when she got up in the morning. Her husband, Jackson Petersson, received the medal after he died in Korea at the Battle of the Chosin Reservoir in the bitter winter of 1950.

Torbjorn also took a framed, handwritten letter off the wall. It was from Captain George McKlane, dated January 26, 1951, written in a hospital in Japan. It explained that Gammy's husband was a Marine Corps hero who saved the lives of many men at the price of his own. Ernestine had ironed the letter and put it in a simple, wooden frame. The heat of the iron turned her tears into permanent age spots on the paper.

"Our family saved this man twice, Gammy."

His grandfather had protected George McKlane in Korea, and Torbjorn Petersson had spared his life in Boca Raton, Florida, less than a year ago.

Torbjorn returned to the grave. He jumped down into it and then gently pulled his grandmother in after him.

His fingers reached out and found the framed letter, which he then placed on her chest.

He could not find the Bronze Star.

He lifted himself out of the grave.

The sun was setting, spreading dark shadows up the mountain beyond the Jackson River. He could hear the river, a sound which had always comforted him, but which now seemed threatening, unfriendly.

In the growing darkness, it took Torbjorn a while to find the medal in the leaves where the framed letter had been. He tossed it into the grave, heard a crack as it broke some glass.

Torbjorn was not a superstitious person. Shattered glass meant nothing.

Although this was the first grave he had ever personally dug, he had filled many others in his life, first as a Marine Corps sniper in Afghanistan, and then later as a professional killer in the United States of America.

He started shoveling dirt into the hole. He did not cry as he buried his grandmother. However, he did make a promise, out loud, in the dark.

"Only rain's gonna fall on your resting place, Gammy," Torbjorn said.

"No lake will ever touch your grave."

A week later, 20 miles away, Martha Krumble and Brigadier General George McKlane II were enjoying their wedding reception. They held it at the Homestead in Hot Springs, Virginia, just as autumn flowered the mountains with a final burst of color.

Over 130 people joined the festivities.

The participants included all three generations of the McKlanes, decorated Marines, although the youngest and the oldest were not in uniform.

The groom was the only son of Captain George McKlane. The Captain had written the condolence letter to Ernestine Petersson.

Martha Krumble gave the best speech of the evening, covering the exploits and the character of the McKlane family with a mixture of wry humor and praise.

She ended her talk with an admonishment as she officially and willingly became part of the history of the McKlane tribe.

"I am no longer a young woman," she told the crowded room. "But, I may yet have a child."

Her new husband, General George McKlane II, raised his eyebrows.

So did his father, and his son, both sitting at the married couple's banquet table.

Something close to laughter nervously rippled through the room.

"This is not a shotgun wedding," her new husband said.

People laughed.

"We might adopt," Martha replied.

Her new husband took his napkin and patted his forehead, causing more laughter.

She waved at the McKlane men surrounding her.

"They all look alike and have beautiful smiles," Martha said. "Some have a few more wrinkles, but they are men of honor, integrity, and bravery."

She reached over and patted the original George, sitting to her left.

Everyone in the room knew the story of Captain George McKlane, the winner of the Medal of Honor in Korea.

Martha Krumble straightened up, looking every inch the Principal Broker of the largest Real Estate Agency in Boca Raton, Florida. "And yet, each of these men has a fatal flaw."

She scanned the room.

People began to fidget.

"Here's the problem," she said. "The McKlanes have shown absolutely no originality when naming their children, none whatsoever."

She looked at each one of the men.

"George, George, and George."

The men smiled at one another.

The crowd relaxed.

"I made a solemn promise to my new husband today," Martha said, reaching to her right and putting a hand over the single star on his left epaulet. "Now, I will make another vow, one of equal importance in the eyes of God."

The minister who had married the couple a few hours earlier shrugged his shoulders and looked a little nervous at his table, where guests on either side of him were whispering pious, curious questions.

Martha waited for silence, which slowly arrived.

"If we have a new son, he will be named Ryan Sean Conor Brendan Fergus Kevin Liam Padraig Quinlan Seamus," she took an exaggerated breath, "McKlane."

The laughter grew with each additional Irish name and then died down.

The guests realized that she was not quite finished. She looked at all three men, then straight ahead.

"And if it's a girl," she said, drawing a lung full of air in anticipation of another onslaught of Irish names, " ... we'll call her George." She sat down to laughter and applause.

"That was very good," her new husband said.

"Thank you, General McKlane," she said, leaning close and whispering in his ear. "I think I'm pregnant."

Brigadier General George McKlane never lost his smile or the look of love in his eyes. He registered no surprise.

"You're forty-seven years old," he said quietly.

"You're a fertile plow, George. When you reach your father's age, you'll have a teenager running around the house. It will keep you young."

He laughed at the thought of it, but it pleased him, and Martha reminded herself yet again why she loved this fierce warrior, this gentle husband.

"A girl named George," he said, feeling proud.

At the banquet table, the nametags placed Sharonda Nelson to the left of Captain George McKlane and next to her husband, Samuel Nelson, a sergeant and an ex-Marine who had retired six months earlier from the Boca Raton Police Department.

He was now a private security guard for Captain McKlane. Sharonda was George McKlane's personal PA, a Physician Assistant with a Master's Degree in Nursing.

The Nelsons had moved into the guest house at George McKlane's multi-million dollar estate at the Royal Coconut Yacht & Country Club in Boca Raton, Florida.

George McKlane became wealthy as a Wall Street trader. After he left the Marine Corps in 1953, he quickly learned how to take advantage of the insider information freely given to him by people who admired him as a war hero. He bugged his home, where he gave extravagant parties that included the wizards of Wall Street and the leaders of America's chief industries. He eavesdropped on private conversations. He recorded people without their knowledge, and he discreetly turned their secrets into a fortune.

What he did was illegal, and he knew it. But he had seen good, brave men die for no reason in Korea, and he had no trouble gaming the system for his own family's advantage.

At the bridal table, Sharonda asked the elder McKlane: "Are you ready for a female George, George?"

"Stop repeating yourself, Sharonda," he answered. "I dislike redundancy." He had grown older since the attempt on his life the previous year, but his mind remained sharp.

Sharonda laughed.

"The three of us are going on a special sightseeing trip tomorrow," George told the Nelsons.

"Where are we going," Samuel asked.

"Are you both packing?" George asked.

"Oh, sweet Jesus," Sharonda said. She looked at her husband. "He's going to start another war." She was smiling as she said this, not worried, knowing that the older man was just having some fun.

"Yes, we are packing," Samuel said.

"We are?" Sharonda said.

Samuel looked at Captain George and said: "I got the concealed carry permits the day before yesterday, as soon as we got up here, Captain George." With his police credentials, it had been no problem.

"You did?" Sharonda asked her husband. "When were you going to tell me about it?"

"Good," said George.

"Stop!" Sharonda said, loud enough to get the attention of nearby guests.

"Huddle up," she said, grabbing both men by their shoulders and pulling them towards her.

Sharonda Nelson was a strong woman.

"What the hell is going on here, George? Samuel? You're starting to scare me."

"We're going on a sightseeing trip," George said.

"Where to?" Sharonda asked.

"Through the Richardson Gorge. It's stunning at this time of year."

"We need guns for that?" Sharonda asked.

"No," George said. She let go of both men, and they sat back, shrugging their shoulders.

Quietly, Sharonda asked, "Then why are we packing?"

"We're going to meet somebody," George said.

"Who are we going to meet?"

"The man who tried to kill me last year," George said.

Sharonda stared at him, suddenly realizing that all of the computer work she had been doing the previous week in Florida had brought them to this moment.

"Petersson," she said.

George nodded.

"You told me he saved your life."

"That's what his grandmother wrote on the back of the picture frame," George said. It had been one of six, returned framed letters, all from the families of men who had died under his command in Korea.

The pictures disappeared from the so-called War Room in his Boca Raton mansion on the night of his attempted assassination. Over fifty thank you notes lined the wall.

Of the six framed letters taken, the thief returned five with Express Mail within days. One had appeared later, with the note from Ernestine Petersson.

In the framed letter of the last one to arrive, a postscript from Ernestine Petersson had said: *"I will pray that you come home to the people who love you."* It was something that her husband, Corporal Jackson "Smartass" Petersson, would never be able to do.

On the back of the frame, in the same neat cursive in which she penned the original note 64 years earlier, she wrote: *"P.S.S. My original prayer was answered, Captain McKlane. Now my grandson has also returned you to your loved ones. Take no one else from my family."*

At the wedding reception, Sharonda looked at Captain George and asked: "You don't believe her?"

"Oh, I do believe her," George said.

"Then why don't we end it right there?" Sharonda asked.

"Because I want to thank him."

"With a gun?"

"Well, he might not view us as a welcoming committee," George said.

"Probably not if we're carrying a bunch of guns," Sharonda pointed out.

"Concealed weapons," Samuel Nelson said.

"I will not be carrying," Sharonda said, delivering as dead a stare at her husband as she could.

"Suit yourself," George said.

Sharonda shook her head at his magnificent smile. Lord, how this man got away with things because of that grin.

He put his hand on Sharonda's shoulder and said: "Don't forget to bring the First Aid Kit."

"Oh, for God's sake," she said

She stood up and walked away, leaving the gun-packing fools to themselves.

Chapter 4

Love and Fear in Appalachia

The Homestead in Virginia

The Youngest McKlane Meets His Match.

George McKlane III, the son of Brigadier General George McKlane II, served two tours in Iraq and one in Afghanistan before he left the Marine Corps as a Major. He did not lose his pay grade or length of service. Instead, he became a Lieutenant Colonel after being handpicked to run the first international anti-terrorism unit at Homeland Security.

It made a mockery of the term "Homeland," a result of the worldwide success of terrorism.

The Lieutenant Colonel's friends called him "Mac," which he preferred to George. He agreed with his new stepmother. Too many George McKlanes filled the ranks of the Marine Corps. His father and grandfather also preferred to use his nickname.

At the wedding reception, he leaned over to Martha after her speech and asked her who the woman was sitting at a table with Angelo Rossellini.

"I'm glad you enjoyed my speech," Martha said to him, following his gaze. "Did you hear any of it, Mac?"

He laughed, looking at her. "Of course, I did, *Mummy*."

Martha laughed. They liked each other and enjoyed one another's jibes. They rarely had a straight conversation, and both of them preferred it that way. Martha knew what he did for a living, as much as anyone could remember, and she understood that superficial conversation represented the best and perhaps the only type of communication he had outside of Homeland Security.

At the table which Mac focused on, a white-haired man, Angelo Rossellini, was surrounded by many of Martha's friends and associates from the firm that she ran.

Angelo owned Accelerated Realty Sales in Boca Raton, where Martha Krumble worked as the Principal Broker. She also had a minority shareholding in the company, Boca Raton's largest real estate agency.

"That's one of Angelo Rossellini's favorite bodyguards," Martha said. "Her name is Holly Smolkes. She's stunning, but she's a marked woman, Mac."

"What does that mean?"

She smiled. "I'm joking and being a little unfair, catty perhaps. I don't know much about Holly Smolkes. She has a scar on her left cheek that you can't see from here. I seem to recall that she got it in a barroom brawl when she was modeling swimsuits."

"That sounds like my kind of woman," Mac said. "Is she attached to anyone?"

"I don't think she's married right now," Martha said, looking at him. "She has a few dead husbands in her past."

"A woman of experience," Mac said. "Excuse me. I think I'd like to meet her." He got up.

"It was a great speech, Martha."

"Thanks," she said. *What was it with McKlane men and danger?* "Be careful."

Mac smiled. "McKlane men last a long time," he said. His father caught that part of their conversation and smiled at his son. Both he and his new wife said, in unison: "I hope so." All three of them laughed.

"You guys have already become echoes," Mac said to his father and new mother. "Old married folk, a good sign."

His birth mother had died in a car accident in Cleveland, Ohio, 21 years earlier.

He turned towards the Rossellini group.

The entire table looked up as he approached. He extended a hand to Angelo Rossellini. "I'm Mac McKlane," he said. "You're the owner of my new mother's real estate agency, and she said I should come over here and suck up to the boss."

Nobody at the table said anything. A few people smiled politely and looked at their coffee cups.

"That was a foolish thing for me to say," Mac said.

Angelo took the youngest McKlane's outstretched hand just as Mac was about to drop it back to his side. For an older man, Angelo had a surprisingly firm grip.

"Only wrinkles separate the McKlane generations," Angelo said. Mac McKlane could not quite figure out if this was an insult or exoneration. "Please, sit down," Angelo said.

The seat next to Holly Smolkes was empty. "You are a lieutenant colonel in the Marine Corps," Angelo told the table, not looking at Mac.

Very few people knew this. Mac's official title did not include the Marine Corps, although his pay grade did. He was a team leader in the Homeland Security CWMD service focused on cybersecurity and antiterrorism both at home and abroad. They called him a director at Homeland.

He could return to the Marine Corps at any time, with no loss of seniority or time served.

"I work at Homeland Security," Mac said.

"Are we all secure?" Angelo asked, sweeping his arms to include the entire table.

"We are tonight," Mac said, smiling.

"I worry more about tomorrow," Angelo said.

"So do I," Mac said. The tone of the table was dropping rapidly. "But tonight we celebrate, and we dance." He turned to Holly and said: "Would you like to dance?"

She had a beautiful smile, but her eyes looked at Angelo, who gave her an almost imperceptible nod.

"I would love to dance with Homeland Security," Holly Smolkes said.

Mac stood. "I guess that's me."

He took her hand and led her to the dance floor. She was a feather in his arms, and he was a skillful dancer. When the music stopped, he asked her if he could buy her a drink.

"I don't drink," she said.

"Why not?"

"I am Muslim," she said.

Without pausing, he said: "*As-salāmu-Alaykum.*"

"And peace be upon you, Homeland Security."

"Please," he said, "call me Mac."

She laughed, and it was a deeper sound than he expected. He liked it.

"Mac," she said.

"Can I tear you away from your table, take a walk with you out on the terrace?"

The Homestead had a great veranda, with oversized rocking chairs and comfortable love seats separated by evenly-spaced, stately, white columns.

"I think I would enjoy that."

As they walked away from the celebrations, she waved to Angelo, and he waved back, smiling.

"He is like a father to me," Holly said. She smiled at Mac. "I have had many fathers in my life."

"I'm not sure I know what that means," Mac said.

"Perhaps you will learn," she said. "I have the feeling that you learn things very quickly."

"What makes you say that?"

"You immediately corrected what you did when you made a fool of yourself at Angelo's table."

"I've had a lot of practice," he said.

She laughed and flopped down on a two-seat lounge chair. Mac followed her lead. They never made it outside to the veranda. They sat next to card tables covered by partially-finished jigsaw puzzles. They were alone.

"Tell me about your multiple fathers."

She smiled, and he could see that she was calculating what she would say, how much truth Holly would share with a stranger she might like.

He felt the heat of her body next to him, and he knew she felt his as well.

She was not quite ready to blow him off and return to the reception, but he knew that it was close. She smiled at him, not with trust, but with curiosity.

"My real father was a Russian major, a helicopter pilot who invaded my country of Afghanistan. He raped my mother, and I was the result. My second father, a CIA operative, helped me kill him with a Stinger missile in 1988. My second father was a good man, he adopted me, he was a true father, and I loved him. His name was Charles Smolkes. Everyone called him 'Red.' He died in Syria nine years ago. My third father is Angelo Rossellini, but his parenthood is one of feeling, not fact."

"Jesus Christ," Mac said.

"I am a Muslim. Jesus has nothing to do with it."

Mac did not know what to say. He floundered with: "You have no accent."

Holly laughed, and Mac smiled, still unsure of himself. It was not something he felt very often.

"I am an American," Holly said. "Nobody with an accent exists in me anymore."

"The scar on your cheek," Mac said. "You got it in a barroom brawl, but — "

"How do you know that?" Holly asked. He saw her eyes narrow slightly.

"Martha Krumble, McKlane, I mean, she told me that when I asked her who you were."

"It's just a scar. It ended my career as a swimsuit model. I am not sure I would have enjoyed that profession."

"Why have a brawl in a bar? You are a Muslim. You told me that you don't touch liquor."

"I don't, but you learn more about people when they drink than when they are sober. I tell Angelo it is like men playing golf to discover the value of other men." Mac just stared at her. She was stunning, and he desperately wanted to connect with her somehow.

"Can I touch your scar?" he asked.

She smiled and moved closer to him. "Of course."

His finger traced the scar down the left side of her cheek. It was a soft, thoughtful touch, and she liked it.

No man had ever done this so early in a relationship with her, certainly not before making love.

"Would you like to touch more of me?" she asked.

"Yes," said Mac. "I would like that very much."

She led him down the corridor to the elevators that took them to her room.

He was a little frantic at first, but she slowed him down. They danced without music as they undressed one another, admiring bodies that they had not seen before.

Afterward, Holly watched him go into the bathroom.

He did not close the door as he washed, and she liked the honesty of that.

Mac came back with a washrag for her. He stood at the foot of the bed, watching her with a smile.

"Do you always do that?" he asked.

"Do what?"

"Tremble all over; your whole body was vibrating?"

She looked at him. He did not get edgy or nervous.

"Why do you ask?" she said.

Mac laughed. She thought it sounded nice. He said: "It's hard for me to control myself when you do that."

She smiled at him. It reached her eyes.

"What do other women do?"

"Bad question," he said.

"Why?"

"This is not a good time for comparisons."

"Yes, it is," she said. "This is a perfect time." She sat up on her knees. The sheets dropped off of her.

They both smiled.

"Okay," he said. "That's probably the best lovemaking I've ever had in my life."

She laughed, threw herself at him, felt his renewed excitement. They made love again, slower this time. Her vibrations still got to him.

Exhausted, he turned his head to her. They both smiled, lips softly touching, their teeth clicking and then softened by their tongues. He fell away from her.

"I'm going to work on my self-control," he said.

"Yes, you should."

"But it will probably take some time."

"I hope so."

Holly Smolkes liked this man, Mac McKlane, and she liked the way he smelled. He might last longer than most.

As Mac backed out of Holly's room the following morning, kissing her passionately and almost dragging her, naked, into the corridor, he ran into his grandfather, Sharonda, and Samuel Nelson, and all dressed in hiking gear.

Holly quickly slammed the door with a deep laugh and an "Oh, Sweet Jesus!"

"That's not very Muslim-ish," Mac said to the closed door. He turned to the hikers and said, with a look of complete innocence: "Well, it seems as if you're all going trout fishing."

"Maybe he should come with us," Sharonda said.

"Nope," said his grandfather. "My grandson is not thinking with his head."

Samuel Nelson laughed.

As they brushed past Mac, holding his dinner jacket from the night before, his grandfather winked at him and said: "Busted." Mac watched them go, smiling.

Sharonda, Samuel, and George had breakfast together in the main dining room at the end of the corridor, next to the fancy stores that sold overpriced wares to vacationers visiting Virginia's autumn foliage. Sharonda was wearing her Glock. Samuel had changed her mind about packing.

They rented a black Lincoln Navigator for the trip. Sharonda pointed out that it made them look like the Feds, probably not a good disguise.

"We have nothing to hide," Captain George said.

"Except for our guns," Sharonda said.

Samuel drove, with George in the passenger seat and Sharonda in back.

They didn't take the usual route to Richardson Gorge. Captain George had planned the trip like a military maneuver. Instead of taking the Jackson River Turnpike and swinging north, then south, they went to Bacova Junction, west of Hot Springs.

They headed north on a smaller road, turning west again at the Mt. Hope United Methodist Church. They stayed on the Richardson Gorge Road, passing a well-kept farm where it met Switzerland Trail.

"You sure this is the right way?" Sharonda asked when the paved road turned into dirt.

"Quickest route," George said.

They twisted their way west with the Jackson River on their right, at times showing a sheer drop of over 120 feet. It would be hard for two cars to pass going in different directions, and pull-off siding areas dotted the route. They drove through a trout club with a modern, metal bridge leading to neat cabins on the other side of the river: The Cold Springs Trout Club.

The road widened and became paved again as they approached the Petersson place. At first, they drove past the entrance, which had a broken sign, barely readable saying: "Leatherwood Farms."

It was almost invisible behind the yellow autumn leaves of Leatherwood shrubs surrounding the entry.

Samuel drove across the metal bridge spanning the Jackson River, turned around, and came back to the Leatherwood Farms' entrance. "I think this is it," he said.

"In we go," Captain McKlane said.

The road to the cabin was a mile and a half long, all dirt. The final half mile started as the SUV came around an elevated bend in the road that dropped down to a large, open metal gate.

They stopped there for a moment and looked at the farm: a big barn beyond some cleared pastures, some storage areas, a hen house surrounded by chickens, a reasonably large pig pen, and a vast field that stretched down to the Jackson River. They saw a few cows, a herd of sheep, and one horse in a pasture. The horse appeared a bit skinny.

Sunlight reflecting off the windows of a two-storied log cabin a half a mile down the dirt road. The cabin nestled into the side of the mountain. Beyond it, they could see a harvested field of something, corn or wheat. On the other side of the Jackson River, bails of hay wrapped in white plastic dotted the edges of empty fields.

Dust from the dirt road in the Richardson Gorge covered the black Lincoln Navigator. The SUV made a racket as it drove across some metal rollers spanning the pasture's entry gate.

The tightly-grouped bars, eight inches in diameter and hollow, 18 of them, were held in place by gravity alone.

The rollers prevented livestock from passing through the open gate.

The metal bars made quite a racket as the SUV passed over the cattle guard.

"So much for our surprise attack," Sharonda said. Nobody laughed or even smiled.

It took a while for the metallic sound to reach Torbjorn as it echoed down the valley.

But he heard it, loud and clear.

He was near the top of the mountain, in a hidden treehouse that he had built 20 feet up an old oak tree. It was big enough to sleep in comfortably, with a small gas stove and running water piped in from a sweetwater stream at the top of the mountain, further west.

He had a good view in all directions, and he could look down the mountainside and see his gravel driveway in front of the log cabin.

Torbjorn usually used the treehouse as a lookout during the deer hunting season.

But right now, he was using it to look five miles down the valley to where the United States Army Corps of Engineers were struggling to put the finishing touches on the Gathright Dam and Lake Moomaw.

The spring floods, less than six months away, would probably fill the lake.

He had his M2010 sniper system with him, but he had not attached the sound suppressor or muzzle brake to the weapon. It would make a tremendous noise if he fired the M2010 with no silencer.

He turned his attention from the Gathright Dam to the SUV trailing dust as it approached his log cabin.

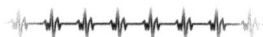

"Okay," Sharonda said, "Mister Petersson and his Grandmother are not at home. I think it's time to leave."

"Got a freshly dug grave over here, Captain," Samuel said as he stepped out from some bushes just off the driveway behind the log cabin.

Sharonda shook her head and made a sign of the cross, although she was not Roman Catholic.

They all walked to the grave. It had a beautiful headstone, which said: "Ernestine Petersson, R.I.P." There were no dates engraved on the stone.

"His grandmother," Captain McKlane said.

He bowed his head and said a silent prayer. Samuel also dropped his head, but. Sharonda kept her eyes open and watched the woods.

They walked back to the SUV. After a few minutes, Captain McKlane said: "We're going to wait for him."

Sharonda and Samuel said nothing.

"We're going to wait for him in the cabin," Captain McKlane said. He pulled on the door. It was not locked.

"Are you crazy?" Sharonda said as George McKlane stepped across the threshold. "You're going to add 'breaking and entering' to trespassing, George? Have you lost your damned mind?"

George McKlane stopped and looked at her.

"Get in the cabin," he said. "We're not breaking anything. We will be safer inside."

"We'll be safer if we all get into the SUV and drive back to the Homestead right now," Sharonda said.

"I agree, Captain McKlane," Samuel said.

"Into the cabin," George said. "I'm not asking, Sharonda. Consider it an order." He watched Sharonda and her husband exchange glances.

"Please," George said, "you need to humor an old man who knows how to stay alive in this situation."

Reluctantly, they entered the log cabin. All three went to the porch, sat down in rocking chairs, and waited.

"It's a wonderful, peaceful view," George said. They heard some cows mooing in the distance. A rooster crowed. After ten minutes, Samuel got up and said: "I'm just going to look around, Captain. I won't touch anything."

"Be careful," George said.

Sharonda was silent, but not with eyes.

Eight minutes later, Samuel came back.

"He's got a helluva computer system in one room downstairs," he said. "And I found this."

He handed Captain George a color copy of the thank you note Ernestine Petersson had sent to him over 65 years earlier. It had a small photograph of Corporal Jackson Petersson in the bottom, left-hand corner.

George looked at it and said: "Smartass."

Sharonda said: "I beg your pardon?"

"That's what we called Corporal Jackson Petersson," Captain George said. "Ernestine Petersson's husband. He was a helluva shot, one of my best men. He also wrote for the *Stars and Stripes*. Get me a pen or a pencil, Samuel."

Sharonda's husband returned with both in less than a minute, taken from the small desk in the bedroom where he found the thank you note.

Five minutes later, as George put down the pen, there was a sound.

It was a bell, nearby, but not a doorbell. All three of them looked at one another. Sharonda and Samuel drew their weapons, waiting.

Nothing happened.

Samuel went to the front entrance, slowly, gun ready. His voice was quiet, urgent.

"Captain, you better come see this."

Sharonda and Captain McLane joined Samuel, looking through the screen door.

On the hood of the SUV, three 3.34-inch Remington 700 bullets pointed at the sky — deadly, copper soldiers, neatly aligned in the sunlight.

"What does that mean?" Sharonda asked.

"Fragging," Samuel said.

"What the hell does *that* mean?" Sharondas asks, chambering a round in her weapon.

"It means that we should go," Captain McKlane said.

"Great," Sharonda said. "Good idea."

"Holster your weapons."

"Bad idea," Sharonda said. She looked at her husband and shook her head negatively. He looked at George.

"Do it," George said, and they did.

"Be careful," Samuel said. "Fragging was when an officer's men marked him for execution in Vietnam."

"Sweet Jesus," Sharonda said, crouching and running towards the SUV.

Soldiers in Vietnam, and other modern wars, often put a bullet next to a commissioned or non-commissioned officer when he slept, a warning not to risk their lives needlessly.

They killed the officer with a fragmentary grenade if he didn't take the hint, hence the term "fragging."

Sharonda ducked quickly into the rear seat, getting down on the floor and praying.

Captain McKlane grabbed the bullets, faced the forest, put his hands holding the rounds together in prayer, and slowly bowed towards the forest.

Then he got into the passenger seat.

The SUV was already running as he closed the door. Samuel backed it around and put it in gear. The stones of the driveway flew beneath the spinning tires.

A loud gunshot burst from the forest, smothering the sounds of the SUV as it escaped from the driveway in front of the Petersson's log cabin.

Something hanging on the side of the cabin exploded, shattered, making a hellish noise.

Sharonda gasped and pressed herself further into the floorboard. She covered her mouth to prevent a scream.

Neither Captain McKlane nor Samuel Nelson ducked, although they both flinched.

Sharonda did not sit up until the SUV clambered across the metal rollers of the cattle guard and through the entry pasture's open gate. No one said anything until they reached the rusted mailbox on the road that headed back into the Richardson Gorge.

Sharonda spoke first.

"Thank God he missed," she said. "Praise the Lord for making that man miss."

"He did not miss," George said quietly. "He was aiming for whatever he hit."

"It was a cowbell," Samuel said.

After 15 seconds of nothing other than the sounds of the dirt road beneath them, Sharonda said: "Ding-a-ling."

They laughed with relief, but not humor.

Chapter 5

A Great Danger Appears in Africa.

Walking Down a River in the Switzerland of Africa

Shadrach Ringer woke up before sunrise without an alarm clock. He slipped out of the king-sized bed in the rondavel, a large circular hut, where he and his wife, Sookie, were on holiday. They were nearing the end of a two-week safari at a luxury health destination in the Drakensberg Mountains in the Kingdom of Lesotho, a landlocked, independent nation surrounded by South Africa.

Their rondavel had been there for half a century, one of 29 identical units at an upscale health spa called the Royal Peacock Resort and Lodge. Each rondavel was the same: a large circular hut with a straw roof and four, huge, evenly-spaced picture windows cut into the whitewashed, curved cement siding. Separated by gardens, strutting peacocks, and flowering bushes, the rondavels surrounded a much larger building, which was also circular. It had steel supports and a sturdy, metal roof.

This central building housed a formal dining area, a dance floor, conference rooms, an exercise gym, two squash courts, and a saloon with a 40-foot mahogany bar.

Each of the 29 guest units had a fully-equipped kitchen, a vast living area, a central wood-burning fireplace, and two or three spacious bedrooms. Shadrach and Sookie Ringer had an entire rondavel to themselves, using only the most enormous bedroom, in which Sookie was still asleep as Shadrach stepped off the rondavel's wooden porch.

Shadrach turned and watched sunlight touch the melting snowcaps of the Drakensberg Mountains.

Morning crept down the peaks quickly. Flowers bloomed everywhere as the southern hemisphere moved into the springtime of October.

Shadrach grabbed his Orvis fly rod and headed to the trout stream, which he had walked down every day for over a week. He had caught and released over 55 trout, many of them newly stocked fingerlings.

He had discovered one lunker that had snapped his three and a half-pound tapered leader twice. The trout had never broken the surface, so it was not a Rainbow. He figured that it was a natural Brown, probably a resident of the stream for many years. It lived in the shadow of a colossal boulder near a cascade that fell into the two acres of relatively smooth water where it lurked.

On the second day of his vacation, he had hooked the fish with a red and black Wolly Bugger. It immediately snapped the nine-foot leader filament at the end of his line.

On the sixth day, using a slightly weighted nymph to get the fly under the water, he had it on his line longer. He never saw the trout. His fishing line stripped out over 40 feet towards the dark boulder. It suddenly went slack.

Now, he would try a third time.

"Today, I get you," he said.

It was a two-mile walk to the pool. Shadrach thought about the first day he had fished the stream, a week and a half earlier. A park ranger had arrested him.

He had walked the brook for a mile before any sunlight flickered on the water.

He had caught a dozen fingerlings, gently freeing all of them back into the water. Then he hooked a one-and-a-half pound rainbow, which he gutted and cleaned. He built a fire in a circle of small rocks, cooking the fish suspended over the coals on a newly cut sapling.

After he had eaten the trout, all that remained was the fish's skeleton, its head, and tail. A voice startled him.

"*Goeiemore, Meneer.* What are you doing?"

The Black person said good morning to him with a guttural Dutch accent, mixing Afrikaans and English. He had a pistol in a brown holster, but he did not look like a soldier. The patch on his arm said: Park Ranger.

"Breakfast," Shadrach said. "I'm afraid I ate it all."

"They are delicious, *Meneer.*"

"Yes. The best. I would have shared it with you."

"You will put out the fire with water and kick in the stones," he said.

"Of course."

"That is good, and now I would like to see your license if you please, *Meneer.*"

Shadrach reached into his backpack, noting that the park ranger's hand moved to his holster.

Carefully, Shadrach pulled out his Tanzanian driver's license, which had his photograph on it. He and his wife, Sookie, were Peace Corps volunteers in East Africa, and both of them were Americans.

The Park ranger looked at the driver's license and said: "You had more hair in this picture."

He handed it back.

"Yes. My wife made me cut it off."

"That is good, you look better, and now I need to see your other license, *Meneer.*"

"What other license?"

"Your fishing license, *Meneer.*"

Shadrach shrugged his shoulders. "I didn't know I needed a fishing license."

They stared at one another for a moment. Shadrach thought about offering the ranger a bribe.

"I must place you under arrest, *Meneer.*"

"Oh, come on," Shadrach said, standing up.

The American was a foot and a half taller than the park ranger, who took two steps back and unhooked the safety strap on his holster.

"Okay," Shadrach said, holding out the palms of his hands. "Should I put out the fire?"

"I will do that," the ranger said, motioning Shadrach to the passenger side of a gray Land Rover hidden from view behind a boulder.

Shadrach wondered why he hadn't heard the vehicle approach. Perhaps it was there from the start, waiting, Africa's version of a cop hiding behind a billboard.

He got into the passenger seat. The ranger handcuffed him to the door handle in a smooth, fluid movement.

"You can't be serious," Shadrach said.

"I am an earnest person," the ranger said. "I will break down your fly fishing rod and secure your possessions, *Meneer.* Then we will go to the police station."

Shadrach reacted calmly, saying nothing as the ranger twisted his rod apart and carefully extinguished the fire.

The ranger picked up the bare fishbone, with the head and tail still attached, and placed it in a plastic baggie, apparent evidence of his crime.

Shadrach begged the ranger to take him to the resort rather than the police station, which the guard agreed to do after a cell phone call in the language of Lesotho, which Shadrach did not understand.

A half an hour later, Shadrach walked out of the manager's office at the Royal Peacock Resort and Lodge, with a Fishing Permit and a promise that they would delete his arrest record in the Kingdom of Lesotho.

He did not laugh at this, although he wanted to.

In the manager's office, the discussion had been lively. Shadrach did not know what they said to each other because they spoke Sotho, which had a lot of tongue clicks and meant nothing to him. He kept thinking of Miriam Makeba, the first artist to popularize African music internationally in the 1960s with the click song, *Pata Pata.*

"Miriam Makeba," Shadrach said during the conversation between the ranger and the manager. "One of my favorite singers of all time. Mama Africa."

They both stared at him.

"She was not Southern Sotho," the ranger said. "She was born in Johannesburg."

"She spoke Xhosa," the manager said with a loud click on the "Xh" of the word.

From that point on, Shadrach remained silent.

The fishing license cost him 40 loti, the currency of the Kingdom of Lesotho, equivalent to the same amount in

South African rand. Wiping his record clean had cost more, 400 loti.

Afterward, Shadrach stood with his wife at their bedroom bay window, explaining what had happened.

"So we've already spent a little over $300 more than we planned," he said. They watched the park ranger depart from the main building with the manager. They were holding hands, a widespread sign of friendship in Africa.

Shadrach watched as the manager gave the ranger a wad of money. Both men laughed.

"We should complain to someone about that," his wife said. "Who can we bitch to?"

"I guess we can send a letter to the King of Lesotho, but don't hold your breath," Shadrach said. "This is Africa."

〜〜〜〜〜〜〜

Now Shadrach was on a quest for the lunker that ruled what he called The Boulder Pool. The water felt like ice from the final springtime snow melt off the mountains.

As he approached the pool, he saw three men in the distance, one of whom appeared to be his buddy, the Park ranger. He waved. They saw him but did not wave back.

Shadrach Ringer put down his backpack and his fishing gear and set off to where the men stood. He was a former United States Marine, Division Recon, and there was something about these men that made him curious.

They might be stocking the river with fish, but they looked and acted like Muslim warriors.

As he approached, the Park ranger got into his Land Rover and drove off. Shadrach Ringer found that odd.

As he came near the remaining two men, he recognized them as soldiers of Islam.

He had known men like these before in his life, some friends, but most enemies. He nodded at them. They nodded back. Everyone's eyes remained empty but on edge.

"*As-salāmu-'alaykum,*" Shadrach said.

"*Wa'alaykumu -salām,*" one of the men said. The second man's eyes darted at the man who spoke and then quickly resumed their dead stare at Shadrach.

Shadrach scanned the area without moving his eyes. He saw no apparent weapons, just massive, metal barrels, three of them, all sealed, lined up on the side of what appeared to be a military truck.

They looked like 50-gallon, stainless steel, beer barrels.

"You have chosen an excellent day for fishing," the man who greeted him said. He had an English accent.

"I hope so," Shadrach said. "There's a huge Brown Trout down in the big pool there. I would guess he weighs between three and four kilos. He's slipped off my line twice in the last week."

"I think today you will catch this fish," the man said.

"I hope so. My name is Shadrach Ringer. I fought in Afghanistan as a Marine Corps Recon Staff Sergeant during Operation Enduring Freedom." He held out his hand.

"Shadrach," the man said, shaking his hand. The other man moved back towards the truck. "That is quite an unusual name, quite biblical."

"My father was an avid reader of the Bible. I think that's where he stumbled across it. I prefer it to Meshach or Abednego." He watched both men's reactions. There were none. "What are you doing with the beer barrels?"

The man he spoke to smiled. The other man showed no reaction at all. Perhaps he did not understand English.

"Well," the talker said, "we poor Muslims are not supposed to drink, so we have to come a long way to satisfy our thirst, don't you think?"

Shadrach laughed. The talker smiled.

"My name is Professor Ahmed Khan," he said, "and I am currently working as a marine biologist with the Suid-Afrikaans Water Conservation Board."

"Pleased to meet you, Professor."

"We are here to make sure that your fishing experience is the most memorable of your life. Of course, I cannot guarantee that you will catch this huge fish you speak of, but I have an excellent feeling that today is your lucky day, Sergeant Shadrach Ringer."

"Thank you, Professor Ahmed Khan."

They would both remember each other's names.

"Well, let's see if Allah respects your wishes," Shadrach said, turning back towards the brown trout that he wanted to catch. "Thank you for the blessing."

He returned to the pool and began stripping out fishing line towards the boulder.

It took a lot of concentration. When he finally fluttered his fly precisely to where he wanted it, he looked up to see what the Muslims were doing. They were gone.

Shadrach watched his slightly weighted nymph disappear beneath the water.

He slowly fingered the fly line into his hand with a slight jig of the Orvis rod.

And there it was, like a stone, tugging the line. Shadrach waited a moment, then set the hook. Let the monster run with it, away from the boulder, back towards it, then to the waterfall, and then back to the boulder.

"I've hooked a submarine," he said out loud.

He fought the fish carefully, knowing that it could snap the filament leader if he pulled too hard.

He gained some fishing line, let it run out again, gained a little more, thought for a moment that he saw it, a massive Brownie, before it made another run towards the waterfall. Then he started all over again, gaining a little line, losing less.

Suddenly he saw it, near the surface, worn out. It was a monster, probably close to nine pounds. He took his net and guided the exhausted fish into it.

"Here you are, my beauty. I think you had a heart attack. Lunch for the entire Royal Peacock dining room today."

He quickly stepped away from the stream, tying the fish onto a line and carrying it over his shoulder as he walked two miles back to the Royal Peacock Lodge, where the head chef would clean and gut it for Shadrach.

He and his wife had become friends with a dozen guests at the resort. They would all enjoy his catch. The chef's specialty at the resort was fish.

"*Allahu Akbar,*" Shadrach shouted. *God is great.* Shadrach knew that the phrase was not as simple as it seemed. In reality, Muslims only shouted it during the bullet-riddled heat of *jihad,* their holy war against the infidels.

In Afghanistan, the Muslim warriors often spat on the ground in disgust when they heard the phrase come out of the mouth of an American soldier.

They considered it an insult by infidels ignorant about the ways of the holy warriors of Islam.

Shadrach liked the phrase, and also the insult.

At lunch, he would tell their new friends at the lodge about his meeting with Professor Ahmed Khan. He would repeat the marine biologist's special and prescient blessing. And he would bore them all with a detailed description of the Battle with the Brownie at the Boulder Pool.

There was one thing that Shadrach did not notice as he returned to the lodge.

At the stream, first a few, and then many fish floated to the surface, dying.

It took a little longer for the fingerlings to expire, but their frantic wriggling displayed deadly discomfort. The older fish came to the surface, gulping for air, and then went belly up quite quickly.

At lunchtime, the chef, followed by two of his assistants, marched the beautifully poached and garnished brown trout through the dining room. The guests applauded.

"He must have lived in that dark pool for years, fed by whatever came over the falls," Shadrach told his table. The Chef stepped up to him and reached for the choicest cut of the beautifully poached fish.

"No, no," Shadrach said. "All my friends first. Please serve Sookie and me last." He looked at the people in the room. "Dig in as soon as you get it," he said. "And do NOT take it all."

By the time the chef got back to Sookie and Shadrach, people were already standing up at their tables, clutching their throats, gasping for breath, falling in agony.

"Don't touch the fish!" Shadrach shouted, but for many, it was already too late.

He frantically looked around the room, shouting for a doctor. Was anyone a nurse? Christ almighty, why hadn't he made the connection between the Muslim soldiers at the river and the men and women dying in front of his eyes?

Shadrach looked at the manager, leaning against the door to his office. He was smiling.

"You!" Shadrach shouted, pointing at the manager. He started to move towards him in the chaos. Out of the side of his vision, he saw military trucks pulling up to the front of the Central Building. The manager disappeared into his office, slamming the door.

Shadrach grabbed Sookie, and frantically pulled her towards the kitchen.

"What's going on?"

"We're about to be slaughtered," Shadrach said.

He entered the kitchen, grabbed a large knife, and stood by the back door with Sookie behind him.

Three men burst through the door, Muslim warriors, heading for the main dining area. Shadrach caught the third one by his tunic, near his neck, as the man's feet carried him forward and then extended in the air.

Shadrach slammed him to the ground, pulled the Kalashnikov AK-47 out of his hands, and thrust the knife through his heart, adding a single twist.

The two men in front of him slid to a halt, turned, and met two short bursts of fire from Shadrach's borrowed gun.

He stepped forward, took the warriors' weapons, and gave one to Sookie.

Shadrach said: "I want you to stay with me, sweetheart. Our lives are going to depend on it."

Sookie Ringer expertly checked that the AK-47 was on automatic, slapped it against her side, and followed Shadrach out the door without saying a word. Nobody was there.

They sprinted through the gardens, came to the end of the manicured property, and continued into the rough terrain beyond. As they ran in unison, crouched low, they could hear bursts of gunfire from the lodge, and then silence, and then more shots.

From a half a mile away, hidden in dense undergrowth, they watched the Muslim warriors go from rondavel to rondavel, checking each one.

Occasional bursts of gunfire drifted up to where Sookie and Shadrach hid.

They watched a young honeymoon couple dragged from their rondavel, naked. The man was on his knees. His head jerked back as they shot him point-blank. His newlywed wife threw herself on his body. They eventually killed her as well, but not right away. She screamed a lot.

"Bastards," Sookie Ringer said. "I wish you had your sniper rifle, Shadrach."

"Me too," he said.

They moved up the mountain. The terrain was rugged, and it took time, but nobody back at the compound noticed them. It would be a cold night, but they had each other, and they knew how to survive, how to stay alive in unfriendly terrain. They were a team.

Shadrach patted his fishing jacket, which he had worn to the luncheon as a badge of honor.

"I have my iPhone," he said.

"Make the call," Sookie said.

"Not yet," he said. "I want to see how much the terrorists miss us first."

"There's too many of them, Shadrach," she said. "We don't have enough ammunition." She knew what he was thinking. He was careful, but he also enjoyed going against the odds.

"I know," Shadrach said. "I just need to settle down a little." Sookie relaxed and stroked his hair. She had been through a lot with this man.

They watched the warriors milling about the compound. They saw them go into the rondavel where Shadrach and Sookie Ringer were staying, and then come out again.

They did this several times.

A man who might have been Professor Ahmed Khan came out of the Central Building. Muslim Warriors dragged the manager and park ranger behind him.

Shadrach recognized the clothing of the manager, and the small stature of the park ranger, even from a great distance. The man he thought was Ahmed Khan gestured at the rondavel in which he and Sookie had stayed. He shouted at the two men, too far off for Sookie and Shadrach to hear. He shook his fist at them. He kicked the ranger, who fell over and then tried to stand up. They beat him back to his knees.

They then battered the manager with an AK-47. He joined the park ranger, falling to his knees. After a while, Sookie and Shadrach heard the shots that killed the ranger and the manager, but they had toppled forward into the manicured grass before the sound ever reached them.

"I guess they miss us," Shadrach said.

"I want them to keep doing that," Sookie replied. "Make the call."

Chapter 6

Poisoning the Well in Africa

Homeland Security Reveals a Weapon of Mass Destruction.

George McKlane III spent the entire next day with Holly Smolkes after his father's wedding reception. Mac McKlane had missed even his father's and his new stepmother's honeymoon departure to a destination unknown. He was with Holly, in bed in his suite, laughing about nothing important, feeling almost in love when his secure cell phone buzzed and vibrated on the bureau.

He grimaced and said: "I have to take this."

He looked at the text message on the screen. It said: "Operation Poison Well: Extraction Request."

Holly watched his face turn to stone, something she had not seen in this man.

She stood and quickly dressed as Mac tapped a number on his cell phone.

His eyes watched her as she slipped on her shoes and headed towards the door.

His face remained expressionless. Holly blew him a kiss and smiled at him, but the iPhone killed sny happiness.

Mac McKlane spoke in single words, separated by answers she could not hear.

"When?" Short pause.

"Where?" Longer pause.

"Who?" He listened and nodded, then said: "I was with him in Operation Enduring Freedom."

He looked up at Holly, guarded in what he was saying.

Holly stepped into the hallway, quietly closing the door behind her. She knew she would see him again.

She liked Mac McKlane.

She also knew that business was business.

Alone in his room, Mac McKlane said, perhaps louder than necessary: "EXTRACT. Do it now. Make them safe."

There are 17 airports in the Kingdom of Lesotho, the largest being the Moshoeshoe International Airport in Maseru, named after the first monarch of Lesotho, who died in 1870. When the king died, the city was a small police camp established by the British.

Maseru had grown into a modern city of over a quarter of a million people.

It was the nation's capital.

A hangar door slowly rolled open in a white, domed building at the far end of the airport, surrounded by restricted signs and 15-foot-high chain mail fences topped with razors.

Three UH-60A Black Hawk helicopters rolled onto the tarmac. Their blades began to rotate.

One of the Black Hawks carried 11 combat troops and their equipment. The other two had six-man crews and M102 howitzers. There were no markings on the helicopters; they had more firepower than a company of boots on the ground. The UH-60A created lightning strikes, not trench warfare.

Most of the uniforms were American, but also some South African and Lesotho troops. They took off and headed northeast towards the Royal Peacock Resort and Lodge.

The United States Embassy in Lesotho knew nothing about this strike force. They might learn something later, perhaps never. No red tape existed in this unit's operations manual.

Only 24 minutes had passed since Shadrach "made the call" to Homeland Security's Central Operations in Washington, D.C.

He had spoken directly to Roberta Macumber, the Assistant Director of "Operation Poison Well." The AD immediately sent the text and opened a secure voice line to the head of the secret unit, Mac McKlane, who was at the Homestead in Hot Springs, Virginia. With the extraction in motion, the Homeland Security unit gathered to discuss critical details of the operation.

"Fifty bucks," Assistant Director Roberta Macumber said to the group in the Comm Room as they watched monitors slowly shift from Lake Victoria in eastern Africa to a small river north of Maseru, Lesotho, in southern Africa.

One man floated a 50-dollar bill into the center of a small mahogany conference table. He had bet on Burundi, probably a tributary leading into Lake Tanganyika.

More fifties followed; some of them crumpled up. Unit operatives had bet on Lake Victoria from all sides: Uganda, Kenya, and Tanzania. Only Roberta Macumber chose South Africa. She plucked a crumpled bill off the table.

It showed a Five, but nothing more when she flattened it out in front of everyone.

"This was you, right? Lake Malawi and the country of the same name?"

"Hey," the man whom she addressed said, "I'm a field operator, not a desk jockey. We try stuff. That's what we get paid for."

He forked over the remaining $45, smiling.

"And I should point out," he said, "that I moonlight for the IRS because of the crummy pay I get here. So all that money better be on your tax return, Boss."

The government paid the agents very well, and they knew it. They were settling in, letting off steam, getting ready.

Assistant Director Roberta Macumber had not bet on Lesotho – nobody had – but she had the under bet of South Africa. In the room, some people thought that Lesotho was part of the Republic of South Africa, not an independent nation born in 1966.

A few of them remembered that the South African military intervened in 1998 after suspicious voter fraud in their national elections. The intercession destroyed much of the capital city of Maseru. They rebuilt and modernized it for the people who survived.

The call placed by Shadrach Ringer did not just reach the headquarters of Homeland Security in America. It also opened a traceable signal. At the Royal Peacock Resort and Lodge in Lesotho, Dr. Ahmed Khan picked it up. Although he could not read the encrypted message, he could pinpoint its source with surprising accuracy. Suddenly, a lot of ISIL warriors were looking far up the mountainside to the exact spot where Shadrach and Sookie Ringer tried to conceal themselves behind rocks and bushes.

"They've locked onto us," Shadrach said.

"Turn off the phone."

"Can't." He was watching the screen. "They're still pretty far away from us, sweetheart."

"Just a couple of klicks," Sookie said.

"Over three, and all uphill."

"They'll be tired by the time they get near us," she said.

"Maybe even dead," he said.

They were quiet for a while, watching the leader of the ISIL terrorist group round-up and instruct his men.

"I love you, Shadrach."

He looked at her and smiled.

"But will you respect me in the morning?"

Sookie laughed, a real laugh, although nerves tempered it. Then she looked back down to the compound.

Men were starting to move into the rough terrain, heading towards them.

"I will love you forever and ever if you help me kill all these bastards," Sookie said.

"That's my girl," Shadrach said.

Then, for a long time, they did not say anything. Sookie watched the ISIL warriors climbing through the terrain.

It had taken Sookie and Shadrach over an hour and a half to climb to where they hid. Sweat soaked them, but it had now started to dry off in the afternoon sun.

"You know, Shadrach, I could never understand why ISIL chose black as a uniform. They must sweat like swine."

"Yeah, well, I don't think anyone joins ISIL to prove they're smart," Shadrach said.

Still, there was no message on his iPhone.

"They have to get a lot closer before they have a chance to tap us," Shadrach said.

"Three fifty," Sookie said. That was the effective range of the Kalashnikov AK-47 in meters, almost four football fields in length.

"We can start slowing them down from twice that distance," Shadrach said. "Be another 20 or 30 minutes."

"We've got three weapons and six magazines," Sookie said. "You probably spent most of one of yours on the dead guys in the kitchen."

Double magazines were taped together in all three of the AK-47s they had taken from the terrorists. The magazines could quickly be flipped and reinserted when one was empty.

Sookie examined all the magazines, popping them out and reinserting them. Each held 30 bullets.

Shadrach watched his iPhone.

"So we have over 150 rounds," she said.

"Make sure that the weapon is not on automatic."

"Roger that."

The AK-47 could fire 100 rounds in 60 seconds. Even on semi-auto, it would spit out 40 bullets a minute.

Shadrach's iPhone pinged. He looked at the screen, then passed it over to Sookie. It said: "15 OUT. TALK."

Sookie handed it back with a smile. "Say 'hi' from me."

Shadrach started speaking into the phone, succinctly describing their situation, their position, the terrain, estimating the numbers of ISIL warriors and their weapons. He had seen no Russian surface-to-air missiles, and none of the military vehicles had anti-aircraft machine guns attached to them.

After he had stopped talking, he waited. No more questions came. A text message said: "12 OUT. TOSS THE PHONE."

At one point in his life, Shadrach had thought about becoming a professional baseball player. He had the arm, but not the speed. He was not accurate enough to be a pitcher. He still amazed people with how far he could throw a baseball or a rock.

The iPhone was in a protected, rubber casing. It could take a beating and keep on sending.

Shadrach reared back and tossed it at the ISIL warriors creeping towards them. It flew a long way, and it landed softly on a patch of grass and bounced onto a rock shelf. He thought that it was probably still functioning.

"So now we've established our perimeter," Shadrach said. Even if the iPhone had broken, he had given enough information to the approaching helicopters to avoid any friendly fire.

He did not see the final message on the iPhone, which said: "RECORD TOSS MATE." The communications officer in the lead helicopter served in the South African Air Force.

At the Royal Peacock Resort and Lodge, a terrorist looked at his monitor and said: "The Devils are moving. They are moving very fast towards our men."

"Like birds," Dr. Ahmed Khan said, watching the screen. The iPhone movement stopped, and he immediately understood what had happened, and also what was about to happen. Khan grabbed his Second In Command, ran outside, and quickly left the area. He did not drive fast. Khan let the

SUV slowly roll out the front gates. He knew, from experience throughout the Middle East, that speed killed. Stealth survived. After about a half a mile, he began driving a little faster.

From their hiding place, Sookie said: "I think we should take a little target practice."

"Well, they're still too far away, but, yeah, you never know; we might get lucky."

They got lucky three times before the UH-60A Black Hawk helicopters roared over the hilltop behind them and swept down the mountainside.

Five miles away, Ahmed Khan watched the destruction of his ISIL unit. He had stopped his vehicle, parking it under a rocky overhang near the road.

He and his driver would wait there until nightfall, which was only two hours off. They would then drive in the dark until they hit the road back to Maseru.

At the Royal Peacock Resort and Lodge, most of the ISIL terrorists were dead or dying. It took Shadrach and Sookie about 45 minutes to reach the compound. Going down was much faster than climbing. Shadrach retrieved his iPhone along the way, smiling at the message on the screen.

"I guess the vacation's over, huh?" he said to Sookie as they approached the compound. She leaned against him. She liked a lot of the people at the resort, and they were all dead.

She and Shadrach had not met the honeymooners. The newly married couple never left their rondavel until their final, terrifying moments. They were French, from Cannes.

A United States Marine Corps major and a South African captain debriefed Shadrach and Sookie, separately in the main building. Then Shadrach and Sookie toured the enemy dead, the dying, and a few prisoners who would begin lengthy interrogations lasting years.

It took several hours to bring the bodies of warriors down from the mountainside. They were lined up on the ground in the courtyard, uncovered.

As the sun started to set, Shadrach said: "He's not here. I'm certain that he was in the compound during the slaughtering of innocent men, women, and children. But he's not here."

The Marine major looked at Sookie. "Do you agree with that, ma'am?"

"I never met him, Major," Sookie said. "And stop calling me, *ma'am*."

"I'm very sorry, Captain," he said.

He knew, from the debriefing, that she was a not-so-retired Army infantry captain, and a well-decorated one, including a Purple Heart.

"I'm the only one who put eyes on him," Shadrach said. "He told me that his name was Doctor Ahmed Khan, and he said that he was a marine biologist with the Suid-Afrikaans Water Conservation Board."

"No such Springbok," the South African Captain said. They understood that he meant the organization was fake.

"Still, that's probably his real name," the major said. "It's strange how they rarely use aliases for their given names."

Shadrach looked at all the dead people, some already zipped into black body bags, although their faces remained visible. The ISIL warriors maintained their dark motif, with black tags attached to each of them.

The innocents all had bright red body bag tags. They were in the majority. Some of the bags held two children.

Shadrach shook his head and asked the major, "Where do we go from here?"

"You're going home," the major said. Shadrach and Sookie thought that this meant returning to the Southern Highlands of Tanzania, to the town of Mbeya, where they had been for almost two years. The major added, "Back to America, to Washington."

"Really?"

"That's the orders cut from Unit Leader Mac McKlane," the Major said.

"I was under his command for eight months in Afghanistan," Shadrach said.

The Major smiled. "You still are under his command."

Shadrach pulled Sookie close to him. "And very thankful for it," he said.

In their Homeland Security command center, the team had watched events unfold, first quietly, then with clenched fists, and finally with cheering.

The Operation Poison Well Unit had already completed three successful terrorist interventions: in Sweden, Spain, and Turkey. The Maseru victory was the first one in which the extraction saved the lives of the agents who "made the call." Previous firefights counted them among the dead.

Mac McKlane received the good news in a Marine Corps helicopter bound for Washington. His cell phone buzzed. He looked at the message: "4-0, RINGERS SAFE."

He dialed Assistant Director Roberta Macumber and spoke to her about the operation. At the conclusion, he asked the AD to put two files on his desk: one for Ahmed Khan and one for a woman named Holly Smolkes, the daughter of a former CIA agent named Charles "Red" Smolkes.

The AD had heard of Charles Smolkes, but nothing about his daughter. She did not ask any questions.

Then Mac McKlane phoned his grandfather, who would not be leaving the Homestead until the following day.

"Captain Gramps," he said, using his nickname for George McKlane, "I had to leave prematurely for, well, you know, business."

"Is business good?"

"Very good."

"Glad to hear that, Mac. Listen, you're probably going to be getting a call from Sharonda saying I'm sliding fast into dangerous dementia, but before you believe what she says, you and I need to have a private talk."

Mac held the cell phone in front of him with a crooked smile, then brought it back to his ear.

"What's up, Captain Gramps?"

"We need to talk. It's about the guy who was supposed to kill me last year, but he ended up saving my life instead."

Mac McKlane was silent for a moment; then he said: "That's important, but I can't discuss it right now because of what's going on at Homeland, Gramps."

"I understand," his grandfather said. "But we need to talk az while. ."

"We will."

"And don't believe whatever Sharonda tells you."

"I won't," he lied.

Mac thought that Sharonda was one of the best things that had ever happened to the McKlane family, and he trusted her as if she were his sister.

He took an iPhone out of his carry-on bag. The device was not secure. He saw that there was a text message from Sharonda. It said: "I LOVE YOUR GRANDFATHER, BUT HE IS GOING TO GET ME KILLED. We need to talk."

Sharonda never shouted with capital letters in any of her text messages.

Mac sent a reply immediately: "I spoke to him. We will deal with it. I'm on my way back to the office. Talk to you tomorrow or the next day. Important."

Then he ordered some flowers online for delivery to Holly's suite at the Homestead in Hot Springs.

He requested an attached note that said: "You and I are 'to be continued.' Love, Mac."

He thought about the next to the last word of the message for some time before settling on it.

"What the hell." He clicked on the "complete transaction" button for flowers sent via iPhone.

Then he sat back and relaxed for the first time since the initial call from his unit.

Shadrach Ringer was safe. And his wife. What was her name? Sookie. Army brass. Tough and nice looking.

And the unit was still batting a thousand: four wins and no losses. And this time, the ground team survived.

Sooner or later, Mac knew they would suffer a setback. ISIL was not stupid.

He thought back to the first day that he had introduced the latest threat from ISIL to his unit at Homeland Security. He called the entire team, only nine men and two women at the time, into the conference room.

They all sat around the table, which spotlighted a black, one-foot cube. One of the agents reached for it.

"STOP," Mac ordered. "Do not touch that box." The agent backed off and sat down quickly.

Director Mac McKlane walked over and very deliberately locked the conference room door.

He closed all the privacy shades on the thick, bullet-proof glass windows. ISIL logos and Arabic slogans covered the black cube. He then took masking tape and sealed the doorway, which took time, and he said nothing.

"I am about to show you the latest ISIL weapon of mass destruction," Mac said. "It's live. It's real. Do not touch it, whatever you do."

Very slowly, he lifted the cube, revealing its contents: a three-quarter-filled glass of what looked like water.

Nobody said anything.

"There's enough poison in that glass to kill every man and woman in this room," Director McKlane said. "And it can do it 20 or 30 times. One drop on your body, anywhere, and you will be dead within eight seconds."

He pointed at the glass, tucking the cube under his arms.

"It will be the longest and most painful eight seconds of your life."

Everyone stared at what looked like water, and most people were leaning slightly away from it.

Director McKlane took the black cube that had covered it and carefully started to lower the ISIL box over the glass.

An edge of the cube caught on the glass, and it spilled across the table. Pandemonium broke out.

People splattered by the poison screamed, men as well as women. Several tried to escape, but the door was locked. Three people reached for their cell phones, two dialing "911" and one phoning her husband.

Four people did not flinch at all, one of them being Mac McKlane. He picked up the glass and drained a few remaining drops into his mouth.

"You bastard!"

"Son of a bitch!"

"That's not funny!"

"Fuck you very much, Mac."

A few people laughed, but none with joy.

"I'll admit it's a bad joke," Director McKlane said. "But with a purpose. The truth is that ISIL has developed a potent poison with which they intend to destroy our water supply."

People calmed down and took their seats.

"Can we get some bottled water in here?" a woman asked. "I'm dying of thirst."

Another agent followed up with: "I gotta call my broker; I gotta buy a lot of shares of Crystal Springs."

Mac McKlane let them decompress; then he said:

"We are all professionals in this room. Consider how we just reacted to what we thought was a deadly poison. Now think what normal civilians will do if they are threatened with ISIL poisoning the water of this nation. Or any of our allies, or even our enemies in the war on terrorism."

"Just the threat itself is a weapon of mass destruction," the Assistant Director said. She was one of the four people who did not flinch when Director McKlane knocked over the glass of poison.

"Precisely," Mac said. "We need to neutralize the threat, the poison, and the bastards who want to knock us back to the Stone Age. We need to have strike forces throughout the world that can react in minutes to this threat, and we need to do it covertly. We need to lie to people and cover our tracks and somehow keep all this away from the media. In the end, we may not succeed in keeping things secret. But we are the first and the last defense against this threat. From this day forward, this team at Homeland Security is the Operation Poison Well Unit."

He paused and looked around the room. "I better not see that moniker in any newspaper or on any televisions, websites, iPhones, or blogs."

"There's going to be an awful lot of Flint, Michigans, out there, boss," one man said.

He referred to the State of Emergency declared by President Obama on the weekend in mid-January of 2016.

Toxic amounts of lead in drinking water exposed thousands of residents to life-threatening dangers in Genesee County, Michigan.

"Not if we can stop them, kill them, and clean up their mess beforehand," the Director told his unit of Homeland Security. "Starting today, starting right now, we will create anti-terrorism cells throughout the world, and I don't want anybody to know about it."

He looked again at each person in the room, locking his eyes on them one at a time. Then he continued.

"It will not be easy. People will find out about us. And we will lie to their faces if we have to, even if they are senators and congressmen. What we do and how we do it will die with every terrorist we kill. We can take prisoners." He paused. "But it will not be a priority."

"Are we all eventually going to go to jail?" a woman asked, raising her hand as high as she could above her head. "I don't think the Constitution of the United States covers this one. Nor does the Uniform Code of Military Justice."

The Director did not answer right away. The silence of the room grew uncomfortable.

Finally, Director George "Mac" McKlane said: "I know that if we do not do this, then our entire world will go to Hell. All of it. Everybody. Everything. Everyone we love."

‑‑‑‑‑‑‑‑�404ᴴᴢ‑‑‑‑‑‑‑‑

The Lesotho News Agency reported the terrorist attack at the Royal Peacock Resort and Lodge north of Maseru 24 hours after it occurred. **TERRORISTS SLAUGHTER TOURISTS** made the front page of the Lesotho *Times*. The Sunday *Express* devoted several pages to the event. Many of the photos were stock shots of radical Islamic terrorists operating in Africa.

The Royal Peacock Resort and Lodge was under repair before any news agency or media ever got there. The physical damage to the resort did not seem significant. Four new male peacocks and two hens were strutting around the compound, the males fanning their tails. A new resort manager suggested that the lodge would re-open in a matter of weeks — he seemed somewhat military in bearing.

Nevertheless, a handful of radical Islamic terrorists had ruthlessly slaughtered 34 visitors to the Kingdom of Lesotho.

The world would mourn those who died at the Royal Peacock Resort and Lodge.

Their families would all be treated sympathetically and with great generosity.

Any additional legal action by the bereaved would result in their reimbursement disappearing into a lengthy quagmire of diplomacy. Everyone settled quickly.

All of the terrorists died, it was reported, at the hands of the Lesotho military, which acted decisively, bravely, and quickly. A military spokesperson confirmed that not a single survivor was available for interrogation, but ISIL was definitely behind the attack.

The Ministry of Social Development lamented the loss of innocent civilian life and assured everyone that the Kingdom of Lesotho was a peaceful, beautiful country, plagued like the rest of the world by jihadist madmen.

The minister praised the heroism of the Lesotho military, not mentioning the police force, which, once again, was at odds with the armed forces. The attempted coup of 2014 had not yet faded into forgiveness.

With no surviving terrorists to interrogate, the Lesotho military brought charges against many so-called insurgents, some of them already under house arrest. Quite a few were members of the Lesotho police force.

A spokesperson promised "the surgical removal of the cancer of terrorism from the Kingdom of Lesotho." Meanwhile, international aid poured into the country from a caring world community that universally condemned what had happened.

Quite a bit of the donated food and money made it through the bureaucracy that usually snacked on foreign aid.

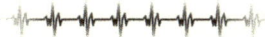

───────────────

In a separate event, two lorries ladened with chlorine had collided on a bridge north of Maseru. Both drivers died.

The contents of the lorries spilled into the river, and the fish kill resulting from it was extensive.

The military would deliver bottled water to towns and villages downstream for many months.

Quite a few civilians would die before the water supply finally returned to normal.

The chlorine company promised generous restitution to anyone who suffered from the unfortunate chemical spill.

The death of loved ones in a society that placed a relatively low value on human life produced an unexpected financial blessing to the family members who survived.

There was quite a spike in the number of deaths among senior citizens, many of whom went swimming in the toxic stream against their will.

Chapter 7

The Price of Falling in Love

An Afghan Hero Makes a Terrible Connection.

Holly Smolkes returned to Delray Beach the same day flowers arrived at her suite at the Homestead in Hot Springs. When she read the love note from Mac McKlane attached to the flower delivery, a noise escaped from her that she had never heard before. She giggled. She did not realize that she possessed such a sound. She glanced around her suite, making sure that she was alone. Mac was gone. She saw no reason why she should stay in Virginia another day.

"You are not a schoolgirl," she told her image in the full-length mirror.

She reread Mac's note. She giggled once more. Okay, so love made you stupid. It felt nice. Then she packed quickly for her return to Delray Beach, Florida, where she lived and operated her charter boat, the *Wholly Mackerel.*

As soon as she got back, she dropped everything off at her condo except for the vase and flowers and went to check the boat. She sat on the deck for a while, trading pleasantries with some of her neighbors. She scanned her social media.

Someone on LinkedIn wanted to hire the *Wholly Mackerel* for three days of fishing, with maybe a run over to the Islands. It was a trip she often made. She grabbed a boilerplate reply from a previous customer saved in her word processor, personalized it, checked that it read smoothly with the necessary name changes, and then she sent it. She did something similar on her professional Facebook page for two different one-day charters.

Word of mouth had an electronic taste in the Digital Age, and Holly loved it.

She got a call from Angelo Rossellini, making sure that she made it back from Virginia with no problems.

"So you liked Mac McKlane?" he asked.

"I think I am in love with him, Angelo."

"Ah, that would be magnificent, but how do you know it is love? It is a huge four-letter word."

"It's I know its only four letters long, Angelo Rossellini. Do you know how I know?"

"You counted them?"

"Stop it, Angelo. Do you know how I know that I love him?" she said.

He waited.

She waited.

"Okay, how?" he finally said.

"He makes my toes tickle."

"Oh, my God," Angelo said.

They both laughed.

She turned off her cell phone, untied the boat, and cruised up through Gulf Stream to the Boynton Inlet, then out into the ocean: light chop, blue sky, increasingly pink clouds in the late afternoon as the sun dropped behind the city. It was a perfect day. Only Mac McKlane standing next to her on the bridge could make it any better.

Her phoned pinged: "unknown number." Out of habit, she opened and closed the line, canceling a nuisance call. Then she thought perhaps it might be Mac. There was no way of telling.

She turned the boat back towards the inlet. After a few minutes, an unknown number pinged again. Holly opened the line. "Whatever you are selling, I don't want any, and I already gave at the office. Who is this?" She made her voice as playful as possible in case it was Mac, but she still sounded severe.

A voice she did not recognize, but one that she knew, said: "*As-salāmu'Alaykum, Malalai.*"

She throttled down the engines, turned off the boat, drifting in the dusk.

In English, she said: "And upon you peace. Who is this?" She felt suddenly cold.

"This is your brother, Ahmed." He spoke with a perfect English accent, in a voice much deeper than the one she remembered from their childhood three decades earlier.

"It has been a long time, Malalai," Ahmed Khan said.

"My name is Holly," she said.

"Your name is Abira Khan," her twin brother said. "And you are *Malalai*. You are a holy warrior of your people, Abira Khan. *As-salāmu-'Alaykum, Malalai.*"

"*Wa' alaykumu s-salām,*" she replied.

—─╫╾╾╫╫╾╫╫╾╫╫╾╫╫╾╫╫╾—

Sitting at his desk at Homeland Security, Mac McKlane put his hand on one of two folders. It was thick. Mac looked at the photo of the subject, and then he started to read every page of Ahmed Khan's dossier. He was just getting to the part about the Abu Kamal raid in Syria in 2008 when his AD, Roberta Macumber, tapped on his open door and stepped into the office.

"Welcome back, Mac," she said. "Everyone in the unit thinks you're a genius."

He raised his eyebrows. "Why?"

"Nobody can quite figure out how you put those two files together, how you made the connection."

Mac McKlane stared at her.

She said: "The Ringers are landing at Andrews in a few hours and we've arranged a Survivors Party for them at four o'clock. I've never met them. What are they like?"

"They're the best we have. We need a lot more like them," Mac said.

"When can we talk about those files?" she asked.

"In a little while, Roberta. I'm not quite ready. I have to think about it."

"Let me know when you're ready," Roberta said.

"Thanks, close the door on the way out, please."

"The unit wants me to tape this to your door," she said. She held up a goofy picture of Professor Albert Einstein and the headline: **GENIUS AT PLAY**.

"Don't do that," Mac said. "You'll know why later."

Roberta Macumber left, closing the door, unsure of the conversation she had just had with the Boss. Director Mac McKlane hardly ever closed his door. Once shut, it would only be opened by a unit member if there was an emergency.

Mac looked at the Holly Smolkes dossier, which was quite thin. He read everything within minutes. Then Mac reread it. He could not believe it, but he did not question the information. Holly Smolkes' original name was Abira Khan, and she was the twin sister of Ahmed Khan, the ISIL leader who had led the terrorist attack in Lesotho. Holly's natural-born brother was responsible for the slaughter of 34 men, women, and children vacationing at a luxury resort in the Drakensberg Mountains in Africa

Mac returned to Ahmed Khan's folder. He read about the Abu Kamal raid in Syria in October of 2008. The only American casualty was Charles "Red" Smolkes, the man who had adopted Abira Khan several decades earlier. Her adoptive father had her name legally changed to Holly Smolkes in 1989. She became a naturalized American citizen the following year.

Mac returned to Holly's file and read it a third time. She had no police record, although she was part of an assault and battery lawsuit that was subsequently dropped by a law firm named Lewis, Herald, Smythe, and Fiddwick.

Her dossier also flagged the file of Angelo Rossellini, a real estate developer who helped various Federal agencies on an *ad hoc* basis.

Mac returned to Ahmed Khan's dossier. He was the probable killer of Red Smolkes. In the helicopter in which Charles Smolkes died, an eye witness had seen an ISIL operative on the rooftop firing his AK-47 at them. The ISIL terrorist screamed "Malalai!" repeatedly, loud enough to be heard over the stealth helicopter blades during the clandestine operation to capture Abu Ghadiya, a crucial logistical kingpin of ISIL in Syria.

The name "Malalai" was a reference to a famous female warrior from an earlier century in Afghanistan. It was cross-referenced to the personnel file of the deceased and decorated CIA agent, Charles "Red" Smolkes.

Mac leaned forward and toggled a button on his desk. Assistant Director Roberta Macumber answered.

"Now we can talk," Mac said. "Just the two of us."

When the assistant director entered his office, he asked her to close the door.

They moved to comfortable chairs around a coffee table that had a full pot and cups waiting. Mac poured out two cups, black with no sugar.

"I have an update on the file," Roberta said.

"Okay."

"We just had cell phone contact between Ahmed Khan and his twin sister. We'll have a transcript in a few hours, but we know that Ahmed Khan initiated the call."

The call came from a village on the outskirts of Johannesburg, South Africa.

The location was a small, nine-acre estate in Witkoppen owned by a German absentee landlord.

"By the time our people got there, Khan vanished," Roberta Macumber continued. "They interviewed a gardener and a cook, but they knew nothing. Neither one of them would admit that they knew Professor Ahmed Khan. The absentee landlord has no record and is under no surveillance by any of our friends in Germany."

"Okay. Fast work, Roberta."

"So please tell me how you made the connection between the two of them, Mac? How did you do that?"

Mac thought about it, considering the danger of secrets, then answered: "In bed."

It was Roberta's turn to say: "Okay. Fast work, Mac."

Mac McKlane did not smile. He told Roberta the entire story, start to finish, leaving out nothing, not even Holly Smolkes' unusual ability at lovemaking.

Although anyone in the Poison Well Unit could lie to someone outside of their group, they had no secrets within the organization.

Every man and woman told the truth about any operation in which they were involved: no politics, no egos, no positioning, no cover-up, and no bullshit. They all understood that their lives, and the existence of millions, depended on it.

When Mac finished, Assistant Director Roberta Macumber nodded and smiled.

"This is fantastic, Mac. You just became a double agent. I doubt if Holly Smolkes has any idea of what we know about her, and even if she does, we can use it to our advantage."

"Did you hear the part about how I thought maybe I loved her?" Mac said.

"I did," Roberta Macumber answered. "You are going to make a perfect double agent, Mac, and with your permission, I will run you myself."

Mac laughed, but it was not a very pleasant sound.

Two hours later, the Survivor's Party for the Ringers took place. Roberta had a private meeting with Shadrach and Sookie afterward.

She asked the Ringers if they would join the Poison Well Unit full time. They were considered stringers, part-time volunteers in Tanzania, seconded to Homeland Security through the Peace Corps. Almost by mistake, they had become the first team to "make the call" and survive.

They both agreed to join the unit immediately.

The assistant director apologized for the absence of Director Mac McKlane in their discussions. Mac had to catch a flight to Boca Raton, where his grandfather George McKlane lived, a veteran of the Korean Conflict.

Early in the morning, Holly left her condo and jogged south a few miles along the beach towards Ocean Dunes Park. Then she turned north again and exited the shoreline at Ingraham Avenue. Holly cooled off slow-jogging and then walking. She approached the Intracoastal Waterway.

Holly moored the *Wholly Mackerel* at The Yacht Club at Delray Beach. As she approached her boat, she saw someone sitting in one of the removable-mounted fish-fighting chairs on the aft deck.

She was confident that she had no charter planned for today. As she got closer, she realized it was Mac McKlane, and she felt her heart in her chest.

She wondered if he had seen the flowers he sent, arranged in the salon, still with his note attached. She had carried them aboard her flight home, upgrading to First Class to make sure the airline did not give her a tough time.

Mac swiveled in the fighting chair and smiled at her.

"To be continued," she said, jumping aboard and wrapping her arms around him as he stood to greet her. "I am sweating from my morning jog, but I swear I don't stink. I never stink. And you make my toes tickle."

"I love sweaty women," he said, holding her tight. He thought for a moment that maybe he did love this woman. And he knew it would not matter in the end.

"I have a wonderful little shower on the starboard side of the salon," she said. "Do you want to take a shower with me, Mac McKlane?"

"Since I've known you," he said, "that's the dumbest question you've ever asked."

They both laughed, and he followed her down a few steps into the salon, and afterward into the stateroom, where she told him to be quiet and not to rock the boat too much because she didn't want the neighbors to start spreading bad rumors about her.

The vessels on either side of the *Wholly Mackeral* were empty, so it didn't matter much when he broke her rules.

Afterward, they sat out on the deck and had some coffee. It was another perfect October day in Florida, although it would probably rain late in the afternoon.

"No butterflies are flapping their wings in Africa," Mac said, and Holly wrinkled her forehead, and then understood.

"A butterfly in Sierra Leone flaps its wings, and a hurricane in Florida is born," she said. "Why are you looking at me like that, Mac?"

He seemed a bit intense.

"I'm memorizing you, inch by inch," he said, realizing he had to be careful.

"Oh, I think I'm going to enjoy that."

Silence lay comfortably between them for some time. Holly asked Mac if he wanted to go out on the ocean for a while, noting that they could always return before any bad weather came.

"Yes," he said.

She jumped off the boat, untied it quickly, jumped back aboard, and climbed the ladder to the bridge. Mac followed.

The twin motors throbbed to life, and she moved the boat smoothly towards the Boynton Inlet, then out into the ocean.

He watched her. She loved what she was doing. She cut back the engines so Mac could hear her easily, although Mac pressed against her.

"Your grandfather was on this boat once," she said.

"Really?" Mac said.

She looked at him. "Yes, and he tried to kill me."

"What are you talking about?" Mac said, stepping back.

She laughed. "It wasn't your grandfather," she said. "But he chartered the boat under the name of George McKlane. He was going to kill me and steal the boat, take it to the Islands, and disappear. His real name was Anthony Silberg, and he stole a lot of money from your father's new wife's real estate company."

Mac McKlane knew the story, but nothing about the attempt to steal Holly Smolkes boat.

"Anthony Silberg," he said.

"That's the guy. He was pretty tough. He came aboard using your grandfather's name. Angelo Rossellini scared him overboard before he could do any damage. Silberg was an outstanding swimmer."

"Angelo is an old guy," Mac said, a little surprised.

"Not when he has a speargun in his hands," Holly said.

Mac shook his head.

"What happened to Silberg?"

"He jumped overboard and swam ashore. Last time I saw him, he was stumbling through the Sea Grapes on that beach way over there."

She motioned to the shoreline of Highland Beach on the border of Boca Raton, south of Delray.

"You've led an interesting life, Miss Smolkes."

"You have a lot to learn about me, Mister McKlane. It might take years." She gave him a very sloppy kiss.

Mac laughed. *Well, I already know a lot more about you than you think, Abira Khan.* He had a hard time deciding whether or not he was enjoying himself.

Chapter 8

The Enemy of My Friend

The Search for a Terrorist in a Forest of Infidels

Captain George McKlane was in the Birdroom, a sunny alcove parallel to the pool and deck of his multi-million dollar home on the Intracoastal Waterway in Boca Raton, Florida. The only birds in the sunroom were 20 original Audubon prints, each one in identical 41x28-inch, vertical, mahogany frames. The beautifully drawn birds lined the interior wall.

Sharonda gently awakened George. Her husband, Samuel, was standing behind her, and Mac McKlane joined the group staring down at the older man. It took the Korean War hero a moment to get his bearings and speak.

With a smile, he asked: "Am I under arrest?"

"You should be," Sharonda said, but also with a smile.

"So, how are you feeling, Captain Gramps?" Mac asked.

"I didn't drink enough Guinness at the wedding. When you're Irish and old, it's better than a blood transfusion. I could use one right now. How are you, Mac?"

Sharonda left to get him a room-temperature bottle of Guinness and a mug. Only George could pour it properly.

"Sharonda said you were trying to get her killed," Mac said. "What's that about."

"She exaggerates."

"Not much," Sharonda said from the kitchen.

"And she has the ears of a cat," George whispered.

"Tell me about it," Samuel said.

"I scratch much worse than I bite," Sharonda said, handing George his Guinness and a mug. Everyone watched the Captain pour the dark brown liquid into his glass. He did not spill any, and he formed a perfect, thin head of foam on the bitter brew, but his hands trembled slightly, something which was new.

They all sat down. Samuel handed Mac a picture taken from the second-floor War Room, where George mothballed the memories of his life.

"Jackson 'Smartass' Petersson," George said. "Jackson was going to be a great journalist after Korea. Best shot in the company. He didn't even need a scope on his M1 rifle to be a sniper. He saved a lot of Marines before he died in a firefight during a whiteout on Hill 1081. Snowed like hell all day long."

"You remember the Hill?"

"Hell, I remember every sound, every shot. Smartass died on December 7th, 1950. He's my Pearl Harbor."

In the War Room on the second floor, 49 framed "Thank You" notes lined one wall, each one containing a letter from the surviving family of a Marine who died under his command.

Mac looked at the frame in his hands, the 50th framed note. He studied the picture of a Marine Corporal in the lower, left-hand corner. He read the carefully written letter from a wife named Ernestine, who was pregnant and would never have a chance to see her child in the arms of her husband. Mac sighed.

"Turn it over," Sharonda said.

On the back was a message in the same schoolgirl cursive handwriting. Ernestine ended it with: "Take no one else from my family."

"She wrote that 65 years after the original message," Sharonda explained.

"Ernestine is dead," Captain George said.

"And her grandson almost killed us three days ago," Sharonda told Mac.

"He missed us on purpose," George said. "Just the way he did when he was supposed to kill me a year ago."

"Do you think he saved your life again, Gramps?"

Mac had heard his grandfather talk about the failed attempt on his life before.

Separately, his father, Brigadier General George McKlane, had also spoken of the incident.

Captain George answered his grandson's question.

"He has spared my life twice. His grandfather did so even more times."

"I'm going to go get a Guinness, and then we're going to talk about this," Mac McKlane said.

He went into the kitchen and returned with the drink and a mug. He poured it perfectly. His hands were rock steady. He took a sip. Then he said:

"I think you — each of you — need to tell me the whole story. We'll start with you, Samuel. Also, I would remind everyone that I am the Director of an extraordinary unit at the Department of Homeland Security."

And just like that, everything became serious.

Torbjorn Petersson shot the cowbell on the side of his cabin from about 100 feet up the ravine.

He had no intention of killing the person who had taken the three 3.34-inch Remington 700 bullets off the hood of the black SUV. He had watched the old guy bow to the forest with the rounds in his hand, clearly understanding the threat of fragging.

Torbjorn knew the name of the old man, and he would honor his grandmother's wishes to protect the commanding officer of his long-dead grandfather, Corporal Jackson "Smartass" Petersson.

Torbjorn had no idea of the identity of the two black people who had accompanied Captain George McKlane on their expedition to Leatherwood Farm.

After remaining in the forest for 15 minutes, Torbjorn walked across the gravel driveway and into the log cabin. On the floor of the entryway, he picked up a copy of the "Thank You" note that his grandmother Ernestine Petersson had sent to George McKlane over 65 years earlier.

On the back, in handwriting that was difficult to read, there was an incomplete message of condolence that included two questions:

"Who ordered you to kill me?"

"Was it Silberg?"

Torbjorn understood how McKlane had tracked him down. The message of his grandmother on the back of the original Thank You note which he had mailed back to Boca Raton a year earlier spotlighted Petersson's involvement in the bungled "hit" in Florida.

McKlane wanted to know who had ordered the murder, but Torbjorn had no idea.

The anonymous nature of his business guaranteed connections remained invisible.

Torbjorn did not know anyone named Silberg, although a few hours in his computer room revealed that a Boca Raton real estate broker with that name had stolen millions in escrow funds from a company called Accelerated Realty Sales. The theft occurred around the same time that he tried NOT to kill Captain George McKlane.

Torbjorn spent much of the night acquiring information surrounding the Boca Raton event. He fell asleep and woke up in the blacked-out computer room. He did not know what had opened his eyes.

He came out of the room slowly, his M2010 sniper rifle in the lead. He realized it was dawn. He heard the rooster crow. He remembered that he had chores to complete: milk the cows, feed the chickens, and throw corn slop into the pigs' trough.

At least all the autumn harvesting was done.

Cautiously, he checked the driveway, expecting to see State Police cars or the Bath County Sheriff's wagon. He saw nothing. He crept out the door and slipped into the woods.

He watched daybreak develop, the fog lifting off the Jackson River.

Everything seemed normal.

He spent several hours doing his chores, always with his sniper's weapon within easy reach, continually looking at the entry to the farm at the top of the farthest pasture.

Nobody appeared. No vehicles rattled across the metal cattle guard at the open gate.

Torbjorn recognized that he might lose control of his life. The money that he had in offshore accounts would not save him unless he fled the country, giving up the farm, accepting the eminent domain that had killed his grandmother. But he remained too angry to run and hide.

He knew that if the authorities put him under a microscope, the best he could hope for would be witness protection. But he had no information with which to bargain for a deal. He might help state and federal agents close the books on quite a few unsolved murders, but in every case, the finger of guilt would point to the same trigger man, himself.

Torbjorn used the rest of the day to expand his knowledge of the Boca Raton incident. When he finished, he had connected many, but not all of the dots.

He knew that Captain McKlane's son, a Brigadier General in the Marine Corps, had recently married the broker at Accelerated Realty Sales, a woman named Martha Krumble. She replaced the crooked broker named Silberg, who had disappeared with all the escrow money. Anthony Silberg remained alive, according to the Federal Bureau of Investigation.

Captain McKlane's son, the Brigadier General, had married Krumble at The Homestead in Hot Springs, Virginia, a few days earlier. That might explain why Captain George McKlane was snooping around the Petersson farm. Curiosity, combined with convenience, was too great a temptation.

Three days passed with no repercussions from McKlane's visit and retreat. Torbjorn relaxed, but not much.

On one of his printers in the computer room, he scanned a copy of the chicken scratches that the older man had written in his note of condolence.

Torbjorn added a single sentence confirming that the instigator of the hit was Silberg and that Torbjorn had no knowledge of the man's whereabouts. He snail-mailed the letter to George McKlane in Boca Raton.

Torbjorn had no idea if what he wrote was right, but its logic might keep authorities out of his back yard.

〜〜〜〜〜〜〜〜〜〜

The reputation of Ahmed Khan among ISIL's leadership faltered after the disappearance of Abu Bakr al-Baghdadi in June of 2016. Some of the funds supporting him also vanished. Baghdadi had been Ahmed Khan's champion.

Khan had achieved notoriety throughout ISIL's commanders as the man who said: "In a forest of infidels every tree looks the same."

Ahmed Kahn would use the talents of non-Muslim malcontents to advance the tactical terror of ISIL throughout the world. Not all of ISIL's leaders found comfort in this approach. Many considered it irreverent. Some went so far as to brand it as blasphemy.

The strikes against Western values that led to the murder of 34 infidels in southern Africa helped repair Ahmed Kahn's reputation and some of his funding as well.

The park ranger who helped Ahmed Kahn set up the operation at the Royal Peacock Resort and Lodge was a Christian who had been forced out of a high-ranking position in the Lesotho Police Force several years earlier.

The manager of the lodge was a Christian landowner who had most of his property confiscated following the 2014 attempted coup in Lesotho.

Neither infidel involved in the Royal Peacock slaughter received credit for the attack.

Both had died at the hands of ISIL warriors. Ahmed claimed he had killed one of them himself.

The credit for the attack fell squarely on the shoulders of ISIL. Ahmed Kahn had predicted this to his leaders in the early stages of planning. The infidel's forces, who subsequently destroyed the ISIL terror cell had managed, however, to minimize the fear of a poisoned water supply.

The existence of the strike force disturbed ISIL. Similar military groups had wiped out successful terrorist cells in Sweden, Spain, and Turkey following the successful slaughter of non-Muslim men, women, and children.

"Now we know that the Devil is waiting for us," Ahmed Khan told the ISIL leadership in Iraq four days after the attack in Lesotho. "We have been slow to learn from their reaction. Yet, it always has been the same. I stand before you because I knew it was coming. You have not given me the weapons our brothers need to turn every counterattack into infidel slaughter. If I had surface-to-air missiles, our success would be far greater."

"And how do we manufacture these missiles?" one of Ahmed's detractors asked.

It was a stupid question, but Ahmed knew that he should not embarrass his critic.

"I have asked Allah for guidance on this," Ahmed said.

"And what did Allah tell you?" another leader asked. He was one of Ahmed's supporters, a Chechen named Omar.

Dropping his gaze to the floor, Ahmed said: "He told me to look to Benghazi, to request the help of our Muslim brothers in Al-Qaeda."

In August of 2013, following the Benghazi attack in Libya, the U.S. State Department shut down 19 embassies in the Middle East. One of the rumored reasons for doing so was the theft of almost 400 surface-to-air missiles, which subsequently fell into the hands of Al-Qaeda.

Many of the weapons had been recovered by American, French, British, German, and Israeli organizations, sometimes operating together, often alone.

By the summer of 2016, over half the surface-to-air missiles had been recovered by NATO allies; they were in friendly hands, although not always returned to America. Terrorists had used a few of them in attacks in Syria. Over 150 of them remained "lost."

The meeting in Iraq went well for Ahmed Khan, and following his closing comment to the leadership, they fully restored all of his funding. They had asked: "Where will our next Devil attack occur?" That was how they referred to the use of infidels in their terrorist acts.

Ahmed Khan looked at each man in the room. Then he spat on the floor and answered with one word.

"America."

They stood. Even the doubters applauded. Ahmed Khan feigned humility, confident that he would soon take his place in the inner circle of ISIL leadership.

Later that night, he sat in front of a computer and digested more information about American citizens who hated their government. He had been doing this, on and off, for many months. The Devil state always organized information correctly, and often publicly, although Ahmed Kahn had no problem hacking resources in America that promised their customers high personal security.

In the summer of 2016, Ahmed Kahn had discovered the injustice of something called eminent domain. It allowed the American government to take a person's property away from him, just as the Lesotho government had stolen the property of the manager at the Royal Peacock Resort and Lodge. That was what led Ahmed Kahn to the soft target of the Peacock Resort in the first place. The fact that the resort advertised a natural trout stream, easily poisoned, sealed the fates of 34 men, women, and children, all infidels. It also killed hundreds, perhaps a thousand people who lived downstream, although ISIL did not get credit for those deaths. By concealing ISIL's water-poisoning approach with a chemical spill, the enemy had stolen the facts, which were justifiably due to the Islamic State.

The eminent domain became a red flag for Ahmed Khan. Most of the people subjected to it lost their property to government buildings, or private railroads, or public highways. Sometimes it was for community safety or public use. Occasionally, water rights entered the picture, but not often, although a push towards a clean water infrastructure might change that.

Ahmed Kahn could not remember exactly when he discovered Lake Moomaw and the Gathright Dam.

Although he did not realize it at the time, his snooping in cyberspace revealed the eminent domain affecting the Peterssons months before the "Virginia Landowner's Bill of Rights" landed in the rusty mailbox at the entrance to Leatherwood Farms.

Ahmed Kahn studied the layout, the location, and the plans for Lake Moomaw. He pored over and printed aerial shots from Google Earth.

The Jackson River snaked through the Petersson farm.

A trout club was just a few miles upstream.

It was a perfect, soft target for ISIL's attempt to poison the well in America.

What made the Petersson eminent domain ideal, however, was the secret emails exchanged among the authorities who had earmarked the property for condemnation. The Tennessee Valley Authority said that it would condemn all but the mountaintops on the 526-acre farm near Hot Springs, Virginia.

The TVA warned Torbjorn Petersson that Lake Moomaw would put Leatherwood Farms underwater.

They were not telling the truth.

Ahmed Kahn hacked all of the undisclosed emails.

He printed them out.

Torbjorn Petersson, in the vernacular of America, was getting screwed, and the farmer knew nothing about it.

Petersson was an ex-Marine who had been a peacekeeper in Afghanistan, the homeland of Ahmed Kahn. The world was a small place. Kahn praised Allah for the opportunity to make it much more dangerous for anyone who was not a Muslim.

He felt quite confident that Allah had revealed to him the right invisible infidel in America's forest of infidels.

Chapter 9
Secret Admirers and Admirers of Secrets

Slipping Through the Cracks in Homeland Security

Holly Smolkes knew that someone was following and photographing her. She called Angelo Rossellini and asked him to find out who. In less than two hours, Angelo confirmed that her secret admirer existed and that he had met with the Homeland Director, Mac McKlane.

Angelo Rossellini wanted to know something.

"Why would the new love of your life have you under surveillance, Holly?"

"I don't know," Holly said. "I guess Mister McKlane feels that our love should have no secrets," Holly said.

"Be careful," Angelo said. He sighed, then added, "I am not in a position to protect you on this, Holly Smolkes. Do you understand me?"

Holly felt something cold inside her. He never used her last name like that. "Are you saying I am on my own?"

"Yes, you are." The words carried a threat that she had never expected to hear from her benefactor. She felt shocked.

"I will never do anything to hurt you, Angelo."

"No, you won't," Angelo answered. He sounded angry.

Holly ended the silence that followed by saying: "You have always been a father to me, Angelo, and I love you."

She cut the call without waiting for an answer, knowing that there would be none. She also knew that her life was probably in danger. Angelo Rossellini had suddenly, and unexpectedly, distanced himself from her.

She had seen him do this with other people when he felt a threat to his empire and his power.

It never ended well for the person offending Rossellini.

Holly had taken several of his designated enemies on their final cruise as part of the "wet" work that Angelo commissioned her to do.

Angelo trusted no one, a lesson he taught Holly. It was the reason that she kept a detailed and secret dossier on him and his activities for many years.

The first entry was 15 years old.

Holly had always been surprised that Angelo shared so much information with her, especially in the last five years.

She documented, for example, where the escrow funds thief, Anthony Silberg, was caught and buried after Rossellini had missed killing Silberg with a speargun. Silberg had jumped off the *Wholly Mackerel* and made it to the beach. He was captured by Rossellini's men in a parking lot as he struggled through the sea grapes bordering the shoreline.

Holly knew that tons of cement hid Silberg beneath the recently completed Rossellini Towers in Miami.

The Feds still thought Silberg was alive.

The government spent a lot of money chasing the phantom of Anthony Silberg. Angelo fabricated and kept the ghost alive, all over the world. It laundered a lot of money.

Angelo ended up with all of the escrowed funds, plus he collected insurance on the loss suffered by Accelerated Realty Sales. Why did Angelo share such information with Holly?

Rossellini often told her that she was "the son he always wanted." His son, Roberto, was a fool incapable of running his father's empire. All of Rossellini's fellow crime bosses agreed with this.

Holly now realized that the information in her secret folder could save her life.

After she had hung up on Rossellini, Holly phoned Homeland Director Mac McKlane on the secret number he had given to her. He answered immediately.

As dispassionately as possible, she said: "You don't need surveillance on me, Mac."

"I think I do," Mac said. He laughed. "But maybe I need a better private investigator following you."

This statement was followed by silence until she asked: "So, are you divorcing me, Mac McKlane? Don't we have to, and I don't know, get married first?"

Mac laughed again.

She was intelligent; he had to give her that.

"Why don't we sit down, and then we can talk about it?" he said.

"Meet me at the *Wholly Mackerel*," Holly answered.

It took him 35 minutes to get there from his grandfather's house in Boca Raton.

She was waiting for him on the deck, with an unopened, slightly chilled Guinness and a mug. He came aboard and sat in the removable-mounted seat next to hers.

"Deep-sea fishermen call these fighting chairs," she said. "Are we going to have our very first fight?"

"I hope not," Mac said.

"Want to take a trip on the ocean?" she asked.

"I'd rather stay here, tied to the dock."

Since identifying Holly Smolkes as Ahmed Kahn's twin sister, her classified folder had grown considerably. It now included the death of all three of her previous husbands, only one of whom the Neptune Society recorded as having been legally dumped at sea.

The other two husbands had simply vanished.

"What should we talk about, Mac?"

There was no point in beating around the bush. Mac said a single word. He had practiced its correct pronunciation and researched it thoroughly.

"Malalai."

Holly did not flinch. She said: "Malalai of Maiwand. An old Afghan saying." And then she quoted the famous Afghan proverb. Coming out of Holly's mouth, it had a slightly sing-song quality. *"If you don't fall in the Battle of Maiwand, by God, someone is saving you as a symbol of shame!".*

Holly smiled at Mac. "Malalai was a young bride who helped her husband beat the crap out of the British about a century and a half ago."

"And in 1988, you became Malalai."

Holly looked angry, then her face relaxed. She did not try to hide or disguise her feelings.

"I used to get very angry at my father, Red, when he told that story to his friends. He stopped doing it. I am an American. I am not an Afghan warrior."

They were silent.

"Do you know how Red died, Holly?"

"In a freak car accident in Syria. I loved Red a lot."

"He died in Syria, yes. But not in a car accident."

Holly said nothing.

"He was a team leader in the Abu Kamal raid in October of 2008 in Sukkariyeh in eastern Syria." Mac watched her face, looking for anything that might hint at something, anything out of place. "We wanted to capture a senior logistics coordinator named Abu Ghadiya, but we ended up killing him instead."

She showed nothing, merely staring at him, waiting.

"Your father was the only American fatality in the Abu Kamal raid."

"Why would the CIA lie to my mother and me about that?" It appeared to be a genuine question. She answered it herself. "Of course they would lie to us. It's what they do. Thank you for telling me the truth."

After a short silence, she looked at Mac and asked: "Why are you telling me this truth?"

Mac watched her closely. He said: "Because it was your twin brother, Ahmed Kahn, who killed your father."

She was either a great actress, an accomplished terrorist, or someone who had just learned a terrible truth that she never wanted to know. Tears ran down her cheeks. Her chin trembled. She leaned forward, covered her eyes with tight fists, and Holly started to sob softly.

Mac sat in his chair, motionless, watching, waiting.

Then Holly Smolkes, Abira Khan, whoever she was leaned back and let out the tormented wail of an Afghan woman. It came from deep within her, a long, piercing, otherworldly sound that drifted across the Delray Beach Yacht Basin, bringing people onto the decks of their boats in search of its source.

Mac stood up, moved towards her, tried to hold her, comfort her.

She repeated the sound twice, then it stopped. Holly slumped, exhausted in the fighting chair. She stood and moved through the salon and into the stateroom. Mac came after her, sat on the edge of the enormous bed, watched her curl up, silent. He wrapped himself around her.

She accepted his presence. She seemed to fall asleep for a while, with steady breathing. Eventually, she stirred, sat up, moved back into the salon.

"This is one of the few times I wished I was not Muslim, and I could drink," she said.

"I know many Muslims who drink," Mac said.

"So do I, but I don't, and I won't." She got a ginger ale out of the galley fridge. "Your Guinness is still on the deck."

Mac got it and returned to the salon. Knowledge had drained her face, turning her normal weathered tan sallow.

"Do you have any more surprises for me, Mac?

"Probably," he said.

"Can they wait?"

"Probably not," he said.

She sighed, slumping into a salon chair, drawing up her knees and squeezing her arms around them in a fetal position.

"I am beginning to regret falling in love with you, Director Mac McKlane."

"When was the last time you had any contact with your twin brother?"

Her answer would be the deal maker. The game would continue whether or not she told the truth, but her reply would dictate the rules of engagement.

She answered immediately.

"I heard from him two days ago."

After a moment of silence, broken only by the slap of water against the hull of her charter boat, she added: "Stop looking at me like that, Mac."

"I'm sorry," he said, "What did you talk about?"

"He forced me to speak Pashto, which was difficult because it has not twisted my tongue for almost 30 years."

"When was the last time you spoke to him?"

"Two days ago, I already –"

"Before that."

"In 1988, when I killed my Russian father in my village in Nuristan before the bastard killed me, but after he had murdered my mother."

Her words came out hard, flat, a matter-of-fact report with no emotion.

"I'm sorry, Holly. What did you talk about when he phoned you two days ago?"

"Nothing. Everything. Ahmed kept calling me his Afghan warrior woman. He talked about ISIL. Ahmed claimed to be an important person in ISIL. He said something about an attack in Africa that he had orchestrated. But mostly, he just kept calling me 'Malalai.' It pissed me off, but I did not tell him that. He said I was a critical Afghan warrior many times. He told me that Malalai of Maiwand had written the destiny of my life."

"What did you tell him?"

"Nothing."

"You didn't tell him it upset you?"

"It would have done no good. Ahmed has become a dangerous jihadist. He is no longer my brother. In the end, I did not even want to talk to him."

"Did he tell you where he was calling from?" Mac had read the transcripts several times and knew that Ahmed Khan had not revealed his whereabouts.

"No," she answered.

"Why didn't you tell me about this?"

"Why would I? In my mind, he is a harmless child who I shared space within my mother's womb. He didn't even show the promise of a goat herder as a boy. He is nobody. Until he called, he was a silent voice from the past to which I have no attachment. None."

"He killed your father."

She hung her head.

Tears rolled down her cheeks.

"If I had known this, I would have talked to you about it. I probably would have told you about my brother, Ahmed, when we were at your father's wedding. I had no idea that he murdered Red."

"Your brother has become an important Islamic terrorist, Holly. He is a key player in the ISIL movement. He is responsible for slaughtering innocent men, women, and children in Africa and Europe."

Holly shook her head. "I suppose he has. And you, Mac McKlane, are a Director of Homeland Security."

"Yes, and so you can understand why I might not completely trust you."

Holly shrugged her shoulders. She looked at him. "Can you love me instead? Can we work on the trust thing later?"

She took Mac by the hand and pulled him, willing, through the salon, into the stateroom. As she did so, she said: "I am not my brother. He is a boy, eight years old. But right now, I love you, Mac. And I need to be held and shown that I

am loved, and that I have hope, and that I can feel. I need to
be loved right now, but softly."

〜〜〜〜〜〜〜〜〜〜〜

Less than seven blocks northwest of The Yacht Club at
Delray Beach, a man stood near the pool of The Astor
condos with a powerful telescope on a tripod.

The unoccupied swimming area was on the roof of a
five-story complex, which consisted of two separate buildings
attached by a third-floor breezeway over Pugliese Avenue.

Holly Smolkes lived at The Astor, in a spacious, three-
bedroom penthouse on the fourth floor of the "pool"
building. Both buildings shared the rooftop swimming and
barbecue area, which was the reason for the breezeway.

Holly's penthouse had a spiral staircase leading up to a
private party area that she never used, next to the pool that
she did occasionally take a dip in, but not often. She preferred
swimming in the ocean.

Her unit was almost out of earshot from the trains on
the tracks splitting the town of Delray Beach. The railroad ran
north from Miami along America's eastern coastline. The
piercing whistles in the night and early morning no longer
bothered her.

The man with the telescope on a tripod had a clear view
of the *Wholly Mackerel* in the yacht basin. He spoke quietly
into his cell phone.

"They are still very close friends," he said. "He appears
to have calmed her down after the initial ... whatever that was.
A police siren on steroids mating with a foghorn. It almost
burst my eardrums through the microphones, Boss."

The man thought that it would not be hard to relocate the listening devices under the fishing pole holders on Holly Smolkes' boat.

On the other end of the line, Angelo Rossellini said: "I am glad they are together. What are they doing?"

"They're making love."

"That is nice. Holly needs to be loved. I want you to go home. It is not yet time to end this friendship. Perhaps Holly will prove useful after all. I'll be in touch."

The man packed up his gear. He stopped on the fourth floor and checked that his key still unlocked Holly's penthouse door.

He opened and closed it, but he did not step across the threshold of Holly's condo.

He re-locked the door before leaving, making sure he carefully wiped the brass doorknob.

—⊬—⊮—⊮—⊮—⊮—⊮—⊮—

As the sun began to set at The Yacht Club at Delray Beach, Mac got dressed and said he had to go back to his grandfather's house for the night.

"Are you going to be all right, Holly?"

"Compared to whom?" she asked, smiling to show that she was feeling better. She quickly added: "Yes."

"I'll call you later."

"Call me tomorrow," she said. "I am going to walk home, and then I am going to sleep for 12 hours."

"Tomorrow," Mac said.

When Mac McKlane got to his grandfather's house, he told Sharonda and Samuel Nelson that he needed more time to think about the Petersson problem. He had obligations at Homeland Security that required immediate attention.

He walked back out, through the Birdroom, to the wooden dock on the canal that led to the Intracoastal Waterway. He sat in a comfortable deck chair.

Using his secure phone, he called Assistant Director Roberta Macumber at Homeland Security's headquarters.

"How's my favorite double agent?" she asked.

"I think she's playing it straight with us," Mac said. "And I think we can turn her to get to Ahmed Kahn. We might even be able to capture him."

"I'm listening."

Mac recapped his meeting with Holly Smolkes, from stepping aboard the *Wholly Mackerel* to getting dressed and going back to Captain McKlane's estate in Boca Raton.

Debriefed, he waited for Macumber's reaction.

Roberta Macumber said: "I am not going to tell you the old joke about a mother looking at her four-year-old son after he points to his peepee and asks her if it's his brain. She tells him, *Not Yet.*"

Mac laughed and thanked her for not telling him a joke he had heard dozens of times.

"I have to tell you something, Mac. When I read the transcript of her phone call with her twin brother, Ahmed Khan, she does not sound like a reluctant sister. She sounds like a potentially willing partner in the act of terrorism. My next question is important, Mac. Did you ask her if she would work with us?"

"No, the, uh, the timing wasn't right."

Roberta was silent.

"Why the silent treatment?" Mac asked.

"It's a pregnant pause, so you and Holly can get your timing right."

Mac burst out laughing.

"I think we need to bug your new lover," Roberta said.

"I agree," Mac said.

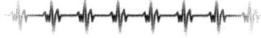

Holly walked home, rejuvenated a little by the bustle of Atlantic Avenue. She talked to a few people she knew along the way.

She took the elevator up to the fourth floor and put the key in the lock. She did not open the door.

She leaned down and retrieved a strand of blonde hair from the hallway carpeting.

"Oh, Mac," she whispered. "You offer so much love, but so little trust."

She stepped into her penthouse. Nothing seemed disturbed, everything in place. She checked the salt shaker and saw that nobody had moved the three grains that were hugging it.

She turned on some music, not loud enough to be noticeable. She carefully checked for cameras in every room as she pretended to dust shelves, nooks, and crannies.

She found nothing suspicious.

Then she discovered three bugs with the help of a security app on her iPhone. She thought about flushing them down the toilet but settled on placing them in noisy restaurants later that evening.

She put them in sponges in a plastic bag.

The sweep took over 15 minutes.

Holly stepped into her walk-in closet, closed the door behind her, and switched on the light, which had automatically turned off. She opened an almost undetectable safe in the wall concealed by neatly hung clothing.

Inside the thick metal security box was a small computer that operated through regional and international proxies, all of which ended with ".edu." They were educational channels.

Holly Smolkes sent an encrypted message: "You must never phone me again. It is not safe. They are watching you."

She signed the communication, *"Malalai."*

Chapter 10

The Hidden Caverns of Bath County, Virginia

The Moomaw Project Almost Caves In.

Torbjorn Petersson knew that a black bear family lived in a cave about 450 yards up the ravine behind his log cabin. He had been dozing up against a tree, squirrel hunting in early May of 2016, downwind, and he smelled the bears before he ever saw the mother and her two cubs pass within 20 feet. He did not move a muscle.

The bear cubs probably weighed 120 pounds each, and the mother looked to be around three times that.

She would stop protecting them before the middle of the summer, sending them off on their own to define their territorial rights.

The bears turned and moved further up the ravine, the cubs playing in the water, but not much. They were almost-grownups. He saw them turn and enter a cave concealed by a lot of foliage. They went into the bear den quickly, just walking through the bushes, so Torbjorn figured it would be a relatively large cavern. He would stay away from it. Black bears were smelly, smaller than brown bears, but dangerous territorial fighters if you cornered them or scared them.

Torbjorn had no idea that his ancestors had lived in the bear cave over 200 years earlier.

At the end of the 18th Century, Gunnar Petersson escaped from the starving poverty of Sweden. Many people abandoned dismal lives to travel to a dream that they called America. Once there, most of the new arrivals journeyed to the Northwest Territory, which would later become Ohio, Illinois, Indiana, Michigan, Wisconsin, Iowa, and Minnesota.

Gunnar Petersson, with a young wife, went south along what would one day be called the Appalachian Trail. He tried to reach the Southwest Territory, which eventually joined the original colonies as the State of Tennessee. The bitter winter of 1798 stopped Gunnar Petersson from ever getting there.

He spent that howling, freezing winter in a cave in the Appalachian Mountains, and he had to kill a bear to do it. His first son was born in the cave. He called him Björn, which later became Bjorn, which meant "bear" in Swedish.

In the spring of 1799, Gunnar watched the valley below the cave turn into a paradise. He and his wife decided to call it their home. An unknown river ran through what his family claimed as their homestead, and they lived in the cave for 18 months as they cleared the land, set up fences, and bought a cow, pigs, and chickens. They started to build a sturdy, two-story log cabin near the bottom of the mountain.

A neighbor named Gathright, a Scotsman who lived further down the river and knew a lot of people, helped Gunnar build a barn. They finished building it before the two-story log cabin had a roof or proper floors, and Gunnar and his wife, and now two children, celebrated the start of the 19th Century sleeping in the barn with cows, pigs, and chickens. Compared to what they had left in Sweden, it was a paradise, and they owned it. The barn was better than living in a cave, a hardship rarely discussed and forgotten within two generations.

Over 200 years later, Torbjorn Petersson rediscovered the cave. Ever since he had received the notice of condemnation from the TVA, he had become a great admirer of caves. From the hidden treehouse that he had built in an old oak tree at the top of the mountain, he watched the Army Corps of Engineers struggle with what they called "The Sponge Effect."

Lake Moomaw would start to fill up, and then it would stop. The Jackson River poured in thousands of gallons of water a minute, but the depth of the lake would not gain an inch. Often, it grew slightly more shallow. Beyond the earthen dam blocking the river's course, water would resume its normal flow.

Another cave had swallowed the Jackson River and then spat it out below the Gathright Dam. Torbjorn would smile as he looked through the considerable scope of his sniper rifle, watching the civilian employees of the Army Corps of Engineers swarm along the river banks, looking for an offending cave. Once they found it, they had to build a road to get their cement trucks to it. They were far behind schedule and way over budget. Hundreds of caves in the mountain kept dipping straws into their plans.

The autumn colors turned brown a week after the cowbell incident with Captain George McKlane and the two black people. Torbjorn made a decision.

He could not fight the eminent domain order, but he was confident that the government would extend the deadline for the turnover of his land.

He would accept the government's money, and he would keep the 40 acres on top of the mountain. It was time to retire, put out a rocking chair on the porch of a modern log cabin, and watch the ancestral farm slip underwater.

He would move the family graveyard to the top of the mountain. He felt sure that he could make a deal with the TVA, perhaps have them pay for it.

He decided to get a lawyer, and he had the money to buy the best one in Bath County, Virginia: Jason Raleigh Newbart.

Jason Newbart looked precisely like who and what he was, right down to his silk yellow bow tie, which he undid at the start of the meeting to prove that he meant business.

When Torbjorn sat across from the pudgy lawyer in his law offices, the counselor expressed astonishment that Petersson had waited so long to challenge the eminent domain procedure.

"I just got the notice a few weeks ago," Torbjorn said.

The lawyer looked down at a large file he had in front of him. "It says here that you got it over a year and a half ago."

"Two weeks ago," Torbjorn said

The lawyer circled something in the folder and slid it towards his new client, turning it upside down so Torbjorn could read it.

It was the same "Virginia Landowner's Bill of Rights" document that had killed his grandmother. The date circled by the lawyer was over 18 months old.

The attorney cleared his throat.

"Now proceedings in this title take precedence over all other civil actions, whether it's for a hearing or a trial, Mister Petersson, but the fact that you have waited so long to dispute the condemnation —"

"I'm not disputing it," Torbjorn said, pushing the folder back across the lawyer's well-polished, mahogany desk.

The lawyer leaned back and said: "Good. That's excellent. Then I think we should go to work on getting you top dollar for every single square foot of your 526-acre property, Mister Petersson."

"You can call me Torbjorn, and it's 486 acres. I'm going to hang on to the 40 acres on top of the mountain, sit in a rocking chair, and watch the Army Corps of Engineers spend all their time spelunking around Lake Moomaw."

The lawyer immediately understood Torbjorn's reference to underground caves. He said: "They are having some problems plugging the holes in Appalachia, aren't they?"

They both laughed politely.

"I want the Army Corps of Engineers to move our family cemetery from behind the cabin to the top of the mountain. And they will build me an access road to the luxury log cabin I intend to put there, a *paved* access road. I doubt if I'll enjoy watching my farm go underwater, but I want to see it happen in comfort."

When Torbjorn drove home, he looked at the "Virginia Landowner's Bill of Rights" document that Ernestine Petersson had brought home from the mailbox a few weeks earlier. Sure enough, it was dated a year and a half previous to its arrival, as was the envelope it came in. Torbjorn could not figure out how he missed that. She must have forgotten about the document for a long time, put it in a drawer perhaps.

Torbjorn smiled. His grandmother lived longer because she misplaced it, and he missed the old girl.

After Torbjorn had left the office of his lawyer, Jason Raleigh Newbart Esquire picked up a phone on his desk and punched a few buttons. He waited for a connection, and then said, in a tone with less authority than his usual, booming courtroom voice: "I think we have a problem."

In Boca Raton, Captain George McKlane was hosting his usual Saturday brunch under the lanai by the pool.

It had rained earlier, and at the last minute, as the sun broke through, they decided to abandon The Birdroom and move everything outdoors.

The group had grown over the years, and the only losses were Dr. Gunther Klein, followed quickly by his wife, Rachel, who always thought she would be the first to go.

Rachel had been Captain George's dietician, and she had tried hard to wean him off Guinness, without success. She did get him to eat more salads, which he either called twigs and sticks, horse straw, or crabgrass, depending on his mood.

Captain George missed Gunther more than Rachel. He and the retired neurosurgeon had shared the Korean War, although they never knew each other at the time.

A year earlier, Gunther got Captain George off a misdiagnosed Prednisone prescription that kept dropping the Medal of Honor winner into blackout flashbacks of the war.

Sharonda Nelson and her husband, Samuel, were part of every Saturday brunch, and they now lived in the guest house attached to the primary residence.

Judge Ralph Broadslate still attended the Saturday brunches, although he seemed to be aging more rapidly since he had finally cut the cord as a silent partner at Broadslate & Barnes in Trenton, New Jersey. Ralph Broadslate was a former federal judge, and the law office continued to honor his name on their letterhead. It was good for business.

Brigadier General George McKlane and his new wife, Martha Krumble, always had a place at the brunch. They had returned from a honeymoon on the Amazon River.

Martha Krumble retained her maiden name. Her real estate reputation as the Broker and part owner of Accelerated Realty Sales demanded no repair, no aliases.

George "Mac" McKlane was the final guest.

"You should have invited that boat captain for brunch," Captain George told his grandson. "Smoking Holly Smolkes." He laughed at his cleverness.

"Captain Gramps, we all have something quite private to discuss today, and it might not be something we'd want to share with a stranger," Mac said, looking at Sharonda and Samuel Nelson.

"Stranger?" Captain McKlane asked. "You call a beautiful woman that you tried to drag into the hallway, naked at your father's wedding, a stranger?"

"Really?" Martha Krumble asked, looking at Mac.

"I knew we shouldn't have left the kids alone," her new husband, General McKlane said, biting into a croissant that failed to hide his smile.

"Buck naked," Captain George said, spreading creamed cheese on a bagel. "Might have killed me, Mac. An older man like me shouldn't see things like that. You might have given me a heart attack."

Even Sharonda smiled. Then she said: "Speaking of killing." She let the sentence hang in the air.

"Oh, for God's sake," Captain George said. "Why don't you just throw me in jail?"

"What the hell is this all about?" Judge Broadslate asked. "You lost me in the naked woman part. Can we go back and discuss that some more?"

The entire table looked at the Judge.

"Please?" the Judge said.

And everyone laughed. Then everyone at the table discussed, quietly, the attempt on George's life a year earlier, and the trip that Captain George, Sharonda, and Samuel had made to the farm called Leatherwood outside Hot Springs a few weeks earlier.

Captain George passed around the note that he had just received in the mail from Petersson.

It was a copy of the Captain's condolences over the death of Ernestine that he had dropped in the hallway of the cabin as they fled.

Torbjorn confirmed that the instigator of the hit was Silberg and that Torbjorn had no knowledge of the man's whereabouts.

"So can we all agree that the shot Petersson took up in Virginia was a warning and not an attempt on my father's life, or Sharonda's, or Samuel's?" Brigadier General George McKlane asked the table.

Everyone looked at Sharonda, the only holdout. Judge Broadslate had an opinion, but he withheld it.

"Okay," she said. "Petersson wasn't trying to kill us. He just made me pee my pants with a huge gun."

"Exactly," Captain George McKlane said, realizing how stupid that sounded before he could seal his lips. "You know what I mean."

Nobody spoke for a while; then Judge Broadslate said: "Here's what I think."

They all looked at the older man, who delivered a quiet monolog, with many years of experience on the bench.

"There can be no doubt that somebody committed severe crimes. I was here when the Feds went through your house, George, after the attempt on your life. I know you think the killer, Petersson, spared your life, and I agree with you on that. I think we all agree that Anthony Silberg hired him. The note Petersson just sent to you says so.

"Some of us knew Silberg as a neighbor here at the Royal Coconut Yacht and Country Club. I had dinner with him a few times.

"He was a scoundrel, and I'm glad that Martha could help save the real estate company from which he stole all the escrow money. I also hope that the Federal Bureau of Investigation catches him someday soon and throws him in prison for a long time.

"But now there's this Petersson fellow. It seems that we have a lot of proof that he was the trigger man, including the note that he just sent to you, George. I don't think he's an ingenious criminal.

"Our justice system does not treat assassins lightly. We don't even have to sit here and debate whether the man was aiming to kill George or not.

"He kills people. That's a fact. That seems to be the business that pays his bills.

"You have two choices. You can decide to put together the paperwork necessary to pursue this person through the criminal justice system and have the scoundrel thrown in prison, or you can whistle happily past the cemetery and hope for the best."

"Thank you, Judge," Brigadier General McKlane said.

"I am not done," the Judge said. "If you decide to pursue Petersson through our criminal justice system, you're going to spend a lot of time doing it. Old guys like George and me may not want to sit down and spend hours with the FBI, giving depositions, and raking over hot coals that appear to have turned into harmless ashes.

"You may not want to spend days or weeks in a courtroom, General. And I know Martha would instead enjoy selling houses. And young Mac here seems to have locked onto a career of chasing beautiful, naked women. If I had known about that job, I would have never become a judge.

"So what I'm saying is this, and it's tough for me to say something like this, and I'll deny it if you ever say I said it, but sometimes it's better to whistle while you work, whistle past the cemetery and enjoy the time you have left."

"Thank you, Judge," Brigadier General George McKlane said once again.

After the brunch, the general pulled his son aside and said: "I know you can get all the information yourself, but if you want me to put together a file on Torbjorn Petersson, I will. I've already taken a look at him."

"I'd appreciate that, Dad."

"He was a Marine in Afghanistan and a pretty good one, a sniper with 14 kills and the nickname of 'One Shot.' He was not an officer, so he's not available for military recall. We can't just order him back into the service. Petersson was a non-com, a staff sergeant."

"Thank you, Dad. I'd appreciate all the information you can get me. I think I'll be visiting him. From the sounds of it, we can own this guy for the rest of his life. And we can keep him off the streets and away from Sharonda."

Both men smiled.

They liked Sharonda, and she was a great protector of the family Patriarch, Captain George.

"I enjoyed the Judge's summation," Mac said. "I"m pretty sure that he would understand the weapons we need nowadays to win the War on Terror."

"I think he'd probably lock our asses up," the general said. "I'll be glad to retire next year."

Throughout history, there had always been weapons like Torbjorn Petersson, trained killers, licensed assassins.

They were hard to find, difficult to control, often impossible to untrain, but precious assets if you could put them on a leash.

"These are tough times," the general told his son. "You know that even better than I. We just have to make sure that we're on the side that wins."

"Amen," Mac said. "And we are."

Father and son, professional American warriors, clenched their jaws at one another, then smiled, and parted.

$$\text{---}\textit{\large ᴧᴧ-ᴧᴧ-ᴧᴧ-ᴧᴧ-ᴧᴧ-ᴧᴧ}\text{---}$$

At the same time, as the Saturday brunch group gathered in Florida, Torbjorn Petersson walked down to his rusty mailbox at the entrance to Leatherwood Farms in Virginia. He carried his sniper rifle and a holstered .45 Colt with him. He hadn't picked up the mail for a few days.

As he opened the mailbox, he heard two shots echo in the valley.

They seemed to come from the top of the mountain behind his log cabin.

He stood still, thinking, and he finally decided that it was probably a deer hunter taking a few shots at a white-tailed buck beyond his posted property.

He reached into the mailbox. He found a brown envelope that looked official, with a laser-printed USPS Media Mail Label on it containing Torbjorn's name and address.

The sender of the brown envelope was an organization that he had never heard of, with offices in Portland, Maine. The correspondent was a marine biologist with the International Water Conservation Board named Professor Ahmed Kahn.

The package contained copies of emails that Torbjorn Petersson would spend many, increasingly angry hours reading.

Chapter 11

Just Another Weekend Down on the Farm

Cyberspace is Always a House of Mirrors.

Jason Raleigh Newbart, widely recognized as the best attorney in Bath County, Virginia, decided to take a drive out to Leatherwood Farms on Sunday, a day he usually skipped Church to play golf on the challenging Upper Homestead Course. He had personally known the great golfer, Sam Snead, who was once the pro at the Homestead in Hot Springs.

That was back in the days when the Engles family from Hunting Valley, a wealthy rural location outside Cleveland, Ohio, owned the famous resort.

Jason had even caddied and shagged balls for the great Sam Snead as a youth.

Jason would walk out about 150 yards with a big metal pail and catch balls hit with old hickory irons by the man who would become famous as Slammin' Sammy.

He never had to move much, sometimes not at all, to hear the metal ping of a successful shot. Sam Snead would give him a nickel for every ball in the bucket, and young Jason always carried some extras golf balls in his baggy pants, which he reclaimed after getting paid.

Jason Raleigh Newbart was born to be a lawyer.

This Sunday, his lower back was bothering him, almost as much as his fourth wife, and he decided to take a solitary drive down Richardson Gorge to visit his client, Torbjorn Petersson. It was a beautiful, peaceful trip, during which he could think further about how to dump his wife with the minimum financial penalty.

The prenup supposedly screwed her, but she would contest it and waste a lot of his valuable time. She was a lawyer herself, and she knew how to do it.

Jason Newbart didn't bother calling Torbjorn to arrange a meeting because he always enjoyed surprise visits. You usually learned something when you showed up unexpectedly.

If Torbjorn Petersson weren't at the farm, Jason would just keep driving down the road to see if the Army Corps of Engineers had made any advances at the Gathright Dam. They were working on weekends, way behind schedule.

The federal, state and county budgets were an all-but-forgotten memory.

Legal costs, however, would always be paid.

Newbart drove past the rusty mailbox and faded Leatherwood Farms sign, and over a new metal, bridge painted light green. His GPS said he had gone too far, and he turned around, found the entry, and drove a mile and a half to the two-story log cabin at the bottom of the mountain.

Torbjorn was standing in the driveway, and he greeted his attorney by holding a gun to the man's head.

"It's a Colt .45, counselor, and it'll blow your brains all over that cute little red Mercedes convertible you're driving."

Jason Newbart's car was still running, and he thought, briefly, about throwing it in reverse and flooring it.

Torbjorn pressed the Colt .45 harder into the side of the attorney's head.

"Do you think the world is going to miss a dead lawyer?" Torbjorn asked.

"What's the meaning of this?" Jason asked. He tried to sound offended, but it came out scared.

"Turn it off and get out of the car," Torbjorn said.

Jason pressed the off button and stepped out.

"Christ, you peed on yourself," Torbjorn said. "You should wear darker pants when you trespass on private property, Newbart."

"This is about trespassing? I should have called Mister Petersson. I'm sorry I didn't call. It was a mistake. I promise I'll call next time. I don't know what I was thinking. How stupid of me."

The words tumbled out of his mouth.

"Shut the fuck up, asshole. I got some milk and cookies in the cabin. We're going to go and have a little chat."

He didn't lower the gun.

He used it as a motion indicator, and Jason Raleigh Newbart followed its instructions, entering the log cabin.

"Don't sit," Torbjorn said.

He reached into a hall closet and pulled out a large towel. He threw it over the bench seat of a long maple wood table in front of a large picture window.

"Now you can sit," Torbjorn said, which the attorney did, with his back to the window. Torbjorn went to the other side of the room and gathered a bunch of paper which he brought back to the table.

"If you try to escape," Torbjorn told him, "I will kill you. You'll never make it to your car. Do you understand?"

"I understand."

Petersson walked through a swinging door into a pantry that led to the kitchen. He opened and closed a few cupboards. Jason Newbart strained to see what was in the papers that Petersson had put on the table, but they were too far away.

Torbjorn reappeared with a bottle of milk, two jelly glasses, and some Oreo cookies. He had holstered his gun, and he sat down at the table, across from the lawyer.

"The milk comes from my cows. Cookies are store-bought. Help yourself."

Jason Raleigh Newbart sat there frozen, moving nothing.

"So, counselor, we have a few things to discuss."

Torbjorn reached for the papers and brought them in front of him, shuffling them a bit. "One thing I want to make clear first, Jason, I hope you don't mind me using your first name. You are my lawyer, and that means everything we talk about is confidential, is that correct?"

"I am here under duress," Jason said.

Torbjorn took the Colt .45 out of its holster, put it on the table, and said: "Yes, you are, Jason. And unless you give me all of the answers I want to hear, you're going to be deader than cowshit. So, do we have client and lawyer confidentiality, yes or no?"

"Yes." It didn't mean anything because he had already said he was under duress, which legally tainted everything.

"Good, and we both know that doesn't mean shit," Torbjorn said as if he were reading the lawyer's mind. "So let me tell you a little bit about myself, Jason. You need to know who I am. I was an excellent sniper, a Marine Corps staff sergeant in Afghanistan, two tours, 14 kills. Just between you and me, it was more than that. I used to go out and practice on my own."

He poured himself a full glass of milk and a half as much for Jason Raleigh Newbart.

Torbjorn nibbled at a cookie and watched the lawyer, who seemed to be dropping into a daze.

Petersson slammed his hand on the table. The Jason Raleigh Newbart jumped, wide-eyed, fearful.

"You need to pay attention to every word I say, Jason. Your life is going to depend on it."

"Yes, sir," Jason said.

"Since I left the service, counselor, I have made my living as a professional killer. The numbers exceed what I achieved in Afghanistan. I have no problem adding you to my list. And believe me, Jason, I know how to make people, and their fancy red cars, disappear. Do you understand what I'm saying, Jason Raleigh Newbart?"

"Yes, sir," Jason said.

"So explain this note to me, counselor." He slid a copy of an email over to the lawyer, who looked at it.

It said that the Petersson property would not be affected by Lake Moomaw, but that Leatherwood Farms would be ideal as a home for the park ranger and his wife and children. Plus, there was plenty of room to construct outbuildings for the equipment and machinery needed to care for the recreational area created.

A few of the lower acres at a fork in the Jackson River might become part of the roughly 40 miles of shoreline that would be created by Lake Moomaw.

"I believe that the property still would fall within the definition of eminent domain, Mister Petersson."

"How about this one," Torbjorn said.

The email suggested that since the Petersson family might successfully dispute the condemnation of eminent domain, it made sense to withhold any notice to them of the proceedings until the latest possible moment.

A reply to the email asked how to accomplish this delay.

The answer suggested backdating the postage meter stamped on the Petersson eminent domain package. The person offering this solution suggested putting it in the Leatherwood Farms mailbox a year and a half after proceedings began. It was signed SLN.

"Where did you get these documents, Mister Petersson?"

"Who is SLN?" Torbjorn asked.

"Sally Leigh Newbart," his lawyer said.

"Newbart. Is this woman related to you?"

"She's currently my wife, Mister Petersson."

"You can call me Torbjorn, Jason. I'd prefer it that way. We're going to be spending some time together. The length of time will coincide with your desire to remain alive. What's the legal term for concealment, Jason?"

"Concealment."

The lawyer leaned forward and took a few cookies, then a sip of milk; he seemed to relax.

Torbjorn spent 15 minutes showing his lawyer some emails related to the eminent domain served on his property. Most of them were signed SLN.

As Jason Raleigh Newbart read each email, he finished his milk and ate all the cookies. Torbjorn got up, went into the pantry, and got more milk and cookies. His lawyer read each email carefully, making sure that his initials appeared nowhere, and that no mention of his guilt in the matter would be evident.

He had seen all of the emails before, and when he got back to his office, he would probably shred the entire Leatherwood Farms folder, leaving only his soon-to-be ex-wife holding the bag. She worked across the street in her private practice.

Jason Raleigh Newbart, Esq., put the final piece of paper on the email pile and said, in a robust and vibrant voice: "You have suffered a great injustice."

Torbjorn's eyes squinted at the lawyer. He said: "When my grandmother saw the eminent domain notice, she died. Right in front of my eyes, she died, counselor."

The lawyer said nothing for a moment. Then Jason Newbart's courtroom voice filled the room:

"We can add a charge of second-degree manslaughter to tampering with evidence, contempt of the court, obstruction of justice, perverting the course of justice, cover-up, and, uh, this is perhaps the most flagrant Spoilation of Evidence I have ever seen. I am appalled and disgusted."

The lawyer's face had turned quite red.

"Wow," Torbjorn said. "You must love your wife a lot."

Jason Raleigh Newbart sputtered some milk that he had just sipped, onto the table.

He almost laughed, but he held it in.

"I withdraw my statement of being under duress during this conversation, Torbjorn. Confidentiality is our bond."

"Until death separates us," Torbjorn said.

"I am your lawyer, sir. You have found your man."

"Have another cookie," Torbjorn said.

At Homeland Security headquarters, Shadrach Ringer tapped on the open door of the Director's office.

"I think I might have another hook into staff sergeant Petersson, Mac."

"What's that?"

"He's losing his family farm to eminent domain, and he'll appreciate anyone who helps him keep some or all of it out of the hands of the Tennessee Valley Authority. We can do that."

After discussing the matter in detail, Mac decided he would fly into Hot Springs on Monday morning, where he would meet first with an attorney named Sally Leigh Newbart, who was managing the Petersson eminent domain case.

After that, he would have a talk, eyeball-to-eyeball, with the man who did not kill his grandfather two times.

Mac's military helicopter landed at the Homestead at 9:30 in the morning.

Less than 15 minutes later, he stood in front of Sally Leigh Newbart, attorney-at-law.

She remained seated behind a desk that seemed a bit too large for her.

She fluttered enormous fake eyelashes at Mac and smiled with expensive teeth.

"I've never dealt with Homeland Security before, sir," she said, Virginia in her voice. She stood up slowly as if she was at a formal dance and held out a limp hand.

"We're a fun group," Mac replied, leaning over her desk and giving her a firm handshake.

"How can I help you, sir?" She pulled back, surprised.

"You have a case, an eminent domain proceeding with a man named Torbjorn Petersson."

"Why, yes I do, Mister McKlane, who works for Homeland Security. How should I address you, sir?"

"Director McKlane," Mac said. "I need to see the Petersson folder."

"I see," she said.

They stared at one another; then Sally shouted: "Marty, can you bring in the Leatherwood Farms file, please."

Some of Virginia disappeared from her voice.

Before Sally Leigh Newbart's assistant could place the file on her desk, the Director of Homeland Security took it from her and put it under his arm.

"What are you doing, Director McKlane?"

"This file and the eminent domain proceeding it defines no longer exist," he said.

"Well, sir, there are private emails in that folder," Sally Leigh Newbart said, glaring at him.

"Yes, there are," the Director said. "And we've already read all of them."

It wasn't the truth, but Mac always enjoyed expanding the mystique of Homeland Security.

He turned to go.

"Wait, I haven't even seen your identification, Director McKlane. How do I know you are who you say you are?"

Mac showed her his official, gold-plated DHS badge, together with his photo ID in a 2-window wallet that had the embossed emblem of Homeland Security burnished into the dark, black leather.

Mac McKlane did not like this woman, and he could not resist dropping what his group called *the bomb* on her.

He repeated the Mission Statement of DHS: "With honor and integrity, we will safeguard the American people, our homeland, and our values."

Then he walked out.

"Sweet Jesus," Sally Leigh Newbart said, collapsing into her leather chair.

"What a Nazi asshole," her assistant said.

"That, too," Sally Leigh Newbart agreed. "Not a Southern Gentleman, but a damned fine-looking specimen." She asked her assistant to leave and to please close the door as she did so.

She sat down and dialed her husband in his office across the street. Jason Raleigh Newbart smiled when he saw her name appear on his iPhone, but, out of habit, he did not accept its Facetime request. Voice only. He had been caught too often doing something he did not wish the caller to see.

"Morning, Sweetie-pie. I surely missed you at breakfast." He looked down at the file that he was about to shred.

She used her latest nickname for him.

"Well, Flubber, that's because I was down the street, humping the eyeballs out of one of your golf buddies." It wasn't the truth. She had come to work early, sneaking out of their home. She couldn't stomach his cement mixer approach to eating pancakes and sausages first thing in the morning. "Don't hang up; this is important."

He almost did. "What's up?" he asked.

"You have a copy of the Leatherwood Farms file, right?

Jason wished he had accepted her Facetime request so that she could see his enormous smile.

"Why, yes, I do," he said.

"Well, shred it, Flubber. Get rid of it."

"Hello?"

"Are you there, Jason?"

Staring at the file on his desk, Jason Newbart asked: "Why on earth would I do that, Sweetie-pie?"

"Because Homeland Security has just ripped the file out of my hands, including all of the emails, everything, and informed me that the eminent domain Proceeding which it defines no longer exists. And the Director of Homeland Security said they had already read every email in that file. Washington has hacked us, Jason. I feel like I'm living in the Soviet Union."

"Homeland Security?" Jason said. "I wonder what Torbjorn Petersson and Leatherwood Farms have to do with Homeland Security?"

Their connection was silent for a while. Then Jason added: "Why *wouldn't* I want to keep a record of all those emails, Sweetie-pie?"

Sally Leigh Newbart said nothing.

"I mean, those are all *your* emails, aren't they? Every single one of them?"

He cut the connection before she could reply. Then he took the Leatherwood Farms folder and locked it in his safe. Five more minutes, and it would have been confetti.

Watching his fourth wife, Sally Leigh, go to jail wouldn't cost him anything.

Of course, as a legally Injured Spouse, he would never stoop so low as to testify against her. Instead, he would publicly hang his head in shame, finding her culpability a crushing, enormously sad revelation.

But why the hell was the Department of Homeland Security involved in Leatherwood Farms?

Director Mac McKlane checked into a comfortable suite at The Homestead for one night, going to his room and reading the Leatherwood Farms folder.

He understood the law. He had a Jurisprudence Degree from Georgetown University, although he had never tried to gain admission to the bar in any state.

He immediately recognized the Spoilation of Evidence involved in the attempt to throw Torbjorn Petersson off the land of his ancestors. He read the emails twice.

He phoned his AD, Roberta Macumber, in Washington and said: "I think this is going to be a lot easier than we thought it would be."

They discussed his meeting with Sally Leigh Newbart, and Roberta laughed when Mac said that the Virginia lawyer had two-foot-long eyelashes and couldn't keep her eyes open.

"Can she help us out at all?"

"I don't know," Mac said. "Don't drop the hammer on her yet. She might be useful for something."

"Understood."

"I'm going to spend the night down here, Roberta. I'll drive out and see Petersson tomorrow. Right now, I need a break. I've got a lot to think about."

"Here's something to add to the pile," Roberta Macumber said. "The love of your life has taken off to the Islands on an overnight trip with a naturalized American citizen named Mohammed Siddiqui. He's Muslim."

"Do we know anything about him?"

"He was a Trauma Surgeon in the United States Navy. Purple Heart. Not sure how you get one of those when you're on the Good Ship Lollipop." That was her nickname for Hospital Ships. "But he has a good record, Mac. He's still a doctor. The only thing that's a little strange is this: he changed his specialty after he got out of the Navy."

Mac was slow on the uptake.

"Maybe he chartered her boat for a fishing expedition."

"Guess what his new specialty is, Mac."

"What?"

Now he was listening.

"Infectious diseases."

The line went silent for a while.

"Data says he's still a surgeon,' Macumber said, "but now he focuses a lot of his time on nasty bugs and stuff."

Mac continued to be defensive about Holly Smolkes.

"I think infectious diseases has more to do with medical antibiotic bag drips to cure cancer and open wounds," he said. Mac had a memory of his grandmother, Agnes, before she died, hooked up to a lot of medical poles that everyone pretty much knew would never save her life.

"We'll find out," Macumber said.

"Yes, we will. Cover for me, will you, Roberta? I need some time off."

"You bet, Mac. Take a break. Give me a call after you sign up our newest recruit."

She killed the connection.

That would be the last time anyone heard from Mac McKlane for four days.

Chapter 12

Fishing in Paradise can be Dangerous.

An Unforgettable Trip to the Bahama's Outer Islands

Hurricane Matthew broke southern Florida's 10-year record of no Category 3 or higher storms tearing into its sandy beaches. But it missed Boca Raton and Delray Beach for the most part. It slid up the coast threatening tidal surges and a Category 4 landfall, but it never made it ashore.

Hurricane Matthew put out the lights for over a million Florida Power and Light customers, and it stole a half a dozen souls before it finally wobbled out into the Atlantic Ocean.

It scared people, but it would never hold a prominent place in Floridian history as a significant storm.

Roofing businesses in southern Florida, expecting a windfall from Hurricane Matthew, continued to go bankrupt every month. It was a gauge that storm watchers liked.

Roofers had enjoyed record profits for years after Hurricane Wilma hit Florida in October of 2005. That tempest ripped the tiles off of condos and homes from Naples on the west coast to Boca Raton on the east.

Dr. Mohammed Siddiqui looked at the clear blue skies over The Yacht Club at Delray Beach and asked Skipper Holly Smolkes if it would continue.

She thought it would.

"You ready for this adventure?" Holly asked him.

"Away with the anchor," Dr. Siddiqui said.

Holly smiled and jumped out, throwing off the dock lines and jumping back on board.

It would be an 85-nautical-mile trip to Freeport, and the weather looked beautiful all the way.

"You want to pray, Muhammed?" He had given her permission to use his first name.

"Am I in danger?"

She laughed. "Of course not, you are Muslim, as am I."

Holly pointed to the east. "Mecca," she said.

"Ah, it's been a while," he said.

He kneeled with her, moved his lips silently. He had almost said: *It's been a while since I've been to Church,* but he caught himself. *Mosque. They worshiped in Mosques.*

Holly climbed to the bridge and expertly moved into open waters through the Boynton Inlet.

Then she let it out. She turned the inboard Volvo Penta D11-725 loose over tiny, three-foot waves. The sound echoed a magnificent roar, a pack of motorcycles on water.

The *Wholly Mackerel* acted like a skipping stone, picking up speed. Holly loved the freedom of flying across a calm ocean as she pushed the throttle to its limit.

It would be a quick trip to Freeport. They'd get there well before sunset.

Meanwhile, Dr. Mohammed Siddiqui was losing his breakfast and his previous night's dinner over the aft railing.

Holly slowed the *Wholly Mackerel* to a crawl and climbed down from the bridge.

"You okay, Doc? I guess you didn't take any Dramamine or Bonine before the trip, huh?"

Mohammed Siddiqui looked miserable.

"Maybe if you could slow down a little," he said.

"Can do, and will, but from the looks of it, you're going to suffer for some time regardless. I have a pretty good remedy that skippers all know about, but it's going to take me a few minutes to put it together."

"Please," he said.

He leaned over the railing and retched again. Holly patted him on the back.

"Good," she said. "That's mostly bile. You're almost running on empty, Mohammed." She reached into a medical bag and gave him a prescription Scopolamine patch. "Put this behind your ear, Doc."

She thought of offering him another patch for his other ear. The sedative, Scopolamine, was used as a truth serum as well as a cure for seasickness.

Holly went into the galley and crushed some crystallized ginger in a small cup with a pestle, together with some water and two Sturgeron tablets.

The UK, Australia, and Canada approved this seasickness medication, but not the United States.

Holly purchased it through an international Web pharmacy that was known by most charter boat owners. She grabbed a bottle of ginger ale and went on deck.

Doctor Muhammed Siddiqui was on the phone.

"Here, take this paste and rub it on your teeth and gums. It's going to be bitter and sting a little, but it'll bring you back to the feeling of solid land in less than 15 minutes. Wash it down with the ginger ale. You're about to feel better, Doc."

Mohammed Siddiqui put down his phone, rubbed the paste in his mouth, and gulped more carbonated ginger ale than he should have.

He jerked around and gagged over the railing again.

As he did so, Holly reached down and pressed the green phone button on his mobile device. She was suspicious, and she wanted to see who Muhammed Siddiqui had called.

Two names popped up, and they both frightened her.

She quickly blanked the phone screen.

The doctor shuddered through a final dry heave, straightened up, turned towards Holly, and tried to smile. He looked a little shaky.

"Well, I'm pretty sure that you blew the cure straight into the ocean, Muhammed."

He nodded.

"I'm going to go make you another batch. And here's another Scopolamine patch to put behind your other ear."

"Okay," he said.

He grabbed the railing and sidestepped his way into one of the fighting chairs.

After two minutes, Holly stepped out of the salon, back onto the deck.

She said: "This will cure all of your problems until the end of time, Mohammed." She paused before adding:

"Or whatever the hell your name is."

She was holding a gun with a silencer pointed between his widening eyes.

At Homeland Headquarters, Sookie Ringer looked at Shadrach and said: "Something's not jiving here."

"What's up?"

"Doctor Muhammed Siddiqui is part of a robotic surgery team at a hospital in Orlando, Florida."

"I think we knew that," Shadrach said.

"Well, he's checked in and helping another doctor yank out some faulty plumbing right now, as we speak."

They didn't expect that. Shadrach and Sookie both headed for Roberta Macumber's office.

"So who's on the boat with Abira Kahn?" Macumber asked. Shadrach and Sookie Ringer shrugged their shoulders.

At Homeland, they had stopped using the name Holly Smolkes unless Mac was there.

He wanted them to use her legal, American name. Openly, the team did not agree.

"Have we got eyes on the boat?"

"No. Just a cell phone location, and that's fading fast."

"Can we hear them?"

"We haven't had time to put ears on the boat. We were going to do that this weekend."

"Can we get eyes on them?"

"Maybe the Coast Guard," Sookie said.

"Make it happen."

As Sookie and Shadrach went through the door to get it done, someone leaned into Macumber's office and said: "She's dead in the water."

The Ringers halted.

They were waved on by the AD, *continue your task.* Macumber stepped into another office and looked at a blue, stationary dot on a computer screen.

"If she had run out five more nautical miles, her cell phone would have been out of range," a technician said. "There are two cell phones there." He pointed at the blinking blue dot. "But one of them's a burner, a throwaway. Neither one is moving."

Angelo Rossellini did have ears on the boat, and he had asked his assistant to turn down the volume as Holly raced towards the Bahama Islands.

"She's running hot," the assistant said, trying to sound knowledgeable about what was happening.

Suddenly, the roar died, and small, disembodied voices started coming out of a speaker triangle.

The assistant quickly turned up the volume, although the sound remained scratchy.

"Who are you?" Holly asked.

Silence, peppered by seagull squawks.

"Keeping your mouth shut will not end well for you, Mister Mohammed Siddiqui, whoever you are."

The man said: "It's a job."

"Whose job?" she asked.

Silence.

"I see two numbers on your cell phone, pal," she said.

Silence. More seagulls.

"My old friend Gregory 'Snake' Richards," she said.

Silence.

Waves slapped against the boat. More seagulls.

"And a man who I have always honored as if he were my father, Angelo Rossellini," Holly continued.

"Point the gun at your head," the man said. "You're a ghost. It's a job. He's listening to every word you say right now, you stupid bitch." Perhaps the truth serum side effects of the extra Scopolamine patch had kicked in.

In his office, Angelo banged his fist on the table. He agreed with Holly when her disembodied voice said: "Well, he picked the wrong idiot for the job, didn't he?"

There was a slight popping sound, a water splash, and then nothing but seagulls and waves slapping against the boat.

Holly spent 12 minutes finding the bugs, using the security app on her cell phone to help her. She discovered four of them. She went up to the bridge and took the boat to full throttle. The speaker on Rossellini's desk vibrated with the roar of the inboard engine.

The assistant reached to turn down the volume, but it suddenly crackled into silence before he could do so.

Holly threw the bugs into the ocean. She thought about saying something before doing so but changed her mind.

In Rossellini's office, Angelo looked at the silent speaker and said: "She found them all."

Then he asked his assistant to leave him alone.

At Homeland Security, AD Roberta Macumber and a technician watched the blue dots disappear from their screen.

"Both phones have stopped giving a location signal," the technician said.

"Get eyes on that boat," Roberta Macumber said. "Give the Coast Guard her position."

Shadrach was already in touch with the Coast Guard, but their nearest helicopter was at least 12 minutes out. By the time they got to the designated coordinates, all they had spotted was unusual schools of blacktip and spinner sharks patrolling the offshore waters of southern Florida. People expected to see schooling like that in the springtime, but rarely in the fall. The Coast Guard crosshatched the area for 15 minutes, finding nothing.

Suddenly, the helicopter banked towards the Bahamas Outer Islands, ordered to continue its search in that direction, looking for a charter boat called the *Wholly Mackerel.*

Holly Smolkes sped towards the Boca Inlet. She would not be taking her boat back to its Delray mooring anytime soon.

There were a lot of boats at the Inlet, mostly going out. She worked her way in, past the Boca Resort Beach Club, under the A1A bridge, and into the expanse of Lake Boca. White pleasure cruisers covered the blue waters, many of them larger than hers.

She moved out of the channel and dropped her boat's Fortress anchor into the sandy bottom.

She brought the *Wholly Mackerel* within a hundred yards of the eastern shoreline of the Intracoastal Waterway. She opened the hatch and disengaged the battery.

Everything in the boat turned off. Holly Smolkes and the *Wholly Mackerel* became electronically invisible.

Huge condos blocked any view of the Atlantic Ocean. She would wait in the Boca Inlet until nightfall, knowing that she had no easy escape.

She kept the phone of Mohammed Siddiqui turned off, as well as her own. No electronic signature would tell anyone her whereabouts, although she thought she might turn on Siddiqui's phone later that evening.

As dusk fell over Boca Raton, people on the boat nearest started shouting at Holly to turn on her lights. She shouted back that she had a major electrical failure, and could someone take her ashore?

She set powerful flashlights on the bow and stern; then, she stepped into her friendly neighbor's dinghy with her overnight bag.

"You want me to take a look at it," the man asked.

"I know what the problem is," she said. "I just need to get home and bring down the new Deep Cycle 75 battery I bought yesterday at West Marine. I made a mistake. I should have installed it right away."

"Great battery," the man said. "Where can I drop you off, miss, uh – ?"

"The Beach Club landing would be perfect," she said.

From there, she took the free shuttle over to the pink Boca Raton Resort & Club. She took a taxi up to Boston's on the Beach at 50 Ocean Drive in Delray.

She paid the driver cash.

She walked into a boutique and bought an ugly floppy hat in which she wouldn't be caught dead. She did not smile at the obvious cliché. She purchased some baggy pants. She walked around a corner, threw the hat and pants down in the street gutter, and covered them with dirt and grime. She shook the hat a few times and put it on; then, she pulled the shapeless pants over what she already wore.

She walked over to the railroad tracks and borrowed someone's old bike, which was unlocked because nobody would bother stealing it.

Hunched over the bike with dirty, sagging pants, carrying her overnight bag on the rusted handlebars, and concealed by a filthy, floppy hat, Holly Smolkes peddled the bike slowly past the Astor Condos where she lived.

They were waiting for her 100 feet down Pugliese Avenue, in front of the side entrance to her building, but they gave no notice to the old bag lady peddling towards whatever cardboard home she might crawl under for the night.

Holly kept going another four blocks, and then she found a park bench to sit on, behind the Delray Tennis Center. The person who was already on the bench stood up and moved away, but not before dropping a dollar bill in Holly's lap.

"Try not to drink it," the person said.

"God bless you," Holly said.

She reached into her overnight bag and pulled out Muhammed Siddiqui's phone.

She pressed the connection to Gregory "Snake" Richards, a Rossellini underboss who had set her up a year earlier with the fake boat charter of Captain George McKlane. It had turned out to be Silberg, the escrow crook.

"What's happening, buddy?" Snake said.

"Hello, Gregory."

Snake said nothing.

"This is Holly."

"I know that."

"You're a dead snake crawling," Holly said. Then she closed the connection and turned off the phone. Holly got back on her bike and moved to another bench, deserted, two blocks away. She waited for 15 minutes. Nobody checked the area where she had been.

She turned on the phone and dialed Angelo Rossellini.

"I've been waiting for your call," he said.

"Here's how this is going to work, Angelo. I have a dossier on you that I can give to my friends at Homeland Security that will shut you down."

"I'm not sure you have friends at Homeland Security," Angelo said.

"This is when you shut up, Angelo. You do not interrupt me, and you do not kill me. I will also send the dossier to the FBI. I might even send it to my friends at the *Miami Herald*. What a story. You will remove your men from the front of my condo, and you will do it now. If they do not go, I will pull the trigger and start sending all this material in 30 minutes. Once I pull the trigger, it's over for you, Angelo Rossellini, *finito Caro Padre*. One more thing. I want you to kill Gregory Richards for me. I hate snakes."

"And if I do all this, how do I know you will not come back for more and more and more, Holly?"

"Because you know me, Angelo. And you know I have always kept my word with you; I have always been loyal to you. Do as I say. You have lost a great friend, a daughter today, Angelo, and our friendship will never return. Ever. But we do not have to kill each other. It is your call. You have 30 minutes. And Angelo, I saw the man on the roof at Astor Condos. They must all vanish."

In anger, she thought of saying, *If you see me, walk to the other side of the street, or I will kill you.* She would not challenge Angelo this way. There was no upside to such a comment.

"Goodbye forever, Angelo Rossellini.," Holly said. "Don't forget Snake. Kill him tonight."

She closed the connection. She pulverized the phone with her feet, picking it up and tearing bits off of it, tossing them everywhere in the darkness.

She felt tears on her cheeks, but they were silent tears.

Angelo Rossellini looked at his assistant, who had just confirmed that the phone signal was no longer live, but he knew its location, he knew where it had been.

"It doesn't matter," Angelo said. "She will be gone. She has learned her lessons well."

He sounded old, which he was. He asked the assistant to leave, go home for the night.

He phoned his men at the Astor Condos and told them to pack it in, all of them, including the spotter on the roof of Astor Condos.

He called a landscaper in a nursery out near the Everglades and told him to take Gregory Richards on an airboat ride and feed him to the alligators, and to do it immediately, tonight.

Then Angelo Rossellini stood up, walked into his bedroom, undressed, and fell asleep watching television. Angelo Rossellini always slept well, although he never understood why.

At the Astor Condos, a bag lady peddled a rusty bike up to the back entrance. She entered the building and cautiously went up the emergency steps to the fourth floor.

She moved slowly from the emergency exit towards her penthouse condo.

The elevator dinged as she entered the vestibule. She raised her gun as the doors opened.

She almost shot one of her neighbors, the incredibly nosy woman down the hall who never had anything good to say about anyone in the building, the woman who always wanted to buy her penthouse condo.

Holly tried to hide the gun.

"What are you −."

Holly straightened up, gave her a huge smile, and said: "Happy Halloween, Betty!"

"Mother-of-God, Holly Smolkes," the overweight woman said, stepping out of the elevator. "Was that a real gun you were holding?"

"Squirt gun," Holly said, "Been to a Halloween party."

"Well, you're a few days early, aren't you?"

"What do you think of my costume, Betty?"

"It's very unattractive, deplorable. I think that was a real gun you pointed at me, Holly Smolkes," she said.

"If it were, Betty, you'd be dead."

She pushed past the woman, realizing that she had possibly made a mistake. She entered her penthouse, quickly moving from room to room, checking every closet, never putting down the gun.

She went to the safe and pulled out the secure computer as well as a large brown envelope, which she put on the kitchen counter.

She put a wad of money in her pocket.

She typed three words on the computer.

"Where are you?"

She showered quickly and took out an emergency rucksack she had always kept in the back of her closet. It was a top-of-the-line, sturdy, black backpack made by The North Face, and she had never had to use it until now.

The computer pinged. Holly looked at the screen. It said: "I'm in a cave in Virginia."

She replaced some clothes in the backpack, then slipped her computer into it. She turned the TV on, loud. She wrote something on the envelope on the counter and left it there. She took the elevator to the parking garage and got into her car, making sure her cell phone had not connected automatically to the vehicle.

As she drove out of the garage, she saw the flashing lights of a police car at the front entrance, two cops, and her neighbor Betty. Holly turned off her car lights, crept north on Pugliese Avenue, then east through a parking lot. She turned on her lights and drove down to Atlantic Avenue.

Then she went west to I-95 and took that interstate corridor north towards Virginia. It would be more than a 900-mile trip.

Chapter 13

Warriors Meeting Face-to-Face

Unexpected Visits to Leatherwood Farms

Torbjorn saw the glint of metal on the northern side of the barn. He calmly brought his sniper rifle to rest across his chest.

He stood in the shadow of an old oak tree at the entrance to his log cabin's gravel driveway. He had been on his way to the hen house for some eggs for a ham and cheese omelet, one of his favorite dinners.

His grandmother had always teased him about how he ate backward. Omelets were for breakfast, not supper. He missed the old girl.

Torbjorn waited, motionless, his shadow slowly stretching eastward with the dying sun. It had grown almost half a foot before he saw the sparkle of metal again.

Torbjorn leaned against the oak tree near his driveway and slowly raised the scope of his M2010 sniper rifle to eye level. He heard the sound of a boot on gravel behind him, and then a voice.

"Please, Sergeant Petersson, put your weapon down."

Torbjorn kept his gun aimed at the barn.

"No harm will come to you, Sergeant Petersson. Please put the weapon on the ground. I am pointing my rifle at the back of your head."

Petersson did not move.

"Please," the voice said. "I am the person who sent you the emails that will stop the theft of your property."

"Then why are you pointing a rifle at my head?" Torbjorn asked, without moving. "And who are the five men jogging towards me from the barn right now?"

"Those are my associates," the voice said.

Torbjorn still did not budge. He had no plan because there could be none. His mind remained calm, waiting.

The voice said: "It is often difficult for warriors to meet one another and not shoot first, Sergeant Petersson. I am going to put down my weapon, and you may turn around and point yours at my head if you wish."

Torbjorn heard the sound of metal on the gravel drive. He listened to the person shifting his feet. He turned around and pointed his M2010 at the man's head.

"The man who sent me the emails was a marine biologist with the International Water Conservation Board in Portland, Maine," Torbjorn said.

"Yes, I know. I am Doctor Ahmed Kahn," the man said, holding out his hand.

Torbjorn did not lower the gun.

"So you travel around with your little army dressed like jihadist warriors while you do what, conserve water?"

The man laughed, showing the palms of his hands.

Ahmed Kahn's five "associates" crunched gravel as they entered the driveway, all of them pointing their AK-47s at Torbjorn Peterson.

"Lower your weapons," Dr. Ahmed Kahn said to his men. "We are all friends here."

The only person who did not lower his weapon was Torbjorn Petersson.

"Please," Dr. Kahn said. "We need to talk."

Slowly, Torbjorn lowered his rifle.

"What are we going to discuss?"

"We are going to talk about changing the world, Sergeant Petersson, so that governments cannot steal from their people."

Torbjorn stared at him, saying nothing.

"My men will remain outside if you wish," Dr. Kahn said. "Although they are thirsty and cold, Sergeant Petersson."

"They can stay out on the porch at the front of the cabin," Torbjorn said.

"Thank you."

"Just you and me inside, Ahmed. Your men stay out on the porch, and you remain unarmed."

"That is fine," Ahmed said.

"You like cookies and milk?"

Torbjorn was trapped and outgunned, and he knew it. He would play along with them. An opportunity would appear. He had to play nice until it did so.

They went inside, and Torbjorn gave one of the warriors two quarts of fresh milk and three large packages of Oreo cookies to take out to the men on the porch.

A sugar high would hit them in 15 minutes, he reckoned. In 30 minutes, their blood pressure would begin to drop. Their focus would wander as well. He just needed an opportunity, and one of their assault rifles. His sniper rifle was good at great distances, but close up, it was unwieldy.

He and Ahmed sat down and talked about what was wrong with America.

Ahmed could not understand why Torbjorn was not particularly upset about his government.

"I sent you all their secret emails so you could see just how corrupt, how evil your government is," Ahmed said.

"Thank you for those," Torbjorn said.

Ahmed failed to comprehend why anyone would condone the theft of a hard-working farmer's land. Ahmed quickly understood that the conversation he was having with Torbjorn Petersson bore no resemblance whatsoever to his discussion with the resort manager in Africa who had his land confiscated by the government of Lesotho.

"I appreciate your sending me those emails, Ahmed," Torbjorn said again. "I had a meeting with my lawyer this morning, and he's pretty certain that he can successfully contest all of the eminent domain proceedings. He will make them disappear, and I'll be able to keep the farm."

Torbjorn Petersson did not tell Ahmed that he had come very close to killing the lawyer when they first met in his driveway that morning.

"You trust your government to give you back your farm? Your government will change its mind so easily?"

"No, I trust the legal system of America to do this. Before it's over, some of the people who tried to steal my property will probably end up in jail."

"Surely you do not believe this."

"I do. Absolutely. I live in the United States of America. Have another cookie," Torbjorn said.

He could see something click over in Ahmed's mind, a new thought that might remain a secret. "Tell me about yourself, Sergeant Petersson. Tell me about your time in Afghanistan as a warrior."

Petersson did. He said he did not like Afghanistan. He served two tours as a sniper, although he did not mention how many Afghanis he had killed. Nor did he tell Ahmed that he enjoyed bolstering his kill numbers in his spare time.

"You're from Afghanistan, aren't you?" Torbjorn said.

"From Nuristan, in the north," Ahmed said. "It looks a little like your Virginia, but rockier, colder, and with different trees. I also did not like Afghanistan very much. I prefer Syria or Iraq, both much warmer, but with a much softer green near the rivers."

"I remember how cold the winters were in Afghanistan," Torbjorn said.

"What do you do here in America?" Ahmed asked.

"Computers," Torbjorn said.

Dr. Ahmed Kahn's eyes widened. "I, too, am computers, Sergeant Petersson."

The two men watched each other. Ahmed shouted something in Pashto, and his men entered from the porch with their guns pointed at Torbjorn.

"I thought they were going to stay out on the porch," Torbjorn said. "You promised me that they would not enter my home."

"I broke my promise," Ahmed said. "I treated it with the same respect with which you have treated my homeland."

"So, I guess you want to see my computers," Torbjorn said. Perhaps in the darkened room, he would have a chance to wrestle away the assault rifle that one of the Jihadists had just handed Ahmed.

"But only you, alone, not your men," Torbjorn said.

"Of course," Ahmed said. "I promise." He said something to his men.

Torbjorn walked with Ahmed into what once had been the main bedroom of the log cabin.

The windows were all blacked out with heavy shades.

Every one of Ahmed's men followed with their guns aimed at Torbjorn.

Ahmed apologized.

"I am terrible with promises, especially with infidels, Sergeant Petersson."

In the dimness, Ahmed Kahn saw a series of rectangular shapes surrounding a huge U-shaped desk.

"Make them work," Ahmed said.

Torbjorn threw a switch, and a generator started to hum softly outside the cabin.

Lights in the molding near the ceiling cast a soft glow throughout the room.

"Turn the computers on," Ahmed Kahn said, prodding Torbjorn with his assault rifle, then stepping quickly back as he watched the muscles in his prisoner's neck tighten.

Torbjorn turned on a bank of uninterruptible power supplies and, once they all showed solid lights and sufficient voltage, he just stood there looking at the terrorists. The monitors remained black.

"Turn them all on," Kahn said.

Why didn't he keep a gun in the computer room?

Ahmed took a step backward and pointed his assault rifle at Torbjorn's head.

"I can turn them on myself, Sergeant Petersson, but I would have to kill you first."

"Then you wouldn't have the passwords," Torbjorn said.

"I am the best hacker you will ever meet, Sergeant Petersson. I assure you that my software can figure out your passwords in less than five minutes."

Torbjorn turned the computer screens on and slowly typed in passwords at each of the computer stations.

One bank of monitors said, "Canada." The others said, "England, Turkey, South Africa, Brazil, and Mexico."

"What do you do with all these computers?" Ahmed Kahn asked.

"I'm a derivatives trader," Torbjorn lied.

He was trapped.

Six ISIL warriors.

Six assault weapons.

Most of the computers had three monitors; some had four. The six primary monitors, one for each computer bank, went through their setup quickly. They were all powerful computers.

As each of the screens filled with apps, Ahmed clapped his hands together twice. "This is where Allah will bring me when I die," he said.

Torbjorn thought that sounded like a good idea, but Allah was taking too much time.

"How about the 70 virgins?" Torbjorn asked.

Dr. Ahmed Kahn looked at him with a wry smile. Then he said: "Screw the 70 virgins."

He laughed at his cleverness. Torbjorn did not.

"You stupid Americans have always misinterpreted that part of the Qur'an," Ahmed said.

"How's that?" Torbjorn asked.

"It was raisins and dates, not virgins," Ahmed said.

"Really? Your Paradise prefers raisins to virgins?"

"You cannot survive in the desert on virgins."

"So your concept of Paradise is a big pile of sand where you prefer raisins and dates to beautiful, young virgins. Now I understand. And you call us stupid?"

Torbjorn's conclusion angered Ahmed, but he let it pass.

Everyone eventually moved out of the computer room. When Torbjorn started to turn off the computers, Ahmed Kahn stopped him.

"Leave them all on," the ISIL leader said.

They returned to the living room, where Torbjorn built a fire, around which they all crowded.

Six ISIL warriors.

Six assault weapons.

Torbjorn was armed with an iron fire poker.

They ransacked his pantry. They found two loaves of bread, a full jar of chunky peanut butter, and blueberry jam, marmalade, and a homemade strawberry spread that his grandmother had made.

"Her name was Ernestine Petersson, and she died because people wanted to steal our farm," Torbjorn said.

Nobody touched the strawberry spread.

He and Ahmed resumed sitting at the dining room table, having a one-sided conversation in which Ahmed tried to learn as much as he could about Torbjorn Petersson.

Torbjorn told him a lot, very little of which was true.

They discussed the Gathright Dam and Lake Moomaw. Ahmed was interested in the trout club further up the river, but Torbjorn said he had never visited The Cold Springs Trout Club. They discussed caves, and Torbjorn quickly realized that Dr. Kahn knew a lot about them, but primarily as defensive safe houses in which to hide from more powerful, better-equipped enemies. Dr. Kahn was fascinated by the Sponge Effect of the Appalachian caves that had stalled the filling of Lake Moomaw.

As night fell, Torbjorn asked Dr. Kahn where they intended to spend the night.

One of his soldiers was already sound asleep in front of the fireplace. Most of the others were having a hard time keeping their eyes open.

Their sugar highs had reversed into sugar lows. But Torbjorn was still badly outnumbered.

"We like to camp out. We have found a wonderful cave up the stream behind your log cabin."

Torbjorn recalled the gunshots that he heard at the mailbox earlier.

"Well, it might get close to freezing tonight," Torbjorn told him. "The cave should offer you good shelter. I think I know the one you're talking about."

They must have shot the mother bear, who would have kicked her cubs out of the den late in the summer. She would have been alone in her cave.

"Yes," Dr. Kahn said. "We don't mind the cold. Although, if you had been Muslim, you would have offered us the warmth of your home."

"I'm a Baptist, Dr. Kahn. Always have been, always will be. You're welcome to sleep in the barn if you want."

He left it at that. If he could just get them out of the house, then he could escape with his sniper gun and kill them one at a time from a safe distance.

Suddenly, surprisingly, commanded by Ahmed, all of the warriors stood, without pointing their guns at anyone. Dr. Kahn extended his hand to Torbjorn.

"Thank you for the Baptist hospitality you have shown us, Sergeant Petersson."

Torbjorn stood, took his hand, suddenly lost his balance, and found himself in a death lock on the floor, with the weight of Ahmed Khan and two other men on top of him.

He knew it was pointless to struggle.

He could not undo the stranglehold of Doctor Kahn.

Oddly, he tried to think what day it was. The date was somehow important, but his fingers turned numb quickly. He had killed two men himself this way.

What a stupid move, he thought.

He suddenly remembered what his platoon leader had told him in Afghanistan when he started his first tour in that godforsaken country.

"You only have to be careless one time to put a bookend on your life," the First Lieutenant said. The man was wise beyond his rank. He had begun his career in the Marines as an enlisted man. Torbjorn could not remember his name.

Friday, October 28.

That was the date. That would be Torbjorn's final day.

"I will not kill you," he heard Dr. Kahn whisper, but it was far away, oxygen-starved, and he did not trust the words.

Mac McKlane drove out through the Richardson Gorge early Saturday morning. The foliage was in its final bloom after a sharp overnight freeze. He found the entrance to Leatherwood Farms without overshooting it because both Sharonda and his grandfather had promised him that he would miss it.

The Leatherwood shrubs at the entrance were in their last shades of autumnal yellow, almost brown. He approached the first pasture visible on the farm, cringing as the heavy Lincoln Navigator clanged across the metal cattle guard pipes at the open gate.

He rolled to a stop in the gravel driveway adjacent to the rustic, two-story log cabin. Sergeant Torbjorn Petersson lived in an old, beautiful place.

He took the folder on the passenger seat and opened it, scanning the information for the tenth time.

He stepped out of the SUV and went to the front door, knocking on it lightly. A man whose face he almost recognized through the screening answered the door.

Mac said: "I'm looking for Torbjorn Petersson."

"I am Torbjorn Petersson," the man said with a slightly English accent.

Mac flipped open the folder and said: "No, you're not."

"Please," the man said. "Come in."

He was holding a gun.

"That's all right," Mac said. "It wasn't important. I'll come back later."

He recognized the face: Ahmed Kahn. But how did he get here?

Mac McKlane turned to go, tasting metal in his mouth.

He started to reach for his Glock, but it was too late. Three men in the driveway were pointing assault rifles at him.

"Please," Ahmed Kahn said, swinging open the screen door, "Come in, whoever you are."

They tied him to a chair, emptied his pockets and put everything on the dining table next to the large picture window with a view of the barn.

Ahmed Kahn sifted through his prisoner's belongings.

He held up the Homeland Security badge and Mac McKlane's ID in its burnished, brown leather case. He smiled.

"Oh, my," he said.

He picked up Mac's cell phone. He saw it was blinking. He quickly shut it down.

"Check his vehicle and make sure that it is not connected to anything electronically," Ahmed said. "Even better, disconnect the battery."

It was a government-issued Lincoln Navigator. When it went off-grid, Mac thought, somebody would have to notice it. But who, and how quickly?

He counted six men, none of them Torbjorn Petersson. They all looked like seasoned veterans of foreign wars.

"So, Mister Director of Homeland Security, how are we doing today?" Ahmed Kahn said.

Mac McKlane remained silent.

Ahmed Kahn moved closer. Incredibly, his breath smelled like peppermint mouthwash.

"What do people call you, George McKlane the Third? You Americans always have pet names, like dogs and cats. What is your pet name, George McKlane?"

"George McKlane, Lieutenant Colonel, the United States Marine Corps, 2028658."

Ahmed Kahn burst out laughing at the absurdity of a military code that required a prisoner only to state his or her name, rank, and serial number.

All of his men laughed with their leader, although they did not recognize anything funny.

Kahn leaned in close to McKlane. "Surely you realize that ISIL, as you call us, does not subscribe to any of the silly treaties or protocols of your Military Code or the Geneva

Convention, McKlane. We truly enjoy torturing and killing infidels, men, women, and children. We are indiscriminating holy warriors. We slaughter all non-believers."

He leaned back, rocked forward, and covered Mac's face with spit.

"You are a great prize," Ahmed Kahn said. "Allah has been extraordinarily kind to us today."

Ahmed Kahn studied the folder which McKlane brought. The detailed dossier on Torbjorn Petersson contained many surprises, including all of the emails that Ahmed had sent in the package he mailed to Petersson from Maine, as a marine biologist with the International Water Conservation Board.

"I see that we hack the same government offices," Ahmed said, shaking the emails about Lake Moomaw and placing them back in the folder.

After a while, he looked at Mac and said: "Petersson is a professional killer? Last night he was a lamb to be slaughtered. If he's the best you have, our victory will come much sooner than I expected."

He kept reading; then, he closed the folder.

"I think, Lieutenant Colonel, I am going to make you a movie star for all of your televisions in America. You offer us so many electronic outlets, the choice of so many media. You are probably handsome to all of your uncovered whores. I noticed that you have very nice teeth. We will keep them in your mouth until we have captured you on camera. I have an entire computer studio available to me here in this cabin, a gift from Sergeant Petersson. Praise be to Allah."

His men became a chorus to his final sentence, spoken in Pashto. The rest had been in perfect English.

Ahmed stood and looked at the Director of Operation Poison Well at Homeland Security, but with no smile.

They kept McKlane tied up in the cabin all day. Nobody spoke to him.

Nobody offered him water when he requested it. The second time he did so, Ahmed Kahn threw a glass of water in his face. Mac managed to catch some of it in his mouth.

"Name, rank and serial number only," the ISIL leader said with a smile, spitting on him again. "You must adhere to the Geneva Convention, isn't that right, Lieutenant Colonel?"

They only approached him to check the strength of his bonds. He could not feel his hands or feet because of the tightness of the ropes securing him.

As night fell, Ahmed Kahn told his men: "Take him to the cave. Pin him to the wall. Guard him with your lives."

The men took McKlane up the ravine behind the cabin. They had powerful military flashlights with them, but the dense foliage that remained on the trees in late October hid their nighttime passage.

If anyone had looked in their direction from State Road 603 a mile off, on the other side of the Jackson River, they might have seen a dull caterpillar of light snaking up a crevice on the northern slopes of Coles Mountain.

A few headlights passed northeast and southwest on State Road 603, but none of the cars slowed down. Campers three miles south might have noticed the lights moving slowly up the ravine.

The hikers were on the Sweet Acorn Trail across the Jackson River, on the mountain just west of Coles, but their night vision had disappeared into their campfire.

Nobody saw anything.

When the men got to the cave, the putrid smell of death overpowered Mac McKlane. He gagged involuntarily. The men around him laughed, covered their faces, and pushed McKlane further into the cavern. They shined their lights into his eyes, blinding him. When he tried to close them, they held them open with their fingers. The military lights quickly stole his vision.

They tied McKlane to the wall with a rope looped through some metal eyelets. *How long had these people been here? How could they equip a cave as if it was a dungeon?* The burning in his eyes slowly faded, but he felt confident that his eyesight had suffered permanent damage. It was the smell that bothered him the most: the rotting, sickening scent of death.

As his sight recovered, he could make out some shapes, but not with any definition.

He assumed that the stench came from the body to his left, lying on the floor of the cave.

He was confident that it was Torbjorn Petersson.

His body jerked when a voice to his right floated out of the darkness and said: "It's a bear."

Chapter 14

Operation Poison Well Almost Panics.

Too Many People Drop Off the Homeland Grid.

Shadrach Ringer stepped into Roberta Macumber's office without knocking. He said: "I think you better come look at this, and I think once you do, you'll want to get hold of Mac." She followed him through the office to an area few people ever visited. The sign on the door said: "Co-Op."

She stepped into the small space, which had monitors nobody wanted, all hooked up to computers that were several years beyond their logical expiration date. Two technicians who were approaching retirement themselves looked up and stood when they realized an assistant director of Homeland Security had entered the cobwebs of their domain.

"Loop it again, and keep the video going," Shadrach said to one of the gray-haired men.

The computer screen in the room, 42 inches diagonally and weighing about 120 pounds, began showing a grainy piece of digital film. Initially, Roberta thought they shot the video in black and white, but in fact, it was an early winter scene in New Brunswick, Canada, just south of Edmundston near the border of the state of Maine. The picture showed six men in black winter clothing crossing the border into America. They were all carrying what looked like Kalashnikov AK-47s and backpacks, but no heavy armaments like surface to air missiles.

They moved quickly through the security camera's field of vision; then, the loop began again. Roberta saw tiny bits of brown and red in the trees, and she realized that the cameras had shot the video in color.

"Exactly where is this?" Roberta asked.

Shadrach had to refer to some notes one of the technicians had given to him in the hallway earlier. "It's in the northeastern section of the Appalachians where Saint John and Madawaska Rivers converge. It's a few miles from Quebec Province and on the border of Maine and New Brunswick."

"When?"

"Uh, six days ago."

"Six days ago? Are you kidding? Is this a joke?"

She glared at the technicians, who quickly took several steps back.

"Well," Shadrach said, "the camera is up a tree in Indian Territory." He referred to his notes again.

"The Madawaska Maliseet First Nation. It's a Federal Indian Reserve. They took their sweet time turning the film over to the Canadian Mounted Police. The Mounties sent it to Co-Op immediately."

"Six days old?" Roberta said, looking at the looping film. "They could be anywhere. I'll get hold of Mac right away."

She looked at the technicians, shook their hands, told them they had done a great job and left with Shadrach. After the door had closed, the two old guys let out sighs of relief; and high-fived one another like much younger men.

"I just can't wait to tell the grandkids about this," one man said.

His partner wagged his finger and said: "Top security, you old goat."

They smiled at each other, just months from retirement.

"What say we cut a CD of this just for our very own, private collection?"

"Good idea," his partner said.

In her office, Roberta phoned Mac on his private, secure phone. She clicked off after 18 rings. She dialed his regular cell phone and got his voice recording to leave a number, and a message that he'd call back as soon as possible.

She got up and walked into the Comm room.

"Where's the Director right now?" she asked.

Three people consulted their screens. One after the other, they all came up empty.

"The Director is in Virginia," Roberta said.

"He's off-grid," they all said, almost in unison.

"How is that possible?"

She wheeled around and almost ran into Sookie Ringer, who said: "Government vehicle. He probably took a G-car up there, don't you think?"

"Good for you, Sookie. Find out."

A few minutes later, Shadrach and Sookie were in her office. Sookie said: "I talked to a corporal named Alvin in Warm Springs, Virginia, where they keep some government vehicles. They delivered a 2016 Black Lincoln Navigator to Director McKlane yesterday."

"Where is it?"

"They don't know. It's off-grid."

"How does an SUV go off-grid?"

"Well," Shadrach said, "it's not easy. Our vehicles kept sending signals even when they blew up in Iraq." It was no time for pleasantries. Something was wrong. "The vehicle would have to suffer a total, electrical failure."

"Or," Sookie said, "you could disconnect the battery."

"Which Mac might do as a signal if he was in some sort of trouble," Shadrach added. "The mechanical version of flying the American flag upside down."

"Or maybe someone else disconnected the battery to hide his car," Roberta Macumber said. "We're in the dark, people." Things were about to get darker.

A member of the team leaned into Roberta's office and said: "We've got a police report out of Delray on Smolkes."

"Is she in jail? Tell me she's in jail," Roberta said.

"Nope, but we could probably arrest her."

"What has she done that I don't know about?"

"One of her neighbors, where she lives, says she pointed a gun at her when she stepped off the elevator last night and threatened to kill her."

"That does not sound like an Abira Kahn move," Roberta said. "She's a lot smarter than that."

"Yeah, well, according to Delray, the neighbor has lodged 14 complaints this year, on track to beat her record number of grievances last year, but, you know, this time it's attempted murder."

Nobody said anything. The man continued.

"We could arrest her, find out why she cut short her trip to the Bahamas with Siddiqui. We still haven't found her boat, but we will unless she pulled the plug on it."

"Where is she?"

"That's the problem," the man said. "Nobody knows. The cops busted into her place when they thought they heard gunfire, but it was just the TV turned up too loud. She skipped. Her cell phone has gone off the grid, but we know the make and year of her car. They're looking for it."

Roberta said: "Something's happening, and we better get on top of it. I want everyone in the conference room now."

The girl with dark hair threw her backpack into the seat opposite him at a truck stop just north of Jacksonville, within 15 miles of the Georgia border. The truck driver paused on his final bite of a Big Mac, mouth open, inches away from finishing dinner.

"Is this seat taken, darlin'?" the girl asked. She had a twang in her voice, but not enough to reveal her exact birthplace. "Good lookin' man like you sittin' here all alone?" Georgia, he thought, maybe South Carolina. He pushed away his paper plate, done.

"Looks to me like you're filling that seat just fine, sweetheart," he said.

"Why, yes," she said with a big smile. "Why, yes, I am. I am fillin' this seat right to the brim, aren't I?"

"You working, young lady?" he asked.

"Workin' and ridin', kind sir," she said. "Gotta get to my momma up in Tennessee. She's sorely ill. Kinda in a hurry."

"Well, I'm sorry to hear that, uh –"

"Betty Louise," she said, blowing him a little kiss.

"I can rig you up as far north as Roanoke," he said.

"Oh," she said, "you're gonna be my knight in shining armor, darlin'." They stood up. He paid his bill.

"Well, will you look at that ruckus out there in the parking lot," the truck driver said. "You just know that poor fella is gonna spend the rest of his life paying for that parking ticket. Whooheee."

The truck stop parking lot full of cars out front and 16- and 18-wheelers in the back, where there were showers for the big-rig drivers.

Four State Police cars surrounded a dark blue Ford Mustang Shelby® GT350 in front of the restaurant as Betty Louise, and her new trucker friend walked out the rear doors.

Two cops had their weapons drawn and pointed at the ground, fingers inside the trigger guard.

All of the officers understood that this was a critical bust since Homeland Security had tagged it as a top priority.

They had no details on the operation other than the color and model of the car and its license plate. They also had a printout of a nice-looking blonde with a scar on her face. She didn't look like a threat to Homeland Security, but that was not their call.

The sirens suddenly whooped out, but the flashing control lights still filled the night with streaks of red and blue beneath all the neon signs advertising food and gift shop franchises inside the truck stop. All the action created a bunch of onlookers.

The state troopers moved slowly through the crowds, elbowing a few people, looking for the person whose face was on the arrest warrant at which they occasionally glanced.

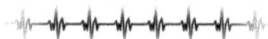

"My name's Jake," the truck driver told his new passenger as they walked out the back entrance and into the truckers' parking area. When they got to Jake's 16-wheeler, he said: "We're gonna have a fun ride, Betty Louise. Up ya go."

He kept his hand on her butt as long as he could as she got into the cab, and she gave him a little wiggle as she climbed in.

He laughed and passed her backpack up to her, which he thought was pretty heavy. Must be a strong girl.

Jake walked around to the driver's side, got in with a grunt, and started the rig up.

"Here we go," Jake said, moving his 16-wheeler out of the lot and smoothly changing gears as the rig slid into the entry lane going north.

In the dim glow of the truck cab, Jake said: "I meant to ask you, sweetheart. How'd you get that scar on the side of your face, pretty girl like you?"

"Aw, heck," she said. "I ran through a glass door when I was four years old, 'cause my momma wanted to give me a bubble bath."

The driver thought about bubble baths as he picked up speed, heading for the border of Georgia, and then north-northwest into the Appalachian Mountains with a destination of Roanoke, Virginia.

Holly Smolkes relaxed for the first time in half an hour. She had walked away from her Mustang five minutes before the State Police arrived. She had come close to leaving her backpack in the car, taking it at the last minute because it held her cash.

"Jake," she said. "I am pretty tuckered out, worrying about my momma and all."

"Well, sweetheart, you just climb into the sleeping berth back there and close your pretty eyes."

"Thanks, Jake," Holly said. "Are you married?"

"Sometimes," he said.

She kissed him on the cheek, laughed, and climbed into the sleeping berth, which had a comfortable twin-sized bed, neatly made, with a soft, stuffed rabbit sitting in the corner.

"Who's this," Holly called out.

"Floppy," Jake said, smiling in the glow of the truck dials on his dashboard.

Holly used the stuffed rabbit like a pillow. Out of nowhere, she thought about Mac McKlane, saw him laughing, naked without trying to cover up, looking at her with something close to love, and she smiled. Then she fell asleep.

They found Holly Smolkes boat anchored in Lake Boca on Sunday morning.

The harbor police quickly figured out that the battery was disconnected.

A boat nearby signaled the police patrol over, and one of the men said he knew the owner.

There were two cops in the harbor patrol boat, with a third one on the bridge of the *Wholly Mackerel*, keeping the ship, now running, stationary in the water.

One of the cops stepped aboard the neighboring boat, looked at the man who knew the owner of the *Wholly Mackerel*, and said: "Then you're probably under arrest."

"Whoa," the man said. "I just gave her a ride in my dingy over to the Boca Beach Club dock. I never saw the woman before in my life, I swear. She told me her battery was dead, and she needed to replace it."

"Battery was fine," the policeperson said.

"I don't know that woman," the man said. "I swear."

"Did she say where she was going?"

The man thought. He made himself look like he was thinking real hard. "West Marine," he finally said. "She was going to buy a new battery at West Marine."

The harbor cop stepped off the man's boat and signaled to his partner on the bridge of the *Wholly Mackerel*. At full throttle, the bow of Holly's boat lifted, roaring towards the Boca Inlet, followed by the Harbor Patrol boat.

"So much for the 'No Wake' rule," the man said.

"She must have been a drug dealer," someone else said.

At Homeland Security, Roberta Macumber treated the discovery of Holly Smolkes' boat as a non-event.

"But make sure they impound it," she said.

She had treated the discovery of Holly Smolkes' dark blue Ford Mustang at a truck stop just south of the Georgia border with far greater interest.

It helped them create a V-shaped flow pattern showing where Holly Smolkes might travel.

Also noteworthy was a thick brown envelope that had arrived on Macumber's desk, delivered in the overnight mail, addressed to George McKlane III, Homeland Security, Classified, Eyes Only.

The Delray Beach Police sent the package to Homeland Security Headquarters, unopened.

They had found it on a countertop in the kitchen of the condo owned by Holly Smolkes. The Police Chief in Delray Beach had spent a lot of time deciding whether or not to open the brown envelope. He finally decided not to mess with Homeland Security property.

It remained sealed.

Roberta was about to open the package, which had been scanned and bore no apparent risk when Shadrach and Sookie Ringer appeared at her door, both dressed in combat fatigues.

"I think you got it right in yesterday's meeting, Boss," Sookie said. "She's headed towards Hot Springs."

Shadrach added: "We just had a report from the Virginia State Police barracks in Roanoke. Looks like she hitched a ride in a truck and then assaulted the driver."

"Tell me everything about it," Roberta said, putting down the package.

––ᐟᶣ–ᐟᶣ–ᐟᶣ–ᶣᐟ–ᐟᶣ–ᐟᶣ––

Jake's 16-wheeler had pulled into a truck stop outside of Roanoke, about six miles short of his final destination. He rolled into a diagonal truckers' parking spot, got wholly undressed, and climbed into the sleeper cab. He hadn't heard any noise from the girl for almost 10 hours. She was tired.

"Time to play, sweetheart," he said. "Wakey, wake – ."

He never knew what hit him, although it turned out to be a black, metal flashlight that held six Type-D Alkaline batteries.

He kept it in a compartment over the bed. It weighed almost six pounds.

He had no idea how long he was unconscious because he couldn't see his watch.

The girl had roped him like a rodeo calf in the center of the twin bed. His head wound was bleeding badly, but it was not that serious. A possible concussion might prove more damaging, perhaps even life-threatening at his age.

It took him almost five minutes to wiggle his way into the driver area of the truck's cab.

When he fell out of the sleeper unit into it, he gave himself a black eye on the big knob of his gear shift. It stunned him for several minutes. He finally positioned himself in the driver's seat, but he had to lie on his back, upside down to reach the rope to blow the air blaster. He couldn't get his hands high enough to grab it, and he had to hook it with his left foot.

Three short, three long, three short blasts, over and over until some truckers finally opened the driver's door and found themselves staring at one of the whitest butts they had ever seen. The soft clicking of their iPhones mixed with their laughter until they saw all the dried blood on Jake's face.

One of the men ran to get the State Troopers that he had seen having breakfast in the truck stop. The truckers untied Jake and cleaned him up with several different First Aid kits.

By the time Jake got dressed, three Virginia State Troopers had worked their way into the crowd around the truck's cab. Jake was begging his fellow truckers not to put the photos on Facebook since it was a hooker that had done this to him.

The State Troopers were not interested in any of the pictures taken by a half dozen of Jake's fellow truckers, although they did smile at them.

The victim explained that he was tied up by a whore he had picked up at a truck stop near the Georgia border. A Trooper bagged the bloody flashlight.

Then the State Police huddled for a moment. One of them showed Jake a printout. "This the woman?"

"That's her," Jake said, recognizing the scar. "But she had black hair, not blonde."

The truckers crowded around to look at the picture. The woman was nice looking, but they all swore that they had never laid eyes on that dark-haired woman during their travels. Some of them would remember the face and the scar from that day forward.

—⧸⧹⧸⧹⧸⧹⧸⧹⧸⧹—

Shadrach and Sookie Ringer left Roberta Macumber's office to catch a helicopter to the Homestead in Hot Springs, Virginia. They were both very well-equipped.

Roberta Macumber finally opened the brown envelope addressed to George McKlane III, Homeland Security, Classified, Eyes Only.

She read it several times, trying to absorb the contents. It revealed an extraordinary list of criminal activities.

Why would Abira Kahn/Holly Smolkes be sending this sort of information to Homeland Security?

She picked up the phone and called Brigadier General George McKlane at the Pentagon.

They needed to talk.

Chapter 15

24 Barrels of Beer on the Wall

The Cold Springs Trout Club Throws a Party.

Long before anyone paved the road that ran through the Richardson Gorge, a quaint and very private trout club had established itself on the shores of the Jackson River, a little over three miles upstream from Leatherwood Farms. Seven families bought property on the river, creating the trout club in the late 1800s. They built rustic fishing cabins to which many of the owners would eventually retire.

They were all friends, and they had a common goal, banding together to keep the Jackson River a natural habitat. The campsites became a barrier to the rest of the world, a place where they could kick back and enjoy the mountain life they all left to make a living. They incorporated themselves as The Cold Springs Trout Club.

As the fishing cabins passed down from generation to generation, some of the children were not friends.

Feuds broke out as to who was responsible for what, and they surfaced in a bitter fight over a swinging bridge that spanned the Jackson River.

The people who had cabins on the "road" side of the swinging bridge fought bitterly over the maintenance charges that the people across the river felt should be shared by all.

The expenses had historically been standard charges, right up to a day in the spring of 2014, when Jonathan Wainwright stood before all the owners and presented a magnificent new bridge that would cost well over $45,000 to put in place.

It led to some severe fistfights between the families, who considered themselves tough mountain people. For several months, men and women would sit in their porch rockers with shotguns in their laps.

The Bath County Sheriff's Office drove through the Richardson Gorge once every day, around noon, with plenty of advanced warning. Nobody got shot and died.

Jonathan Wainwright had many influential friends in Covington, Virginia, less than 15 miles down the Jackson River. On many mornings, he could smell his friends, who either owned or were involved with the paper mill down in Covington. The sulphuric stench drifting up the valley when the wind blew just right was the sweet odor of money to Jonathan Wainright.

He had learned about the go-ahead for the Lake Moomaw project long before it became common knowledge, although plans for the flood-stopping dam had been alive since World War II.

Wainwright's father had been friends with old Tom Gathright, and Jonathan knew that the George Washington National Forest would swallow all of the Gathright properties after the older man died. It would make for a spectacular recreational destination, and the values of the properties located within The Cold Springs Trout Club would triple, quadruple, perhaps more.

Wainwright was a little worried about the Leatherwood Farms property further down the Jackson River because a hotel speculator might make a move on that acreage. Wainwright had friends who made sure that the eminent domain Condemnation process included the Leatherwood Farms spread.

That's when Jonathan Wainwright spent some money on architectural drawings at a firm in Covington, which he then presented to the members of The Cold Springs Trout Club as their new $45,000 bridge over the Jackson River.

In the months that followed, the people who rocked on their porches with shotguns disappeared. One by one, they all agreed to sell their properties to Jonathan Wainwright, who assured everyone that he only wanted peace and happiness in the Richardson Gorge.

The people on the other side of the river proved to be more of a problem. They had all voted for the $45,000 bridge and liked where they lived.

Unexpectedly, several of their homes burned to the ground when they were not there.

In the end, Jonathan Wainwright kindly purchased their scorched properties for more than the insurance companies were willing to pay the original owners.

Of course, he did cut his costs by profiting from the reduced payments made to him by the insurers.

At the end of 2014, Jonathan Wainwright owned 100% of The Cold Springs Trout Club.

He modernized and rebuilt all of the cabins, adding a few more on property lines that no longer existed. He built an oversized log cabin that would serve as the main lodge for The Cold Springs Trout Club.

Then he planned a Grand Opening ceremony, which he had to delay repeatedly because the Army Corps of Engineers kept screwing up as they tried to fill Lake Moomaw. It didn't make any difference to Wainwright whether or not they filled the lake. His trout club was at least a mile above what would eventually become the top of the recreation area.

Finally, he decided to squeeze his Grand Opening into the first week of November, just after Halloween. Jonathan Wainwright was sitting on a lot of assets that were producing no profits, and he was tired of seeing his money going out, with nothing coming in.

The archery deer season would still be going full blast until the middle of November, and the trout season lasted all year long. Wainwright had lined up a series of do-it-yourself programs in the main building, covering everything from fly tying for people who fished to making whiskey venison jerky strips for those who did not.

He licensed a few log cabin builders to set up kiosks in the main building. He owned a lot of property throughout Bath County.

He had permits to sell for hunting on private lands. He made sure the Catchable Trout Stocking Program, which started in October, regularly dumped a bunch of good-sized Rainbows and Browns both above and below The Cold Springs Trout Club.

He had a liquor license, and he built a beautiful bar in the large main cabin.

He ordered hand-made beer kegs mounted into the cabin wall. They were false fronts, into which industrial, 50-

gallon, stainless steel kegs would fit. He ordered a dark beer and a light lager online, and the website guaranteed delivery on the first day of November.

Jonathan Wainwright personally placed the order on a website called The Beer Bust. They never saw the request, because Pakistani members of ISIL hacked the site. The order was filled and confirmed, and ISIL even gave Wainwright a "first-time buyer" discount.

Although his order was for a half a dozen beer kegs, the truck that left a small chemical factory in Hunterdon County, New Jersey, contained four times the number of stainless steel, 50-gallon barrels.

Only two of them contained beer.

⼀⼁⼀⼁⼀⼁⼀⼁⼀⼁⼀⼁

At Leatherwood Farms outside Hot Springs, Virginia, the ISIL warriors forced Mac McKlane and Torbjorn Petersson to pull the putrid, maggot-covered body of the bear out of the cave and downwind, which meant lower on the mountain. A breeze usually followed the ravine towards the Jackson River.

The ISIL terrorists doused the bear with gasoline that they suctioned out of McLane's black SUV. Then they set the bear on fire.

"Perhaps this will be your fate," Ahmed told his prisoners as his men threw deadwood on top of the bear. "If you are fortunate, and I feel kind."

The smell remained in the cave, and Ahmed Kahn's soldiers brought up every cleaning solution they could find in the cabin. Their cache mistakenly included maple syrup, which Torbjorn and Mac drank. It was their only food.

After Mac and Torbjorn swabbed and scraped the floor of the cave, they were tethered once again to large metal eyelets screwed into the cavern's wall. They whispered.

"Someone might see the smoke," Mac said.

"The fire rangers would just assume it's from my cabin," Torbjorn said, "unless they start a forest fire, and these people are not stupid."

"I came here to meet you," Mac said.

"Your timing sucks, whoever you are."

"Mac McKlane. You did not kill my grandfather twice."

Petersson said nothing.

"I'm a Director of Homeland Security," Mac said. "I can't see much because they blinded me with their flashlights when they dragged me in here."

Torbjorn looked over at him, still whispering: "They did the same thing to me, but my eyes have almost recovered. Yours will probably come back, Director of Homeland Security. But I think you're still in pretty deep shit. You're going to be the prize bull."

"How long have they been here?" Mac asked.

"Since the day before yesterday. They showed up in the early afternoon on Friday. They may have been here longer. Their commander is a guy named Ahmed Kahn, and he's supposedly a marine biologist with the International Water Conservation Board."

Director Mac McKlane had heard a similar title when he was debriefing Shadrach and Sookie Ringer after their return to Homeland headquarters from Lesotho.

Ahmed Kahn was a marine biologist with the Suid-Afrikaans Water Conservation Board. A danger similar to the one in Africa now unfolded in the United States of America.

"How the hell did they outfit this cave?"

"They didn't," Torbjorn said. "I guess that it's been here for a long time. Someone probably lived in this cave once upon a time. Maybe some of my ancestors from Sweden. I'm just guessing."

They both watched one of Ahmed Kahn's men tapping on a portable computer just outside the mouth of the cave.

"My place is hard-wired," Torbjorn said.

"What does that mean."

"The signal my computers send out are all hard-wired into their routers, and proxy addresses cloak every one of them. WiFi is available on every router I own, but I never use it. My computers may not be invisible, but they're damned close to it unless someone understands what I'm doing and how I'm doing it."

It seemed unlikely that Ahmed Kahn's fighter would be playing a stand-alone computer game on his portable device. That would not require a link to the Internet. Instead, the ISIL warrior appeared to be using the computer to get information, in which case he was using the WiFi available through one of Petersson's routers.

Mac asked: "So you think he's sending a signal?"

"Probably. The satellite dish is at the top of the ravine."

"Kahn said he's going to make me a star on TV using your computer system. Can he do that?"

"Sure. Easily."

"How can I stop him from doing that?"

"Walk up to the top of the hill and slice the cable on the satellite dish," Torbjorn said.

Torbjorn leaned his head against the wall of the cave. Then he looked back at the man typing on his laptop.

"You got anyone looking for you?"

"Yes, I do. Quite a few people, I imagine."

"Well, they better get here pretty damned quick."

As Torbjorn said this, the darkened cave suddenly filled with dazzling light.

Both Mac McKlane and Torbjorn Petersson instinctively shrank from the brightness, thinking it might be a bomb dropping on top of the cave.

There was no explosion, only a slight hissing sound.

"Don't be afraid," Ahmed Kahn said as the Coleman lamp he brought up from the cabin cast shadows over the two captives trying to cover themselves in their corner of the cave. Torbjorn had three of these powerful lamps, and soon they erased the darkness in every corner of the cave.

"What is this place?" Ahmed Kahn asked Torbjorn, kicking him hard to get his attention.

"I have no idea," Torbjorn said. "I knew the cave was here, but I always left it to the bears."

The cave had once been a home. It had shelves dug into the walls. In the back of the cave, a few things were strewn across the floor: old, broken furniture, perhaps a crib and a useless two-legged stool.

In another area of the cave, broken wooden rods and torn cloth under a thick layer of dirt covered what might once have been a bed.

The metal fasteners in the cave's wall that held Petersson and McKlane were old, but not very rusted. They were probably used to tether animals.

"Somebody lived here," Ahmed said.

"A long time ago," Torbjorn said.

"Who?"

"I don't know," Torbjorn said. "My ancestors came here almost three centuries ago. Maybe they lived here before they built the farm in the valley."

"Your ancestors?" Ahmed asked.

"They came here in the late 1700s," Torbjorn said.

"Your ancestors," Ahmed repeated, smiling. Torbjorn looked at him, instinctively knowing what the ISIL commander's repetition meant.

Torbjorn pulled as hard as he could on his bonds, ripping the metal fastener attached to his right arm out of the wall, but the left eyelet did not budge.

He swung the free fastener out like a whip, narrowly missing Ahmed Kahn.

Another terrorist stepped in and delivered a hard blow to Petersson with the butt of his AK-47.

Torbjorn fell to his knees, his head down, knowing what was coming. He looked at Mac McKlane and whispered: "The Dish." Ahmed Kahn shot him in the head, twice.

"What did he say?" the ISIL leader asked McKlane.

"A prayer," McKlane answered.

"Good," Ahmed Kahn said. "That may help his journey to his ancestors."

An ISIL terrorist cut the rope holding Petersson's left arm to the eyelet sunk into the wall. He untied Mac and forced him to drag Petersson's body out of the cave to where the bear continued to burn.

"More firewood," one of the terrorists said to McKlane, in English. *So Ahmed Kahn was not the only linguist in the pack.*

Later, the ISIL leader returned to the cave, and he crouched down in front of McKlane. Two eyelets in the wall secured the prisoner.

"He murdered your people for money, Director McKlane. Surely you will not miss this savage, but I am curious. Why did you come to visit him?"

"One of his ancestors saved my grandfather's life a long time ago, in the Korean War."

"Ah, I know about this war of aggression that the infidels fought against the people of Korea. If I remember correctly, and I always do, you did not do well in that war. Isn't that right, Director McKlane?"

"George McKlane, Lieutenant Colonel, the United States Marine Corps, 2028658," McKlane said.

Ahmed laughed.

"Well, I am certain you will have more to say tomorrow in front of the cameras," Ahmed Kahn said. "Although even the stupidity of your name, rank, and serial number will capture the attention of America, don't you think? I wish you had worn your uniform, Lieutenant Colonel McKlane of the United States Marine Corps. They are quite pretty, with lots of trinkets on them displaying false bravery, and shiny fake gold buttons."

"George McKlane, Lieutenant Colonel, the United States Marine Corps, 2028658," McKlane repeated.

Ahmed spat on him and said something to his men in Pashto. They came and checked his bonds.

─────※※※─────

"Thanks for the ride," the hitchhiker said at the entrance to Leatherwood Farms. As the car that she exited from disappeared over the green metal bridge, she turned to begin the mile and a half walk to the cabin, which she knew about through an earlier computer message. She had used Google Earth to look at the farm when one of Ahmed Kahn's men texted its location to her.

Holly Smolkes tossed her black wig into the bushes. She walked up the road a few hundred yards and then stepped off it, walking towards a tall oak tree.

An ISIL terrorist stepped out from behind it, and he bowed to her, saying "Malalai," followed by a greeting in Pashto. He briefly looked at her face and then stared at the ground, embarrassed by his curiosity.

She replied in Pashto, but with the vocabulary of an eight-year-old, for which she apologized. "Speak English," she said. "I have forgotten the language I was born with."

His English was poor. He gave her an AK-47 and handed her a scarf with which to cover her face.

"I am Malalai," she said, hanging the veil loosely around her neck.

"You must cover yourself," the ISIL warrior said, looking away from her.

Holly Smolkes looked at the man.

"Malalai was the daughter of a shepherd, who took off her veil on her wedding day and used it as a flag to lead our holy warriors to victory."

The man refused to look at her.

"Let's go," she said, cradling the AK-47 and returning to the dirt drive leading into Leatherwood Farms. For almost half a mile, the man tried to get in front of her. He needed her to walk at a proper distance behind him. Every time he did so, Holly would trot into the lead and say: "Malalai *leads* holy warriors to victory in battle; she does not follow them."

Eventually, the ISIL terrorist stopped trying to lead her.

As they walked across the metal rollers at the gate to the first pasture at Leatherwood Farms, her guide pointed to the cabin in the distance.

"Our leader waits for you," the man said.

Then the ISIL soldier ran into the woods.

⎯⎯⎯⎯⎯⎯⎯

Roberta Macumber stood as Brigadier General George McKlane stepped into her office without knocking.

Her first thought was, *so that is how Mac will look thirty years from now, not bad.*

The General smiled and took a seat.

"Where's Mac?" he said.

"In Virginia," Roberta said. "But we don't know where he is. Have you heard from him since last Friday?"

The General's face hardened. "Not since Thursday," he said. "What's going on?"

"General," she said, "I don't think you have security clearance for Homeland Security."

"I have clearance for concern about my son, Assistant Director Macumber," he said.

"Yes, you do, Sir. I cannot tell you about the operation, and I certainly do not have to explain to you the capabilities of your son to survive in difficult situations. But in the interest of National Security, I am not at liberty to offer you any details whatsoever about his current operation. I wish I could, General. But all of that information is classified, sir, and you understand what that means."

They stared at one another for almost 15 seconds; it seemed much longer.

"General, this dossier was sent to us by the Delray Beach Police Department."

She pushed it across the desk to him.

"The police found it in a condo owned by Holly Smolkes, and she addressed it to your son here at Homeland Security, General McKlane."

The General picked up the envelope. He did not take his eyes off of Macumber.

"I have read the dossier twice, General. It has nothing to do with Homeland Security. It does have a great deal to do with the real estate brokerage that your wife runs in Boca Raton. Roberto Rossellini owns that company together with your wife."

"He was at our wedding a few weeks ago."

"Yes, sir."

"How much danger is Mac in?"

"We'll know more in a day or two," Roberta said. "It's important, General, for you to get your house in order."

"Does Mac's operation have something to do with a man named Petersson?" the General asked.

"I'm afraid that name does not ring a bell," Roberta said. "Who's Petersson?"

She knew all about Torbjorn Petersson, and she hoped the slight twitch in her face gave nothing away.

"He's a hired killer who tried to kill my father, Captain George McKlane, last year. People say that he missed on purpose, and I believe it. Petersson's grandfather fought in Korea with my father. It's complicated."

Roberta stood up. "You're going to find that dossier very interesting, General. If I hear anything from Mac, or about Mac, I'll let you know."

It took a few seconds for the general to realize that the meeting was over, that he was there to pick up a file addressed to his son and nothing more. Macumber continued to talk as the General slowly stood.

"We have not made duplicates of the contents of that dossier, Sir." They had made triplicates. "Other copies may, of course, exist, but that would be the doing of Holly Smolkes, not Homeland Security. I have given the complete file to you as a professional courtesy."

The general moved towards the door. What did this woman mean about getting his house in order? He opened his mouth to ask when one of Macumber's staff suddenly leaned into the office, an excited young woman.

"We have a signal from Virginia," she said.

Chapter 16

A Folder Opens That Needs to be Closed.

Royal Coconut Yacht & Country Club

Shadows of Doubt Creep Into the McKlane Marriage.

Brigadier General George McKlane flew into Boca Raton Airport and drove to his father's house to celebrate Halloween with his new wife, Martha Krumble. It was early evening, and the gathering around the table on the lanai included his father, his wife, Sharonda, Samuel, and Judge Ralph Broadslate. A giant pumpkin with two teeth flickered at the gathering from its perch on the outdoor bar that defined one end of the lanai. Trick-or-treaters would be out in numbers in some areas of Boca, but not at the Royal Coconut Yacht and Country Club, where the only youngsters were grandchildren living elsewhere.

"I have an announcement," Martha Krumble said. "I am two months pregnant."

It surprised everyone, except for General McKlane, who smiled politely and received assurances that a teenager in his house would keep him young when he was in his mid-Seventies. Everyone wanted to know if it was a boy or a girl. Martha's answered, "We don't need another George."

"I will break the stranglehold of that moniker on the McKlanes if it's the last baby I have."

She smiled at the General.

At which point, General McKlane said something extremely odd.

"I hope our child is not born in prison."

At first, everyone just stared at him, and then they realized he was saying something that required a little more information to understand his statement.

"What in the world are you talking about, darling?" Martha asked. "Why would our child be born in prison?"

"What do you mean, boy?" Captain George asked.

Sharonda, Samuel, and Judge Broadslate looked at General McKlane but were quiet. The General looked at Martha Krumble.

"You are running a criminal enterprise, Martha," he said, placing the dossier given to him by Homeland Security in the center of the table. "When the information in that file is released, I guess that the Feds will shut you down overnight. Prison time will become the least of our family's concerns."

Ralph Broadslate had already leaned forward and grabbed the file.

The federal judge started thumbing through it. He did not get far before he said: "Holy smokes."

"What in the world are you talking about?" Martha said. "Explain yourself immediately, George McKlane."

"Don't get mad at me, Martha Krumble," the General said. "You're the one that has been using Accelerated Realty Sales as Florida's premiere money laundering enterprise."

"I have NO idea what you are talking about, George McKlane. NO idea. NONE!"

"How much of Accelerated Realty Sales do you own, Martha?" Judge Broadslate asked, lowering the tone a bit.

"Five percent," she answered. "I never really paid anything for it. Roberto said it was a 'sign-on' bonus."

"How well do you know Roberto Rossellini?"

"Well enough to be his grateful partner," she said. "He saved the company by pouring his own money into it when Anthony Silberg ran off with the escrow account last year."

"How was he repaid for that extraordinary generosity?" the judge asked.

"I have no idea," Martha said. "I am the broker of record. I deal with the buying and selling of residential properties in Palm Beach. I read the account statements; I don't create them."

"How about land development?" the Judge asked. "Were you ever involved with the building of places like, uh," he looked at the file in his lap and flipped back a few pages, "Rhondo Condos, for example?"

"No, although I might have assigned a few agents to a sales office, once that development was built and had show units. But that would not include Rhondo Condos. That was before my time."

"Rhondo Condos," her husband said. "That was where the scum Silberg killed that real estate agent before he got away from the Feds. I remember that. I was up there just after the shooting."

"She was married to Roberto Rossellini's son," Sharonda said. "Their marriage was annulled. I liked her. She was a spunky little white girl. She tried to hide the fact that her father knew you, Captain George. I don't know why. I think Silberg made her do that."

"She was the daughter of Sergeant Raymond Chapman," Captain George McKlane said, sitting at the head of the table. "He's the man who saved my life in Korea." He looked at Martha. "Barbara Rossellini. She was born when Sergeant Chapman was an old man, even older than your husband."

"Did you know anything about the money-laundering scheme going on at Accelerated Realty Sales, Martha?" Judge Broadslate asked.

"I still don't know anything about it," Martha said.

"Okay," Judge Broadslate said. "Sharonda, did I hear a rumor about you making some of your famous pumpkin pie for Halloween?"

"Nope," she said. "That's Samuel's famous pumpkin pie, Judge. It may be the only reason we're still married." She smiled at everyone at the table. "That's a joke, folks. You white people need to lighten up a bit."

Everyone finally laughed. Even the brigadier general relaxed. He was starting to realize that his wife was probably an innocent pawn.

"Well, bring all that pie out here, because I am going to go through this entire 12-page file as if it were a federal indictment, which is probably exactly what it will become."

He did, and it took a lot of pumpkin pie to get to the end of the report. As the Judge analyzed it, the federal indictment could include money laundering, homicide, manslaughter, bankruptcy fraud, drug trafficking, mail fraud, wire fraud, embezzlement, bribery, conspiracy to defraud the government, extortion, forgery, computer fraud, insurance fraud, arson, obstruction of justice, and racketeering.

"So," the federal judge said, looking at Martha Krumble, "you've been a very busy girl."

Everyone laughed, including her husband.

"How could I not have seen any of this?" Martha asked.

"Does Rossellini have people on your payroll that you know nothing about?" the judge asked.

"Yes," Martha asked. "About half a dozen of them, all in commercial sales and land development. Our monthly sales figures do not even include them."

"I rest my case," the judge said. "The worst you can expect, General McKlane, is a wife who testifies on behalf of the government to put a mob kingpin behind bars."

Nobody spoke for a moment. Then Martha asked everyone at the table an important question.

"Doesn't that make me an endangered species?"

Only Captain George went to sleep at a reasonable time on Halloween. Sharonda made sure that he was comfortable, properly medicated, and a little sleepier than usual with the help of an extra PM tablet. Then she went back downstairs and joined Martha, General McKlane, Judge Broadslate, and her husband, Samuel. After a brief discussion, she changed her employment agreement with the McKlane family.

"Okay, we'll do it," Sharonda said. "From now on, Martha, Samuel, and I are Captain George's bodyguards."

She looked at the General.

"I will add a few of my men to Martha's detail," he said.

They worked on their plan for much of the night. The following morning, calls went out for a mandatory emergency meeting of most of the people who worked at Accelerated Realty Sales. The real estate agents were surprised by calls made before sunrise. Angelo Rossellini's people received no prior notice of the gathering.

The meeting started at 9:30 a.m., and not everyone was there, although quick calls made by those Realtors® who did attend swelled the ranks to about 80 percent of the staff.

Martha stood on a podium at the front of the Bull Pen, a large open office area where the company's 74 Realtors® spent time in front of computer screens calling customers, arranging meetings, home showings, and closings.

Brigadier General George McKlane stood to one side of the podium, joined by four armed members of a Marine Corps Raider Regiment at Parade Rest. Samuel and Sharonda Nelson stood on the other side of the platform, both carrying visible, holstered Glocks. Another man, in a suit, joined the group. A few people in the crowd vaguely remembered him from a meeting a year earlier: FBI Special Agent Scott Larsen.

"I have always believed in transparency," Martha began. "And this morning, it is going to cost everyone in this room their job. Effective immediately, Accelerated Realty Sales is closed, permanently out of business, and all real estate activities halted."

She let this sink in. A lot of the real estate agents were already on their cell phones, many talking in hushed tones to other real estate firms to which they were willing to bring their existing expertise and business.

"I have surrendered any ownership I have in this company and voluntarily suspended my Broker's License," Martha said.

Special Agent Scott Larsen of the Federal Bureau of Investigation noticed that some of the employees who were in the back of the room were moving into their offices, an area called the Goldfish Bowl, where the top producers in the company sat in spacious, glassed-in enclosures. Larsen spoke into a lapel button on his nicely-tailored suit.

Martha continued.

"For many years, unbeknownst to most of you or me, this company has conducted illegal, dishonest, and criminal activities which include ... "

Martha Krumble read the list given to her by the Judge.

Most of the real estate agents hung up their phones as Martha enumerated the unlawful activities involved.

They realized that what was going on was an event that might have a profound effect on their lives, one which might taint their futures in the business.

The Rossellini people, including one woman, had a different reaction. They grabbed their belongings and headed for the exit at the rear of the building. Members of the particular unit led by FBI Special Agent Scott Larsen greeted each of them as they hurried out.

Angelo Rossellini was in silk pajamas when he received the first phone call. It came even before Martha Krumble addressed the people at Accelerated Realty Sales.

His sources were deep inside the federal government.

Angelo was never a man to show anger, but the betrayal of Holly Smolkes broke him.

A sound came out of his mouth, filled with anger and angst and the wounds of betrayal and disloyalty, a guttural growl of horror that grew in intensity until it reached a point of no return.

He hurled his cell phone through his bedroom window. He ripped open his pajama top and tore the white hair off of his chest. Old age had turned his skin thin. He bled.

The people working on his palatial estate in a private enclave west of Boca Raton ran to his bedroom. They saw a man they had never seen before, breaking lamps, hurling heavy objects into mirrors, tossing priceless, leatherbound books off a bank of shelves inset in the wall.

His voice had disappeared, silenced by anger, leaving only a wild-eyed, bloody-chested maniac with an open, silent mouth searching for something to destroy.

No one approached him.

Some people were on their cell phones, but nobody dialed 911. They knew better. No cops.

Rossellini collapsed into the middle of an expensive Persian carpet, a personal gift from the supposed offspring of a Sultan in the Ottoman Empire, with whom Rossellini had once done business in Turkey. The anger in Angelo had no appreciation of the irony of the rug's Muslim origins.

He sat there in a heap, a ruined man who knew that no escape existed. His voice returned as a whisper: "She was a daughter to me. The son I never had. The only person I ever trusted. I should have killed her."

Rossellini's real son, Roberto, was close enough to hear this. He walked out of the room, angry and hurt, Angelo's rejected son, talking rapidly into his iPhone.

Within the hour, several limousines pulled into the white, gravel drive of Angelo Rossellini's estate. Important men got out and entered his home.

After about 15 minutes, they left with Rossellini in their care. His son, Roberto, tried to go with them. A man held his hand on the son's chest, shaking his head almost imperceptibly. Roberto backed away, rejoining the entourage gathered at the front entrance. The limos drove off quickly.

Within another hour, black SUVs turned into Rossellini's gravel drive. They had blue and red flashing lights in their windows, but no blaring sirens.

They, too, were looking for Angelo Rossellini.

Nobody knew where he was.

Someone mentioned a breakfast meeting at The Breakers in Palm Beach, but they weren't sure.

The Feds had a search warrant, which had taken some time to get. They combed the house for hours but found nothing, although some household workers were in the master bedroom on the second floor, cleaning up a mess someone had made.

One of the federal agents noticed the broken glass in the window through which Angelo Rossellini had earlier hurled his cell phone.

"Burglars," one of the housekeepers said.

"On the second floor?" the agent asked.

"Vandalism," Angelo's son, Roberto Rossellini, said. "Kids have no respect anymore."

The limousines that included Rosselini as a passenger drove to the Palm Beach Kennel Club in West Palm Beach, which was unexpectedly closed.

Five men, including Rossellini, exited from two limousines and walked into a private room. They sat down at a poker table.

A man entered the room with a dealing shoe filled with cards. He placed it on the green felt table and started to sit down in the dealer's chair.

Then he realized that all of the players, except for Rossellini, had their hands on the table, palms up. The dealer quietly backed out of the room without being asked to do so.

Each man had a half a million dollars in poker chips stacked in front of him, black $10,000 chips, blue for $5,000, and green for $2,500. There were no chips of lower value.

"You have turned into a hazardous, foolish old man, Angelo," one of the men said.

Another man passed around copies of the dossier, which Roberta Macumber of Homeland Security had given to Brigadier General George McKlane.

"This is a gift given to me by a close associate in the Federal Government," the man said. "It is a dossier put together by Holly Smolkes, who all of us know. She is the bodyguard with a scar on her face."

All of the men silently read the 12 pages, looking up and glaring at Rossellini as they did so.

"How could an outsider know all of this, Roberto?"

"There is more information in this folder than I know myself," another man said. He turned and spat on the floor.

"Why, Angelo?"

"Why?"

"Have you lost your mind?"

"Do you know what you've done?"

Angelo looked up. He looked at each of the men. He said: "She was going to take my place when I died."

"I have met this Holly Smolkes person," someone said. "She was your bodyguard, Angelo. She has none of your blood in her veins. *She's a fucking Muslim.* She would not even drink with my men. Have you gone crazy?"

"She was the son that I never had."

"Were you fucking the son that you never had?" another man asked.

Angelo looked at him. Something close to anger showed in his eyes. "No," he said.

One man picked up some poker chips and threw them at Angelo, who did not flinch. They fell harmlessly on the table and the carpet.

"No," the chip tosser said. "You are a man of honor, aren't you, Angelo Rossellini. You would only fuck all of us, your associates, your friends." He spat on the floor again.

"I tried to kill her," Angelo said.

"Yes, and you bungled the job if you ever tried at all. You failed, just as you did on the removal of that war hero McKlane a year ago. You're a useless old fool."

A man at the table pulled out a gun and pointed it at Angelo. The man next to him put a hand on the gunman's extended arm.

"Don't be as stupid as the man you wish to kill. We are reasonable men, except perhaps for Rossellini."

The man replaced the gun in his shoulder holster. Then he spat on the floor a third time.

"We have decisions that must now occur. We must use a firm hand. We must create fear among those who would harm us. This woman who has destroyed the Rossellini Empire, this real estate Broker – "

"Martha Krumble," another man said.

"Yes, this Martha Krumble. She must not enjoy her betrayal." They agreed that she should disappear.

"And the original hit on the man, George McKlane, should be fulfilled. We agreed on this a year ago, and I think we should all agree on this again, now."

After talking about blowback and possible repercussions, they all agreed that teaching lessons and showing a firm hand would take precedent over the cowardice of doing nothing. They needed to prove they were in control.

Everyone put Holly Smolkes at the top of their hit list.

"So, here we are, and the only good news I can see is that most of this folder deals with the Rossellini enterprises. Some of it reaches into our legal affairs, but we can defend against this."

"Our legal bills will be huge, protecting ourselves from this lunatic," another man said.

He flipped his hand at Rossellini, a gesture of disrespect which might have cost him his fingers on both sides if he had done it a day earlier.

"So here we are," someone else repeated.

"Deal the cards. One last hand, Angelo. The last bit of pleasure you will have in your stinking, traitorous life."

"Texas Hold-em, no limit," a man said, pulling the dealing shoe towards him. He expertly slipped three cards in front of each person at the table, the final one face up.

"I'm all in," Angelo said without looking at his cards.

"Indeed you are," the man who was dealing said.

Everyone pushed in their chips and turned over their hole cards. The dealer slid out the remaining cards without stopping. The only sound in the room was the almost imperceptible sound of the cards coming out of the shoe. Each one snapped as the dealer flipped it face up in front of its owner. The man dealt the final card.

Angelo had a Full House, Kings over Threes.

The closest anyone else came to that were two pairs.

They piled all of Angelo's winnings in front of him.

One of the men pulled a small bottle out of his pocket. They got a shot glass off one of the mahogany shelves, placing it in front of Angelo and his mountain of chips.

Angelo smiled thinly at the men and asked if he had time to stack the chips properly.

Nobody laughed at his bravado.

"It would be a waste of time," the man said, filling the shot glass with a slightly yellow liquid. "As are you, Angelo."

Angelo breathed deeply. He took the yellow liquid and held it up to them, spilling none of it.

"*Salute.*"

No one replied.

Angelo tipped his head back and swallowed it all. His final words, as he pitched forward into his mountain of poker chips, were: "*Sono sempre stato fortunato a carte.*"

He got the entire sentence out, which surprised some of the onlookers, before convulsing in death.

"I was always lucky at cards."

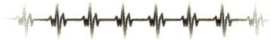

A journalist arrived at the scene of Angelo Rossellini's death long before a stream of black SUVs with blue and red flashing lights disgorged Federal agents at the dog track.

The journalist had been covering crime stories for almost two decades.

He had an upfront and personal view of the Mob because both gambling and drugs haunted his own life.

The forces of darkness owned every word he wrote.

That night and throughout the following day, media from newspapers to crime blogs ran his syndicated column under the heading: "Mob Boss Dies at Dog Track."

The story began: "When crooks go to the dogs, this is how they want to do it." A detailed history of Rossellini's empire followed.

The story ended: "Surrounded by millions of dollars in poker chips, competing against five beautiful young women, all of whom had lots of skin in the game, Angelo Rossellini died face down on a poker table holding the winning hand, a Full House."

All of the women, wearing bikinis that barely covered their assets, told the aging newspaper reporter the same story which they later repeated to federal authorities.

Rossellini had given each of them half a million dollars, and they had played cards for six hours straight. Angelo had won all of his money back, and he had given each of them a $10,000 black chip for their efforts, which they discreetly placed in the front of their bikini bottoms.

Then Rossellini had a massive heart attack and collapsed face down in his pile of chips.

"He was a wonderful, kind gentleman," one of the girls said. Several of them managed to produce tears.

None of them changed her story, not even when the Feds tried to scare them. All of them understood that not sticking to the bought and paid for facts would be a lot more frightening than any threats the Feds might make. Several of the girls had fun with the agents, holding their hands over their heads and asking the agents to examine their $10,000 gift chip personally, up close.

FBI Special Agent Scott Larsen demanded to see all of the videos from the parking lot and track entrance cameras.

"There's nothing there," the head of security at the Kennel Club told him. "The track was closed."

"What difference does that make?" Larsen asked. "That's when you need security the most, isn't it?"

"The track was closed," the man said.

"So why turn the cameras off?"

"Management is cutting costs, pinching pennies," the head of security said.

"And that's why the chorus line gets ten grand stuffed in their bikini bottoms?"

Feigning offense, the head of security said: "That was Mister Rossellini's decision, may the good Lord bless and comfort his soul."

He had one hand in his left pocket, slowly rubbing a couple of chips together.

"The track was closed," he repeated.

Chapter 17

Some Old Habits are Hard to Kill.

A Muslim Woman Meets the Stone Age of ISIL.

Holly Smolkes walked into the driveway in front of the Petersson family cabin. Her brother still looked like an Afghan goat herder, but older and well-armed. Two other ISIL warriors were with him, neither of whom looked at her.

"It's a nice day for a walk in the woods," Holly said. "Who would have guessed I would find my baby brother who I have not seen for almost 30 years." She spoke in English.

She watched Ahmed Kahn's face darken. She had always teased him when they were children: she was the firstborn twin, and he would forever walk in her footsteps, follow her shadow. Her teasing often made him cry when they were children. That was during the Russian occupation, a time of enlightenment when Afghan women briefly enjoyed surprising equality under the rule of their Soviet puppet masters. Many women during that period attended university, openly competing with men in politics as well as business. It only lasted a decade.

"Malalai," Ahmed said.

"Malalai," his warriors repeated, not looking at her.

"Brother Ahmed," Holly Smolkes said.

"Cover yourself," Ahmed said.

"I choose not to," Holly said, smiling.

He struck her hard, unexpectedly, with the butt of his AK-47. He slapped her to the ground, taking away her weapon as she fell under the weight of her backpack.

Holly did not move.

She stared at the gravel next to her face.

Ahmed's men backed away, surprised but not shocked, with their weapons pointed at the woman on the ground.

"Have you become an American whore?" Ahmed asked. He crouched down next to her. "Who has given you this scar on your face?" His finger traced the wound.

Suddenly he was on the ground, his fingers in enormous pain, his AK-47 pressed against his throat.

His men backed away, confused by the unexpected fight in front of them.

"I am Malalai!" Holly Smolkes said in English. "It is MY choice to lead Muslims into battle against the infidel, with *nothing* covering my face. As your mother martyred herself, Ahmed Kahn. Uncovered. Your own mother! Can you not see her every day of your life disappear in the red dust of Russian bullets as she ran towards the river?"

She released him.

He stood up slowly, angry, careful. Holly picked up her weapon and handed his back to him. For a moment, she thought he might try to kill her, but it passed.

"We need to talk," he said in English. In Pashto, he told his men to go back to the cave and guard their prisoner.

"And say nothing of what has happened here," Holly Smolkes said in the Pashto of her childhood. "Nothing. It is Malalai who speaks to you."

They understood, still not looking at her.

Ahmed and Holly Smolkes went into the cabin and spoke for a long time. They did so mostly in English.

Things had changed in the Muslim world of terrorism, and Holly listened carefully to understand what Ahmed and ISIL believed in, and what they were doing in America. She quickly realized that much more than 30 years separated her from her brother. But she could learn, she would adapt.

She asked him if he had killed her father.

"Of course not," he said. "I saw you destroy the devil yourself with a surface-to-air missile, Abira."

"I mean the man who called himself Red, who gave us the weapons we used to destroy the Russian helicopters."

"The man who took you away?"

"Yes," Holly said.

"I tried to kill him in Syria when the Americans murdered Abu Ghadiya eight years ago. I shed my tears on this great martyr. The devil you call 'Red' was in the helicopter that slaughtered our people. They surprised us."

Holly Smolkes looked at him, then she smiled. "You succeeded, Ahmed. You killed him."

"Good, may he scratch at his throat forever in a land with no water." Ahmed smiled at her revelation. Holly turned away and took a deep breath.

"Yes," Holly finally said to him. "He pretended to be my father for many years."

"Is he the man who put the scar on your face?"

"No."

"Did he treat you like the Russian treated our mother?"

"Never."

"He slaughtered the martyr Abu Ghadiya in a stairwell in Sukkariyeh. My tears fell on this great martyr's bullet-riddled, bloody body after the Americans murdered him."

"So you said," Holly replied. "He is in Paradise."

And so was the father that she truly loved, Red Smolkes. They were quiet for a while.

"Who has given you this scar?"

She looked at Ahmed and said: "A man that the Devils call Mac McKlane."

Ahmed stared at her.

"McKlane is a Director of what the Devils call the Department of Homeland Security," she said.

"Lieutenant Colonel George McKlane of the United States Marine Corps," Ahmed Kahn said. "Would you like to see him, Malalai? First, allow me to show you where you will slit his throat."

"This is the man I want to kill more than any other Infidel on the face of the earth," Holly Smolkes said, feeling her heartbeat hard in her chest. Her brother grinned like a simple goat herder, she thought.

Ahmed Kahn led her into the computer room built by Torbjorn Petersson.

A simple wooden chair in the center of the room stood against a backdrop of ISIL's black banners and slogans.

"This afternoon, I will get some photography lights delivered. It is so easy to order things with overnight delivery on the Internet in this country. Tomorrow morning, we will put on a great show for the people of America. The entire world will watch it, Malalai," Ahmed said.

"How did you build all this? Where did you get all these computers, all the monitors?" Holly Smolkes asked.

"It was a gift from the farmer who lived here, a man named Petersson. He left it all to me when he suddenly died yesterday, may he scratch at his throat forever in a land with no water."

Terrorism was a thirsty business.

The beer truck had a hard time getting into the delivery parking area behind the main log cabin at The Cold Springs Trout Club. Two men who said they were Pakistani drove the vehicle, and they spun the back wheels of the large beer barrel hauler until it sunk into the earth, deeply mired beneath the gravel surface.

When Jonathan Wainwright arrived, the Pakistanis were arguing with the chef and two waitresses about the best way to pull the beer truck out.

"They're idiots," the chef told his boss.

"I don't think these boys even speak English," one of the waitresses told Wainwright.

The other waitress said: "They're digging it in deeper."

The Pakistanis had produced a pair of shiny new shovels that they unexpectedly had in the truck's cab, and they had managed to dig the overburdened vehicle further into the ground until the truck's rear axle was level with the gravel drive. It would not budge.

"Let's at least get the beer kegs into their slots so that the guests don't think Virginia is a dry state during our Grand Opening tomorrow," Jonathan Wainwright said.

The Pakistani's immediately understood this, opening one side of the truck, selecting two barrels, and rolled them to their appropriate spots.

They set the 50-gallon barrels expertly in place. Wainwright returned to the main cabin, tapped the kegs, and returned to the parking lot.

Two members of his staff followed him with official Cold Springs Trout Club beer steins on silver-plated trays.

The Pakistani lead driver was talking rapidly on his phone in a language understood only by his fellow driver.

"We tapped the kegs, and we'll worry about the truck tomorrow," Wainwright said. "Drink up lads; this is an official toast to the future success of The Cold Springs Trout Club. No point in being a stick in the mud, eh?"

All of the people who worked for Jonathan Wainwright looked at the stuck truck and laughed at his joke.

The Pakistanis politely declined to join the festivities, pointing out that their religion did not allow them to drink alcohol. They were Muslim.

The lead driver said: "We shall come back tomorrow, unload the lorry, and pull it out with a tow truck. We have, as you can see, many other deliveries we must make. I trust you'll forgive this unexpected inconvenience, Guv'nor."

He spoke with a perfect British accent. Wainwright's people stared at him, dumbfounded.

"We have a lift waiting for us up the road, so we'll be off. We shall see you tomorrow, Mister Wainwright."

They spun about, locked the sliding roller doors on their truck, and walked off in the direction of Road 603.

"Well, I'll be danged," one the of waitresses said. "I didn't think he spoke any real, proper English."

"Cor, Blimey," the chef said in a fake accent that he had acquired as a Mess Sergeant with the United States Air Force at the RAF Croughton airbase in England.

Jonathan Wainright looked at the beer truck, shook his head, and started walking back to the main cabin.

"If I didn't know better," he said, "I'd think those idiots tried to bury the truck on purpose."

Shadrach and Sookie Ringer were in an office in Warm Springs, Virginia, a few miles from Hot Springs. The military outpost they were at usually served as a motor pool.

They had set up the room as a command post, but they were the only people carrying assault rifles, which they stacked in a corner.

Sookie, Shadrach, and some local military reservists leaned over a table, studying topographical maps of the area.

The similarities to the attack on the Royal Peacock Resort and Lodge in Lesotho were obvious. ISIL was going to poison the Jackson River and destroy a fancy trout club just above Lake Moomaw in the process.

If the ISIL terrorists followed their Lesotho footsteps, they would poison the river first.

It would destroy the river's ecosystem and kill thousands of Americans. It would terrorize millions more when the news got out. But where were the terrorists?

Also important, but strategically less significant, where was Mac McKlane?

Shadrach's iPhone buzzed. It was Assistant Director Roberta Macumber. "We had a signal," she said.

She gave them the coordinates.

They traced it on the map.

The signal came from the top of a mountain several miles downstream from The Cold Springs Trout Club, on the southern ridge of the property line that defined Torbjorn Petersson's Leatherwood Farms.

"Do you think that's where Mac is? Did the signal come from Mac's phone?" Sookie asked.

"No," Macumber said. "It was an online Internet order for photo lighting umbrellas from Torbjorn Petersson."

"Do we know Torbjorn Petersson?" Shadrach asked.

"Yes, we do," Macumber said. "He tried to kill Mac's grandfather a year ago down in Boca Raton, Florida. We know a lot about former Marine Corps staff sergeant Torbjorn Petersson."

Roberta Macumber paused for a moment.

"We're just not sure whose side he's on."

"I'll bite. Why the hell would he be on ISIL's side?" Sookie asked.

"Because the Tennessee Valley Authority condemned his family farm through eminent domain and he might have gotten pissed off about it. Mac had gone up there to tell him it was not going to happen. Homeland Security could put a stop to the condemnation, which was suspect on most counts. According to Mac, it was probably a corrupt land grab that involved the people who own something called The Cold Springs Trout Club."

It took the Ringers a few seconds to absorb all the information, which Sookie jotted down on paper.

"So why wouldn't he be on our side?" Sookie asked. "He must know by now that we can save the farm."

"I don't know. We have too many questions and not enough answers, and from the looks of it, not a whole lot of time, either."

"Where did Petersson serve?" Shadrach asked.

"Two tours in Afghanistan," Roberta said.

"What was his MO?"

"Sniper, and a good one, nicknamed 'One Shot.' Mac was going to try to recruit him. I want you to put together a plan, Ringers. You're the only team we have that ever survived one of these attacks. Call me with your program, and I will approve it. You have an hour." She killed the call.

The Ringers called back in 45 minutes, and Roberta Macumber okayed their decision.

Homeland Security contacted the seller of the photo lighting umbrellas to find out how Torbjorn Petersson would receive the delivery. It was coming via UPS. Homeland immediately organized proper, brown uniforms for Sookie and Shadrach. In the meantime, they were driving out to inspect The Cold Springs Trout Club.

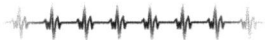

───〜〰〜〰〜〰〜〰〜───

Charlton Tremwallis sat at a red light on the way out to Bacova Junction to deliver a package to a cute neighbor of his who he never had the gumption to ask out.

Suddenly his UPS truck was surrounded by Marine Corps Reservists, all pointing guns at him.

His initial reaction was that the Marines would shoot him because he was having extremely inappropriate thoughts about his pretty neighbor.

He had a painful hard-on.

He shook his head like a dog coming out of the water. That was just plain stupid.

A Marine Corps staff sergeant stepped through the sliding door on the passenger side, which Charlton Tremwallis always kept open on his UPS truck.

"Hello, Charlie-boy," he said.

Charlton recognized a friend of his father.

"Y'all takin' up hijackin', Squirrel?"

That's what his father called this man, known as the best squirrel hunter in all of Bath County. His wife made a squirrel stew with a secret recipe handed down for many generations.

"That a new gearshift, you got between your legs, son?"

Charlton Tremwallis turned red, and his mountain quickly turned into a molehill.

"You got a package in the back for Torbjorn Petersson out at Leatherwood Farms, son?" the sergeant asked

"I believe I do," Charlton said.

"Well, we gonna take us a little detour over to Warm Springs first," the sergeant said. "Yes, sir," Charlton said.

Charlton Tremwallis didn't know what was happening, but he figured he was going to have a first-class story to tell that pretty neighbor of his when he finally got to deliver her UPS package.

She might even invite him in for, well, who knows what? Charlton Tremwallis wheeled the UPS truck around and headed for happiness.

◦〜⊹⊹⊹⊹⊹〜◦

Cars crowded into the parking lot of The Cold Springs Trout Club as people arrived to celebrate its Grand Opening.

Sookie and Shadrach started to exit their vehicle on the southern side of a magnificent new bridge over the river when Shadrach's iPhone buzzed. He answered the call immediately.

"The package is here, and the UPS truck is in the pool, sir," said the sergeant who commandeered Tremwallis' truck.

"Shit," Shadrach said.

"Beg pardon?"

"It's not you, Sergeant. We're running out of time."

Shadrach Ringer held the phone to his stomach and looked at Sookie.

"We go back, get the truck, make the delivery, and then we get all these people the hell out of here." Sookie nodded. Shadrach spoke into the phone.

"We'll be back at the motor pool in 20 minutes, Sergeant," he said, putting his iPhone on speaker so that Sookie could also hear the conversation.

"Make sure that we have UPS uniforms for Captain Ringer and me."

"That's already been taken care of, Shadrach," Sergeant Squirrel said.

"Good. And Sergeant, I want to stress how important it is NOT to talk about this to *anybody*. It is Homeland Security you are dealing with, and I promise you I will personally put any loose tongues in prison. And they may not all be attached to their owners when I do it. Is that understood?"

"Yes, sir, it is."

"How many troops can you put together and arm in the next hour, Sergeant?"

"I, uh, we talkin' live ammo, sir?"

"Yes, we are."

Shadrach rolled his eyes at Sookie.

"Well, uh, I'm not sure how much live ammo we have, to be honest, sir."

Shadrach shook his head. The Marine Corps Reserves: they were a useless band of weekend warriors.

Then Sergeant Squirrel said: "Would it be alright if some of the lads brought their guns, Shadrach? I know that they got a ton of firepower if we let them."

Shadrach smiled. "That would be fine, Sergeant."

"Well, then we got us about 20 men and women who could shoot the nuts off a gray boar squirrel during their mating season, sir, and they got itty-bitty nuts. Can't even see them most of the year."

"Ooh-rah!" Shadrach said.

"Hooah!" Sookie said, proving with her slightly different shout-out that she had been a captain in the United States Army, and not a master sergeant in the United States Marine Corps like her husband.

"See you in 20 minutes, Sarge."

Shadrach closed the call.

He and Sookie smiled tightly at one another and headed back to Warm Springs.

Chapter 18

A Not-So-Peaceful Night in Boca Raton

A Traffic Stop and a Home Invasion

Samuel Nelson drove the large KIA owned by Martha Krumble. His wife, Sharonda, sat in the passenger seat, while Brigadier General McKlane and Martha sat in the back. Both the Nelsons were armed, as was General McKlane. At his request, Martha had applied for a carry permit.

The authorities had not issued it yet.

The four of them were returning from a Delray Beach shooting range where Martha had proved that she was far more comfortable selling real estate than shooting firearms.

"Martha," her exasperated husband had said at the firing range, "you don't sign real estate contracts with your eyes closed, and you can't close your eyes every time ... "

"Stop it, George McKlane."

"But ... "

She fired three quick shots at the target twenty feet away with her eyes slammed shut. No holes appeared in her target.

"Let's try —

"

"George McKlane, if you teach me how to use this gun properly, your own life could very well be in danger. I intend to be a loving wife and mother, not one of your gun-toting Marine Corps Rangers."

Both Samuel and Sharonda tried not to smile.

They all left the firing range and started driving back to the Royal Coconut Yacht and Country Club.

The six Marine Corps Rangers assigned to protect the General's wife had remained at the patriarch's home at the Club. Everyone agreed that Captain George needed a defensive shield, as well as Martha Krumble.

Captain George's name had appeared several times in the folder handed to General McKlane by Roberta Macumber at Homeland Security.

Special FBI Agent in Charge Scott Larsen had already phoned Martha and spoken to her and her husband about the death of Angelo Rossellini.

"A heart attack playing poker with bikini-clad girls?" the General had asked. "Was it strip poker?"

Martha gave him a look, which he shrugged off.

"All the girls give us the same story, almost word for word," Agent Larsen said. "Which means that what they're telling us is probably false. But I guess that the coroner's autopsy will support their story. They were playing for around three million dollars, and Mister Rossellini won it all."

"And had a heart attack and died," Martha said.

The General almost said, "*Who wouldn't?*" but he held it in, asking instead: "Does that mean we can reduce the security around my wife and my father?"

"I wouldn't," Agent Larsen said. "First of all, there's the possibility that they murdered Angelo Rossellini, although we may never prove it. Secondly, that dossier is creating a lot of unrest among the crime families on our radar. They may want to prove to their friends and neighbors that they are still running things. Now is most definitely not the time to relax, General McKlane."

As Samuel Nelson turned off I-95 at the Palmetto Park exit, to head east toward the Royal Coconut Yacht and Country Club, a Boca Raton police car that had been following them lit up its red, white, and blue roof lights.

It whooped its siren and pulled them over in a mostly deserted area.

Looking in his rearview mirror, Samuel did not put both hands on the steering wheel.

He unclipped his Glock and concealed it under his left arm, with his left hand resting lightly on the steering wheel in front of him.

"Gun up," he said, and Sharonda mirrored his actions on the passenger side, bracing one arm against a handlebar above the dashboard, adjacent to the front window.

Two cops got out of the Boca patrol car and approached either side of Martha's 4-door KIA.

As the first cop got up to the driver's window, he leaned down slightly and indicated that Samuel should roll down his window. Samuel hit the automatic control to do so. As the window opened, he shot the cop twice, once in the chest and once in the head.

"Go!" Samuel yelled, and Sharonda opened the passenger door, rolling out and into the recently-mowed roadside grass.

The second cop got off one shot into the dirt before she hit him twice in the chest and once in the head. Later, she would remember smelling the freshly cut grass.

Samuel was out of the car and sweeping the area.

He approached the police car and turned off the red and blue lights, seeing no communications gear in the front or back seats.

It did not look like a Boca Police, Sheriff's, or State Trooper's vehicle.

Brigadier General McKlane was standing next to his opened rear passenger door with his pistol out of its holster. Martha McKlane remained in the KIA.

The few cars that were on the road crept past the scene and then hurried onward, seeing the man lying in the street and people with guns.

Everything had happened in less than two minutes.

"Dial 911, General. Shots fired a half a mile east of the Palmetto turnoff from I-95," Samuel said.

"Should I say 'Officer Down'?" the General asked.

"No, Sir," Samuel said. "Neither one of these men were cops, General McKlane. They were going to kill us."

"How'd you know that?"

"I was a Boca policeman, remember?" He pointed at the dead man on the driver's side of the car. "That guy's badge was a fake and not even a good one. And their vehicle is a poorly put together counterfeit. Those are clip-on flashers on the roof, General. We don't use stuff like that at the Boca Police force."

"But their guns were real," Sharonda said, leaning against her husband and holding him hard.

Soon, they heard police sirens converging on the area from every direction.

Samuel Nelson would probably know most of them, and so would Sharonda.

Everyone holstered their weapons.

General McKlane leaned into the rear passenger side of the car and said: "We're probably going to be delayed a bit getting home, mother of my child."

"At least we're going to get home," Martha said.

The General smiled and began to straighten back up after leaning through the rear passenger door.

"And, George?"

He leaned once again into the car. "What, dear?"

"It works just fine."

"What works just fine?"

"I kept my eyes shut the whole time."

Originally people called them Rum Runners: small, fast boats that could outrun the United States Coast Guard.

They usually carried liquor, often Cuban rum, from ships beyond America's territorial waters, sneaking into hidden harbors to pump alcohol into the veins of an unwanted Prohibition.

In the early 1960s, Canada and the United States renamed the boats because of the new smuggled contraband between their water-bound borders: Cigarette Boats.

Eventually, they became the gas-guzzling toys of wealthy offshore powerboat racers, although they also discovered new life in the Caribbean drug smuggling trade.

Several of the associates of Angelo Rossellini, recently and tragically deceased, owned sleek, extremely powerful, black Cigarette Boats, more often referred to as "go-fast" boats. They moored them in Fort Lauderdale, and they never used them for racing or pleasure.

Each one was a 50-foot Marauder SS, with a Mercury Racing twin-turbocharged power plant that generated 1350 horsepower. Two people could sit comfortably in the cockpit. Four more squeezed into the enclosed, windowless cabin located forward.

Only one of the sleek, black Marauders raced up the coast to the Boca Inlet, where it slowed to 5 miles per hour, carefully observing the "no wake" rule for boats.

At that speed, it still released a deep, guttural sound in the early evening darkness. It moved south down the Intracoastal to the canals that stretched into the Royal Coconut Yacht and Country Club.

George McKlane, who did not particularly like boats, had a 150-foot wooden dock on the canal bordering his estate. He never used it, although an occasional visitor might.

Captain George McKlane's gardener cared for the dock meticulously, planting seasonal flowers along its edge and arranging the deck chairs in slightly different patterns once or twice a day.

As the sleek, black Marauder approached 13752 Coconut Palm Court, where George lived, the pilot cut the engine, switched off the fore and aft lights, and let the 50-foot Cigarette glide silently into the dock.

One man jumped off the boat and secured it with ropes. His clothing matched the Marauder, all black. The hatch opened, and four more men joined them. The pilot remained in the boat.

The five men moved silently over the grass to the edge of a darkened swimming pool that stretched in front of the estate's terrace.

Suddenly the pool lights turned the water a bright, crystal blue. Powerful floodlights lit up the entire back yard.

A loudspeaker announced: "Put down your weapons, gentlemen. My name is Lieutenant Rogers of the United States Marine Corps. You are surrounded by Marine rangers who will kill you in five seconds if you do not put down your weapons and lie flat on the ground, four, three, two –."

All of the men threw down their guns and dove for grass before the count reached "one."

Most of them had their hands locked behind their heads, waiting for handcuffs without being asked.

Marine Corps Rangers stepped out of the shadows and quickly secured them with plastic wristbands.

The pilot of the boat turned on the powerplant, wondering if the Cigarette could rip free of its moorings, but he quickly shut it down when a Marine ranger in combat gear appeared on the dock with a rifle aimed at his head. He crawled out of the cockpit and joined his fellow trespassers.

It happened so quickly that the neighbors across the canal hardly noticed. One of them thought that George McKlane was having a belated Halloween party.

The Marine Rangers turned off the bright lights and herded the six invaders around the side of the house and into the well-lit driveway of Captain George's estate.

Within 15 minutes Special Agent Scott Larsen and his men arrived with blue lights flashing and took all of the men into custody. As he was doing so, Martha Krumble's KIA rolled into the crowded driveway with a Boca Police escort.

General McKlane stepped out of the rear passenger seat, returning the salute of Lieutenant Rogers, who said: "It's not a good night for the bad guys, Sir."

Sharonda and Samuel went into the house to check on Captain George. He was enjoying his second Guinness of the evening with several of the Marine Rangers, who wanted to know more about the Korean War from a man who won the Medal of Honor during a brutal, 17-day battle known as the Chosin Reservoir Campaign. It was called the most celebrated retreat in the history of the Marine Corps. With other UN troops, the Marines effectively destroyed seven Chinese divisions that tried to stop their escape to the port of Hungnam. The Marine Corps suffered combat losses of 836 dead. Estimated casualties for Chairman Mao Zedong's communist forces numbered 35,000 dead. It was a Pyrrhic victory for the Chinese leader.

"I got the Medal of Honor because one of our tanks knocked me off a mountain during the retreat, and my NCO, Sergeant Raymond Chapman, saved my sorry ass," Captain George told them.

"Can we see the medal, sir?" one of the rangers asked.

"Sure," George said. "You guys walk up the staircase, and I'll take the elevator. I'm old. You all need exercise."

Sharonda went with George, and they all spent some time in George's War Room. Captain McKlane had hidden the Medal of Honor on the back of a center island in what originally had been a substantial walk-in closet. None of the rangers were surprised by this act of humility. They had met other retired Marines who concealed their bravery because they never thought of themselves as heroes.

Later, one of the rangers would discover the original citation and tell his comrades that a skidding M46 Patton tank tossed Captain George McKlane and Staff Sergeant Raymond Chapman off a cliff on December 10, 1950. They survived and tried to reconnect with the column of retreating Marines but realized that they could save hundreds and perhaps thousands of their fellow soldiers by digging in at the top of a hill above a North Korean power plant.

Their position prevented the Chinese Communist Forces from using a shortcut that could have led to the slaughter of the retreating troops.

Marine Commandos reinforced their blockade and airlifted both severely wounded men to safety. Hundreds of dead Chinese Communist soldiers piled up in front of their position. Sergeant Chapman received the Silver Star, admitting in private that he would never have dug in at the top of the hill. He would have kept going.

In Captain George's War Room, the Marine rangers read the framed letters mounted in columns on one of the walls. There were fifty of them, with stock photos of a Marine in each lower, left-hand corner.

These were men who died in Korea under the command of Captain George McKlane.

All of the letters on the wall were thank you notes from the families to whom Captain McKlane had personally and painfully written during his recuperation in an American military hospital in Japan.

George stopped at one frame and tapped on it. He said: "Corporal Jackson Petersson. We called him 'Smartass' because Jackson knew something about almost everything. He was going to be a great journalist one day, and he was also the best shot in my company. His grandson saved my life last year, right in this room."

None of the Rangers understood what Captain George McKlane was talking about, and Sharonda said it was time for the old warrior to go to bed. They all snapped to attention and saluted the hero as she led him out of the War Room and into the main bedroom.

"Yeah, yeah," he said to their salutes, waving casually.

In the bedroom, in his pajamas, George looked out at the moonlit canal from the small alcove where he often enjoyed having breakfast.

"Whose boat is that?" he asked, looking at the menacing Cigarette moored at his dock.

"Right now," Sharonda said, "I think it belongs to the Federal Bureau of Investigation."

"The FBI? Well, tell them to get it the hell out of here."

George was getting old.

Sharonda tucked him under the covers, and he quickly fell asleep, hoping that he would have another dream about the woman in the portrait on the wall facing his bed, Agnes, his beloved Agnes.

Sometimes he struggled to remember her name, and that bothered him until he forgot about it.

〜〰〰〰〰〰〰〰〜

The grandson of Corporal "Smartass" Petersson was dead.

Mac had to drag his body out of the cave. They made him throw it on the smoldering remains of the black bear that the terrorists had killed earlier.

Mac McKlane's eyesight had recovered, as Torbjorn had suggested it would. After dragging out the man's body, the jihadists tied George to the wall of the cave again.

He could not budge the metal eyelets screwed into the rock wall.

He watched the ISIL terrorists squatting together at the entrance to the cave. Suddenly they all stood, holding their weapons in the air, shouting *"Malalai, Malalai."*

She stepped into view, her face and head covered by a *hijab*, but he immediately knew that it was Holly Smolkes. She looked into the cave and saw him sitting with his arms stretched by his bonds, and his feet splayed out on the floor of the cave in front of him, then she turned away and kept talking to the terrorists. They laughed at something she said. She disappeared from view.

"Holly?" Mac shouted.

No answer returned.

His captors spit into the cave, speaking in a language that Mac did not understand.

"Water," He said.

No one replied.

"Water."

His captors by the fire at the cave's entrance laughed about something.

Nobody even bothered to spit at him.

Chapter 19

Homeland Security Tries to Get Its Eyes on ISIL.

UPS Makes a Delivery to Leatherwood Farms.

Sookie drove the UPS truck, and Shadrach rode shotgun, but without any weapons. They discussed it at length, and in the end, they decided that they had to make the trip unarmed. And they both knew that they would be taking a terrible risk. Roberta Macumber, on the phone, did not agree with their decision.

It was too dangerous to drive into an armed jihadist terror cell carrying nothing more hazardous than photographic lighting equipment.

"They will search the truck," Shadrach said. "They will kill us if they find a slingshot."

"Just tell them this is America, and UPS drivers are cowboys," Roberta said.

Sookie answered: "That's a difficult argument to have if someone is pointing an AK-47 at your head."

Roberta Macumber backed down. It was their call.

"You're the only team who has ever survived one of these attacks," the Homeland Security assistant director said.

"Yes, we are," Shadrach said.

"Let's keep it that way," Macumber said.

"We're going to give it a shot," Sookie said.

In her office, Roberta Macumber rolled her eyes at the pun. She liked this team.

Shadrach snorted at Sookie after the call.

"Give it a shot."

"What, you don't want to go out with a bang?"

"Stop it, Missus Ringer." They were both smiling, but neither felt very comfortable.

Before they got into their UPS truck, Shadrach had called over the Reservist staff sergeant, who everyone called Sergeant Squirrel.

"What's your name, Squirrel?" Shadrach asked.

"Squirrel," he said.

"Your real name, Sergeant," Sookie said.

"Squirrel. Harry Trumble Squirrel, if you want the whole danged thing," he said.

"I'll be damned," Shadrach said before he could stop himself, quickly adding that it was an excellent name.

"It's worked okay for 41 years," the sergeant said.

"Sergeant Squirrel," Shadrach said, holding his breath a moment so he wouldn't laugh. "You know where I want your men to station themselves out at the whatever they call that fishing club."

"The Cold Springs Trout Club," the Sergeant said.

"That's it. And I don't want anyone to know you're there, Sergeant." All the men and women standing around at the motor pool were wearing camouflage clothing, very little of which had been issued by the Marine Corps.

"Sergeant Ringer, I don't think the leaves on the trees will know we're there."

"Good, and don't go shooting anyone unless they're wearing black and carrying AK-47s or rocket launchers. Homeland is sending you photos of their clothing and weaponry. Make sure all your men understand what they're looking for."

"Yes, sir."

"And Sergeant, I want you to remember that the ISIL terrorists can shoot the nuts off a galloping camel. They're good at what they do."

"Yes, sir. But I bet camels got big ones. They're an easy target. Not itty-bitty ones like squirrels."

Shadrach sighed. "You know what I mean."

"Yes, sir. We'll be careful."

"And Sergeant, that pimply-faced boy standing over there with your platoon, the one we took this truck from?"

"Yes, sir, that's Charlton Tremwallis, Jake Tremwallis' boy," the Sergeant said.

"Is he in the Reserve? He looks kind of young."

"No, sir, he's not, but that boy can shoot the whiskers off a Fairy Diddle running across a split rail fence."

A moment of silence followed this.

"What the hell is a Fairy Diddle?" Sookie asked.

"You'd be calling that a red squirrel, Captain Ringer."

"Well, it sounds good to me," Shadrach said, scratching his head a lot harder than necessary. "We'll be on our way."

As the UPS truck started to roll out of the motor pool, they heard the sergeant yell to his squad leaders.

"Clyde, Duck, Fishbait, Tadpole, get on over here. We got us a job to do."

"Jesus," Sookie said, laughing as they picked up speed. "It's a zoo."

"It's a lucky thing that his daddy's name was Squirrel and not Fairy Diddle," Shadrach said.

Sookie laughed, and then they got serious.

They drove out to The Cold Springs Trout Club. Their UPS truck was about to pass the fancy new bridge spanning the Jackson River.

"Stop," Sookie said.

Shadrach slowed to a stop on the side of the road.

Sookie said: "Didn't you tell me the terrorists in Lesotho had things that looked like beer barrels when you met them the day you caught that killer fish?"

Shadrach twisted his mouth at her.

"Sorry," she said. "Bad joke. But look over there behind the big building. What do you see?"

"Looks like a beer delivery truck, Jersey Brewers."

The truck panels displayed the name, with the "J" in Jersey as an artistic, oversized bottle opener.

The truck appeared stuck in the parking lot; its rear wheels were barely visible.

Sookie phoned Homeland Security and received a quick answer. No such company existed anywhere in the world.

"So that's their delivery, ready and waiting to be dumped in the Jackson River," Shadrach said. "And we can't blow it up because that would just make us their delivery boys."

He called Sergeant Squirrel and told him that nobody, under any circumstances, should put a bullet in the Jersey Brewers delivery truck behind the main cabin at The Cold Springs Trout Club.

If they did, Shadrach explained, it would be considered an act of treason by Homeland Security.

Sergeant Squirrel did not reply.

"I know that sounds a little heavy-handed," Shadrach said. "But it's crucial, Sergeant. It's a matter of life or death for thousands of people living downstream."

"I think I understand," Sergeant Squirrel said. "None of my men will put a bullet anywhere near that truck. And if we see anyone who might try to do that, we'll light him up before he ever pulls the trigger."

"Thanks," Shadrach said, closing the call.

"You need to cool down," Sookie said

"I know," he said. "I feel naked without a weapon."

"So do I," she said.

He looked at her and wiggled his eyebrows. She laughed. They were ready.

And then, suddenly, they were not.

"Jesus," Shadrach said. "Stop the truck. How stupid can I possibly be?"

"What are you talking about?" She was about to turn into the Leatherwood Farms entrance.

Shadrach was on his phone to Homeland Security in Washington. Roberta Macumber picked up.

"If this is the same terrorist leader as the one in Lesotho," Shadrach said, "and everything sure looks and feels the same, then I am about to come face-to-face with Ahmed Kahn, and he knows me. We met above a waterfall at the trout river I fished at the Royal Peacock Resort in Lesotho. We shook hands. We joked about Muslims going a long way to drink a little beer. He knows my name, and he knows my face. He'll recognize me."

Roberta Macumber said that Shadrach was probably right on every count. Then everyone was silent.

Sookie was the first to speak.

"He doesn't know me," she said.

Shadrach tried to cover the phone so that Macumber wouldn't hear her. It was instinctive.

"He doesn't know Sookie," Roberta repeated, followed by a long silence.

"I can do this, sweetheart."

"She can do it, Shadrach."

"Don't I know it," Shadrach said. "Shit."

As Sookie wheeled the UPS truck into the drive, Shadrach stepped into the Leatherwood bushes at the entrance, hoping that the ISIL terrorists did not have any sentries watching the road.

It felt like the longest 15 minutes of Shadrach's life, and then he heard the UPS truck rumbling back towards his hiding place. He waited until the vehicle stopped at the entrance to the main road, making sure that a terrorist was not driving it.

He could feel his heart beating in his chest as he stepped into the vehicle.

"Ahmed says 'hi' honeybuns. Or actually, he said '*As-salāmu-'alaykum*.' And it was him. Also, I saw Mac McKlane's black Lincoln Navigator sitting in the driveway. But there was no sign of the Director. Ahmed Kahn was a very charming gentleman with a slightly English accent, and he thinks buying stuff on the Internet is the future of humanity. He introduced his sister to me as well, Abira Kahn. I thought she was a little weird because even though she was wearing a *hijab,* I could see she had very blue eyes and blonde hair. She spoke like an American. Not a trace of an accent. And I saw three other guys trying to look like casual weekend terrorists leaning up against the cabin. One of them even had a piece of straw in his mouth, like a hick farmer. And what the hell are you crying about?"

"I missed you," Shadrach said, wiping his face and feeling wonderfully foolish.

"Aw, that's so sweet. Now let's go get some guns."

Sergeant Squirrel and his platoon, which was not quite the size of a real one, took the old route out to Richardson's Gorge. It was a ragtag group of Marine Corps Reservists and hunters who had all owned weapons as soon as they were old enough to shoot them. In most cases, that was when they were between six and seven years old, although Squirrel himself had hit his first bullseye with a single-shot .22 one month shy of his fourth birthday. He still had the target, framed and under glass, hanging in his workshop.

Every one of the 18 men and five women had a military backpack, neatly rolled, containing a sleeping bag and some netting to keep away the bugs, although that was not much of a problem in the first week of November. Keeping warm without sweating too much was important. The local weather report said it would be a cold night, with the temperature dipping close to the freezing line.

They parked their vehicles on a family farm owned by the man they called Tadpole. He was probably the best bullfrog catcher in the group, although frogs legs would not show up on the menu on this night. They were about three miles, as a crow flew from The Cold Spring Trout Club. They would climb over a relatively small mountain to get there, spreading out in the forest.

Most of the troops had a few cans of beans, a bag of pre-cooked rice, and some candy bars, figuring it would be a one night bivouac at the most. Some of them had whiskey, but not much.

They carried a lot more ammunition than food.

They moved into the woods as the sun was setting, and they continued in the moonlight for the last mile. They had no problem walking through the woods at night, and they made very little noise doing so.

They were comfortable in the mountains.

They set their perimeter around The Cold Springs Trout Club about 250 yards outside its well-lit cabins, where people seemed to be having a good time celebrating the Grand Opening. Squirrel's platoon spent a lot of time watching them through their rifle scopes as the night got darker and colder.

At one point, a man and a woman walked out onto the empty veranda of the big cabin, deserted because the temperature had dropped quickly after sundown.

The man tried to grab the woman, and she slapped him. He hit her hard, and she stumbled. The man appeared to be drunk, wobbling over her.

He started to unbuckle his belt. You could hear a few rifles clicking softly in the woods.

The woman suddenly kicked the man hard in the crotch, and he bent over in pain. He almost hopped off the veranda, holding his nuts. She stood up and brushed herself off, not knowing that she might have saved his life.

The veranda door opened, and another man walked out. The woman fell into his arms, pointing at the man bent over in pain at the railing. They separated, and the second man walked over to the first, who had straightened up.

A hard, quick punch abbreviated whatever the first man tried to say, sending him over the railing and into the grass, a few feet below the porch.

In the forest perimeter, Fishbait whispered to Duck about 12 feet to his left. "This shit's a whole lot better than watching TV."

"Don't have to freeze your ass off at home," Duck said.

Most of the troops had gotten into their sleeping bags with their boots on, trying to keep warm. A few people dug small, deep holes. They cooked baked beans over Sterno cans dropped into the bottom of the holes.

No light escaped into the night.

Just after 12:30 a.m., a black Lincoln Navigator pulled into the parking lot of The Cold Springs Trout Club.

Throughout the perimeter, weapon checks blended with the sound of crickets.

A few people had to wake up.

Then 23 rifles scoped the SUV.

In the cave above the cabin at Leatherwood Farms, Mac McKlane shivered in darkness. The small fire burning at the entrance, surrounded by four terrorists, offered no heat at the back of the cavern.

He remained tied, tired, cold, thirsty, and hungry.

The entrance brightened gradually, and then Ahmed Kahn and Holly Smolkes appeared with another man who carried a Coleman lamp into the cave, placing it on what once might have been a table. Several more men appeared and leaned weapons against the wall. Mac's eyesight, fully recovered, immediately recognized them as ground-to-air missile launchers.

Ahmed kneeled in front of McKlane. Holly remained near the cave entrance.

"You have raped, and you have disfigured the face of my sister, Abira," Ahmed Khan said.

Mac was surprised that no anger attached itself to the words of the ISIL leader. He spoke very calmly.

"We are a kind and generous people," he continued, "and we show our hospitality and our mercy even to our enemies, even to infidels such as yourself, Lieutenant Colonel George McKlane of the United States Marine Corps."

He motioned to his twin sister standing quietly at the entrance, her head bowed.

His sister came and knelt beside ISIL's prisoner, wearing a *hijab* that concealed her face, but not her identity.

Like all the other warriors, Holly Smolkes dressed in loose, black clothing.

Only her *hijab* was colorful, a pale yellow that hinted at her nose and mouth, and the scar.

"I forgive you for raping me and cutting my face with a knife, Lieutenant Colonel McKlane. I am only a simple, Muslim woman, but I am also a great warrior who can forgive her enemies."

Ahmed Kahn smiled and stood. His sister added: "But my forgiveness will only come after I kill you."

Ahmed Kahn said: "Malalai brings you food."

When he said the word "Malalai," the men at the front of the cave raised their weapons and chanted: "*Malalai!*"

Holly Smolkes reached into the loose, black clothing she wore and produced something for the prisoner to eat.

"Peanut butter and jelly sandwiches," she said. Mac thought he could see her smiling behind her *hijab.*

"Water," Mac said, the word rough in his throat.

Holly looked up at her brother.

"Water," he told his men.

Mac drank greedily from the metal cup that Holly held to his lips. "More," he said.

They refilled the cup. Twice. McKlane had not had anything to drink for two days. He threw up some of the water but asked for more. They gave it to him.

Holly Smolkes slowly fed him pieces of two peanut butter and jelly sandwiches. She said nothing to him, but her eyes never moved from his face. He considered chomping down on her fingers, breaking them, but he did not.

Ahmed Kahn remained standing next to them. He crouched down as Mac finished the second sandwich.

"Tomorrow morning," the ISIL leader said, "You will become a movie star, McKlane from Homeland Security. All of America will greet you and mourn your death."

Ahmed looked at his sister and said: "He looks a little rough, don't you think? A shave, perhaps?"

"If you give me a straight razor, I will slit his throat right here, right now," Holly said.

Ahmed laughed and stood up. Holly stared at McKlane.

"Remember, dear brother Ahmed," Holly said without taking her eyes off McKlane, "it is only I who will rip open the throat of this man in front of the cameras tomorrow. He raped *me*. He disfigured *me*. It is only I who can spill the blood of this Infidel."

"Only you, Malalai," said Ahmed. The chorus at the front of the cave chanted: *"Malalai!"*

She never stopped staring at McKlane. She lowered her *hijab,* and, for a moment, Mac McKlane thought she would kiss him.

Holly spat in his face with her hands, braced on his legs, up close and personal. Ahmed laughed, and his men joined in.

"Only I can kill you, Lieutenant Colonel McKlane." Still kneeling, she pulled a long, curved knife from the folds of her clothing, holding it in her left hand. It flashed in the light of the Coleman lamp.

"I will cut your throat with my left hand," she said. "A great insult, although you infidels do not understand this."

Muslims never greeted anyone with their left hand, which they used for sanitary purposes before the invention of toilet paper.

Mac shook his head, cleared his eyesight. He was about to ask her: "But where's the love?"

But he did not say it.

He felt Holly Smolkes shove something under his thigh with her right hand.

And then she winked at him.

She winked at him twice.

Chapter 20

What You Think You Know Might Kill You.

Homeland
Security

*<u>Can Homeland
Security Find the
Puzzle Pieces?</u>*

Roberta Macumber and
the Operation Poison
Well Unit sat around
the conference table
and spoke about what
they knew and what
they didn't know.
Sookie had gathered an enormous amount of boots on the
ground information in the five minutes she had spent
delivering photo lighting equipment to Ahmed Kahn.

She had seen Mac's car, but not the director himself.

She had seen three additional terrorists leaning up
against the cabin.

And Holly Smolkes or Abira Kahn as most members of
the team had started calling her, had joined her twin brother.

She was a one-person sleeper cell whose alarm had
finally gone off.

"But why did she send a file about Roberto Rossellini to
Homeland Security?" Roberta Macumber asked.

"A diversion," one of the team members said.

"I don't think so," another person said.

"Why not?" Roberta asked.

"Look at what happened." They all knew about Rossellini's death and the failed attacks on the McKlane Clan. "I think Holly Smolkes or Abira Kahn or whoever the hell she is, I think she was protecting herself. I think she knew that Rossellini was going to whack her. We gave her the protection she needed."

"So it's a red herring?" someone asked.

"It's a bloody herring," Roberta said. "I like the thought process. Let's throw out the Rossellini file. It's confusing us. But it does teach us how clever Abira Kahn is."

"So now the Terror Twins are going to destroy the Jackson River with a beer truck full of lethal poison that's stuck in the mud behind a high-class, trout fishing club."

"After they slaughter all people at the, uh –"

"The Cold Springs Trout Club."

"Right. Just like Lesotho."

"So we need to get the people at the trout club to pack up their fishing rods and go home."

"Immediately," Roberta Macumber said. "Even if we have to get them out of bed."

She dialed the Ringers.

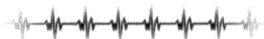

At The Cold Springs Trout Club, the driver and passenger doors of the black Lincoln Navigator opened at the same time. The rifles scoping them from Sergeant Squirrel's perimeter split down the middle, some choosing the left door, some the right.

Shadrach got out of the passenger door, Sookie exited from the driver's side, and 23 people in the forest stopped holding their breath. Their cold fingers moved away from their trigger guards and into gloves. A few of the men and most of the women snuggled into their sleeping bags. They went back to sleep with their boots on.

Sookie and Shadrach walked into the main cabin carrying their assault rifles, with Glocks on their hips.

Everyone at the bar had at least two things in common: they were all men, and they were all pretty drunk, including the bartender who tried to pour some Jack Daniels into an imaginary shot glass on the bar.

The bartender had done this twice, and everyone thought it was hysterical.

Shadrach had an urge to fire a quick burst into the ceiling, but this was not a movie. It was for real.

"I need to speak to a Jonathan Wainwright," Shadrach Ringer said.

Jonathan Wainwright almost fell off the far stool at the bar, managed to right himself, and shouted: "The Goddam Marines have landed."

"Are you Jonathan Wainwright?"

"I speaketh," Wainwright said.

"Jesus Christ," Sookie said.

"He's not here," someone said.

Everyone thought this was probably the funniest thing they had ever heard in their lives.

"I'm glad she didn't ask for the Virgin Mary," another man said.

This wisecrack was perhaps even funnier. People were pounding on the bar.

"Stand behind me," Shadrach said.

"Don't do this," Sookie said.

"Behind me, sweetheart."

She stepped behind him.

He put his assault rifle on semi-automatic. The sound was deafening.

The mirror behind the bar shattered. The top rows of expensive liquor burst, first on the left, then to the right, and the bartender froze in place, unable to hide, although his kidneys performed flawlessly.

Only the occasional breaking of glass as bottles teetered and fell behind the bar interrupted the silence that followed.

All of the men, still drunk, watched the warriors in front of them. Nobody moved a muscle, although several of them had concealed weapons.

"You are all about to die," Shadrach said.

"Don't," Sookie said, seeing one of the men reaching inside his jacket. He dropped his hand immediately.

She stepped from behind Shadrach and moved five feet to his right, with her assault rifle pointed at the men. She put her weapon on semi-automatic, but she kept her finger on the side of the trigger guard.

"You are all about to die," Shadrach repeated.

They had all done bad things in their lives, but nothing that might warrant summary execution.

"You will die unless you listen to what we say and follow our instructions perfectly," Shadrach said.

He had their undivided attention.

Shadrach's cell phone buzzed, and he looked at the caller. "We're okay, Squirrel. But I may call you back in a few minutes with a special request."

The entire perimeter, which had moved closer to The Cold Springs Trout Club in a matter of minutes, stood down.

They returned to the warmth of their sleeping bags, which they had abandoned 50 yards back.

"Bartender?" Shadrach said.

"Yes, Sir?"

His voice managed to reach an octave that he did not know he possessed.

"Start making lots of coffee."

"Yes, Sir."

It still came out as a squeak.

"Gentlemen, stand down from the bar. There will be no more drinking of alcohol. Sit down at the tables. This young lady next to me is Captain Ringer. My name is Shadrach Ringer, and you will listen to everything we say."

He slapped his Homeland Security credentials on the table at which he took a seat.

Sookie said: "We work for Homeland Security, and we are here to save your lives. And believe me, they are all in danger right now."

She remained standing, but she lowered her assault rifle.

Several people who had heard the ruckus had left their cabins and returned to the central unit. As they came through the door, those already in attendance quickly silenced them and told them to take a seat.

"Mister Wainwright?"

"Yes, Sir," he said, moving forward and taking a chair at the same table where Shadrach Ringer sat.

"The Grand Opening is over," Shadrach said.

"Well, I can damned well see that for myself."

Jonathan Wainwright took a look at Shadrach Ringer's credentials. Sookie threw hers on the table. Special Agents. The Department of Homeland Security.

"A grateful nation will generously compensate you for any damages you suffer because of this," Shadrach told Jonathan Wainwright. It sounded to Wainwright like he was going to get a medal, and he nodded his head gravely. He was on their side.

The room was quiet.

"A combat company of the United States Marine Corps has the, uh, The Cold Springs Trout Club surrounded as I speak. They are here to protect you, not harm you."

He had almost forgotten the name of the place, and he had conveniently taken the Reservist platoon, which was already short a few troops, and tripled its size into a company of combat veterans.

"Terrorists are likely to attack this area within a matter of hours," Shadrach said. "They intend to slaughter every person they can find. Now, here's what we're going to do about it."

At Homeland Security, Roberta Macumber was in the communications room with her entire team. Nobody went home. Nobody would.

It was 5:00 a.m.

A tech assistant leaned into the room and said: "You have a call, sir, ma'am."

He held out an iPhone in Macumber's direction.

The assistant director patted her pockets. She had forgotten her secure phone on the desk in her office., and she shook her head. She was losing her focus.

The tech had heard her phone buzzing as he walked past her door. It would keep doing so until answered or until the caller hung up. No message answering services ever existed on Homeland's secure phones.

The tech had not answered the phone. It kept buzzing as it passed it over to Macumber.

The phone ID said: "Holly Smolkes."

"Hello? Holly? How did you get this ph – ?"

"I thought you were on vacation," a deep whisper said.

Roberta Macumber held the phone away from her ear, hit the speakerphone, and said: "We thought you were dead, Director McKlane. Welcome back."

The room burst into applause, smothering whatever Mac said. It quieted down quickly.

"We missed what you said, Sir."

"I said, I may be dead quite soon." They could barely hear him, and one of the men maxed the volume. "Here's what you need to know. Do not interrupt me." He was whispering. The entire room leaned in towards the speakerphone as a dozen pens started scribbling.

"There are probably between eight and 12 terrorists. The leader, Ahmed Kahn, is going to videotape me getting garroted by Holly Smolkes tomorrow; I do not know when. Kahn plans to broadcast this videotape over the Internet to the entire world. There is a satellite dish on top of the mountain behind Petersson's cabin. Torbjorn Petersson is dead, killed by Kahn. I assume they are going to poison the well at about the same time as they kill me, possibly before, using the Jackson River. I am expendable, you all know that. And Roberta?"

"Yes, Mac?"

"They have surface-to-air missiles, at least half a dozen of them. You need to be careful with air support."

"Jesus, Mac, where did they get the SAMs?
"Hello?
"Mac?"
The call was dead.

After Holly Smolkes had winked at Mac, she stood with the knife in her left hand and tested the ropes securing him to the metal eyelets screwed into the cavern wall.

When she tested the one securing his left hand, she sliced through most of the rope with her knife, hiding her movements with her dark, loose clothing in the shadows cast by the Coleman lamp. She did not sever the cord completely, and she quickly exited the cave with her brother, Ahmed.

She said nothing to Mac, who remained on the floor, his legs splayed straight out in front of him, tired but no longer thirsty or hungry.

Three men remained at the entrance. One of them stood, walked over to the Coleman lamp, and turned it off. He spat in the direction of Mac, not coming close to hitting him, and returned to the warm embers of the campfire smoldering at the front of the cavern, at least 35 feet away.

All of the men stood up when the sound of firecrackers drifted down the valley sometime before 11:00 p.m. Like Mac McKlane, they knew the echo of distant gunfire. One of the men spoke into a cell phone, then they all sat down again. Mac heard him mispronounce "Halloween" to the others.

Mac himself knew it was gunfire, but he did not know how or why it had occurred. He did understand that the terrorists were not the source of it. Otherwise, they would all be on alert, and the strange word "Halloween" would never have crossed their lips.

McKlane fell asleep, dropping into a dreamless state of exhaustion. He woke slowly, carefully, not knowing what time it was, although he did know where he was.

The embers of the fire were almost out. The men around it were faint outlines at the front of the cave.

Mac squirmed around a bit, trying to see what Holly had pushed under his butt. He could no longer feel it. Everything below his waist felt numb.

He tried to pull himself into a less uncomfortable position, and the rope securing his left hand came undone. His arm flopped to the ground, making a faint noise.

For 15 minutes, he did not make any movements. The men at the cavern's mouth remained there. Slowly Mac felt under his thigh. It was a cellphone.

He almost turned it on and then realized it would quickly arouse his captors. He very slowly turned around, making no noise as he did so. He pulled his shirt over his head, with his back to the terrorists. He pressed a button. The brightness of the iPhone had set low. He dialed Roberta Macumber's secure phone, quickly turning off the sound as it began to ring. It rang 63 times before she finally answered.

He counted every ring.

He spoke fast, quietly. When he was near the end of what he had to say, he heard something. He wanted to tell Macumber that Holly Smolkes might be on their side, but before he could, he killed the call, stretched his neck back through his shirt, and stood up, slowly turning around to face the front of the cave. One warrior stretched his body at the entrance. Mac could not tell if he was looking in his direction.

He threw the phone to his right, deeper into the cave. It made almost no noise wherever it landed. Mac moved his free hand back up to the eyelet, holding it as if it still restrained him.

The stretching man sat back down. There was no way they could see Mac in the darkness of the cave. He could barely see his hand. He slowly turned and reached up to his right hand, undid his bonds, and then he tied himself to the eyelet again, but with a slip knot.

He turned and faced the front of the cave, spread eagle with his free hand on the eyelet as if he remained in bondage. He slowly went through his body, flexing first this muscle, then that, arms, legs, thighs, calves, toes, trying to turn his stiffness into preparation for what might be his final fight.

⎯⫟⫠⫟⫠⫟⫠⫟⫠⫟⫠⎯

At The Cold Springs Trout Club, all the celebrants were drinking coffee in the main cabin. No guests remained in their units. A dozen of Sergeant Squirrel's men, including himself, joined the group.

The people who were too drunk to drive themselves, which was 90 percent of the guests, were escorted to their cars and chauffeured to the Homestead in Hot Springs, where comfortable suites awaited them, compliments of the Department of Homeland Security.

Their alternate choice was to remain at The Cold Springs Trout Club and die in a terrorist attack on America. Everyone chose a trip to the Homestead.

The guests from The Cold Springs Trout Club all signed nondisclosure agreements, which guaranteed trials for treason if anyone violated them. Homeland Security personnel had already flown into the Homestead from Washington with the necessary documents.

Two of the guests from The Cold Springs Trout Club were high-powered lawyers, still a little drunk. They read the documents, which increased their levels of sobriety and suggested everyone sign them unless they wanted to go to Guantanamo and live with a bunch of terrorists. It was an overdramatization, but they were semi-famous trial lawyers given to hyperbole. Nobody was fooling around. Everyone signed the nondisclosure agreements and went to their suites to finally get some sleep.

All of Sergeant Squirrel's "chauffeurs" were driven back out to The Cold Springs Trout Club by a squad of Marine Corps Rangers who were there to beef up the defense of a beer truck full of poison.

Unlike Sergeant Squirrel's platoon, the Combat Rangers didn't joke around, and they all wore camouflage war paint.

Chapter 21

The Bloodbath at Leatherwood Begins Before Dawn.

Bloodthirsty Terrorists Make Poor Farmers.

Mac McKlane watched as daybreak defined the front of the cave. His body remained stiff, but his circulation was back, and he thought he might be able to put up some resistance when they came for him. He stood on one foot and then the other, realizing that his balance was poor. His left leg felt numb. He probably could not run well. But if he could wrestle a weapon away from one of the terrorists, then there would be no need to run.

The sound of a single gunshot suddenly echoed up the ravine. Two of the ISIL terrorists disappeared from view, but the third remained, facing McKlane from the cavern's entrance. The ISIL warrior was thirty feet away. Mac knew that he would be dead before his second, shaky footstep. He remained spread eagle on the wall.

"Water," he said.

The ISIL guard spat in his direction, stepped out of the cave, and looked down the ravine towards the gunshot.

The rifle firing was not repeated.

In the pasture below, men gathered at the barn.

Nobody had milked the cows for days, and their swollen, painful udders led to constant mooing in the small herd. The cows crowded around the door to the barn, where the milking equipment waited for them.

They banged on the door with their heads.

A terrorist, who had been sleeping in the barn, had grown tired of all the mooing. He shot one of the cows.

Ahmed Kahn had raced from the cabin to the barn as the shot echoed down the valley. He was upset.

"You are an idiot," Ahmed said to the man, who was considering shooting another troublesome cow. "Why not just go up to The Cold Spring Trout Club and announce your arrival. Are you crazy?"

The man did not shoot the second cow.

"Who here has been a farmer?" Ahmed asked. Two men raised their hands.

"Do you know how to milk cows?"

They nodded.

"Then milk these cows."

"It is the work of a woman," the man who had killed the cow said, spitting on the ground.

Ahmed struck him hard in the stomach with his AK-47. The man bent over in pain, falling.

"Perhaps you should teach this idiot how to milk a cow," he said to the farmers in the group.

The man on the ground was angry, humiliated.

He stood up slowly and then started to lean over to pick up his AK-47.

"Leave it on the ground," Ahmed said. "Sit back down, Muhammed Abdelrahman."

The man crouched, and Ahmed squatted next to him. He looked at the other men and told them to take the cows to the barn and milk them.

"You are my greatest warrior, Muhammed," Kahn said when they were alone. "You are much calmer in battle than you are when you are waiting for it. You will lead the Holy Warriors of God today."

"You honor me," Muhammed said, still a little angry.

"Remember to kill all of the infidels. The farm animals will die soon enough."

There was laughter in the barn. When the jihadists had opened the doors, the cows had gone to their allotted stalls and waited for the milking equipment to be attached to their teats. One of the men came out and told Ahmed that the cows were teaching them how to milk them.

Ahmed smiled. "So you see, Muhammed? It is not the work of a woman. It is a cow's work." They all laughed and went to watch the milking machines operate.

"Release all the animals," Ahmed said afterward. "And no more shooting, only infidels. Today we will grant freedom to the horse, the cows, the chickens, the sheep, the pigs –"

The rooster crowed in the hen house.

"Even the rooster," Ahmed added, and they all laughed.

Then Ahmed Kahn became suddenly, noticeably quiet. He held a finger to his lips, the universal signal for silence. Nobody said anything.

"By tonight, all of these animals will be dead. Everything in this valley will be dead. Except for us, the Holy Warriors of Islam, led by Muhammed Abdelrahman." He put his hand on the shoulder of the man he had struck for shooting the cow.

"Bring me McKlane," Ahmed said to his men.

At 5:45 in the morning, Shadrach received a phone call from Roberta Macumber.

"Here's what we know," she said. They estimated the number of ISIL terrorists at a dozen or more.

They were going to execute the director of their unit at Homeland Security on camera and show it to the entire world. Holly Smolkes was the designated terrorist who would slice Mac's throat.

There was a satellite dish at the top of the mountain that would broadcast the event worldwide.

Macumber told Shadrach that the terrorists had SAMs, but that they might be ground-to-ground weapons as well as ground-to-air.

"They're well-equipped," she said. "The destruction of that satellite dish is a top priority. The only thing more important is to make sure that no one releases the poison in that beer truck into the Jackson River."

They were silent for a moment.

"Dead or alive?" Shadrach said.

"Who?"

"The Terror Twins."

"Doesn't much matter," Roberta said. "Alive would be nice. It might be useful to squeeze some information out of — I like that moniker — the Terror Twins."

"Any preference?"

"I think that Ahmed Kahn would be more useful alive," Roberta said.

"Okay, we're on it. And thanks for the extra Marines, although I have the feeling that Sergeant Squirrel's group, operating in their terrain, might be the best weapon we have. They performed perfectly last night."

After he had cut the call, he looked at Sergeant Squirrel, who stood next to him on the veranda.

"Who are the Terror Twins?" Squirrel asked.

"Ahmed and Abira Kahn," Shadrach said. "They're twins, an Afghan man, and woman, ISIL terrorists. Who's the best runner in your pack, Sarge?"

Squirrel answered immediately, putting his hands on the shoulder of the boy listening to them: "Charlton Tremwallis. This boy can chase the wind. He's good at long distances, too. I reckon he's just about the best-danged runner Bath County ever had, aren't you boy? I swear you should have tried out for the Olympics they had in Brazil, Charlton."

"And you can, uh, shoot the nuts off a chipmunk, right?" Shadrach said, looking at the boy.

Embarrassed, the youngster looked down, moved back. He seemed shy.

Sergeant Squirrel leaned in towards Shadrach and whispered: "Don't ever tell anybody this, but I believe that boy's a better shot than I am."

"Does he know anything about the Internet, about how cable dishes work?"

"Now that you mention it, yes, he does. Set up a lot of us with our Internet stuff. This boy's clever with computers."

"Why the hell is he driving a UPS truck?" The youngster had moved away, out of earshot.

"That boy hasn't quite found himself yet," Squirrel said, loud enough for Tremwallis to hear. Then Squirrel lowered his voice again. "To be honest, I think he needs to get laid. It might help clear up his complexion a bit, too."

Shadrach shook his head, smiling. He liked these people.

"Well, get him back over here. He's about to do the most important thing that he's ever done in his life. And if he gets through it, every girl in Virginia is going to take a crack at wiping the pimples off of his face."

Squirrel shouted: "Hey, Tremwallis, get your butt over here, boy, I just got you the Deal of the Century."

Shadrach looked at Sookie and asked her to see if someone could find some heavy-duty wire cutters out in one of the toolsheds. She found them herself.

Using an iPad and Google Earth, Shadrach showed Charlton Tremwallis the approximate location of the satellite dish, which wasn't visible under the treetops.

"It's probably right near the top of this ravine," Shadrach said, tracing his finger up the screen.

"Naw, it's about fifty feet further over," the fastest runner in Bath County said. "I saw it when I was deer hunting on the other side of the mountain. Mister Petersson, he's got his place posted real good, so I'd never hunt on his land. But I saw the satellite dish up there."

"How long would it take you to get from here to there?" Shadrach asked. "And you have to be careful, and you have to stay in the woods, no running on the road, and you're carrying your gun, ammunition, and this, too." He handed Tremwallis some large wire cutters, probably weighing about five or six pounds. "And you have to get there fast."

"I reckon about 40 minutes, maybe 50 minutes tops. Ain't too hard once you get up on the ridge."

"You have to cut the cable."

"They'll do it," he said, hefting the cutters.

"Get going," Shadrach said.

"Run with the wind, son," Squirrel said.

"Yes, sir."

Charlton Tremwallis jumped off the veranda and started to move away in a low trot, bent over a little, his legs running smoothly and gradually faster.

"That boy can run," Sookie said.

"Yes, he can," both men answered as Tremwallis faded into the early morning darkness of the forest.

Four of them came for McKlane at 6:15 in the morning. The dimness in the cave required the lighting of the Coleman lamp. Two ISIL warriors remained at the cave's entrance as one lit the lantern. The fourth approached McKlane with his rifle slung over his shoulder.

As the brightness of the Coleman lamp spread through the cave, Mac jerked his right arm free, and the slip-knotted rope that had held him whipped across the face of the terrorist in front of him. Mac's left hand, free of bondage, grabbed at the AK-47 slung over the ISIL warrior's shoulder.

Both men tumbled to the ground.

For a moment, Mac had his hands on the assault rifle, searching for the trigger.

Then he felt a crushing blow to his face as the terrorist who had lit the lantern stepped in to help his comrade.

Both of the terrorists at the mouth of the cave joined the fray. They pummeled McKlane's body with the butts of their weapons. Mac lost consciousness for a moment, and then he was leaning up against the cavern's entrance, his hands securely tied behind him.

McKlane fell several times as they started down the ravine to the cabin.

The second time he narrowly missed crushing his head on a boulder at the side of the stream. His captors suddenly realized he was probably trying to kill himself. Dead men could not talk in front of a camera.

Two of the terrorists carried McKlane the rest of the way to the cabin.

He kicked and struggled at first, but he eventually gave up, exhausted. The terrorists carried him across the driveway and into the cabin.

"What have you done to him?" Ahmed asked, upset at the damaged goods he had received.

"He tried to escape."

McKlane's left cheek was already swelling. Holly touched it, and he winced with pain.

"I think they broke his cheekbone," she said.

Ahmed looked at him and said: "Maybe he looks better this way. Can you talk, McKlane?"

"George McKlane, Lieutenant Colonel, the United States Marine Corps, 2028658," McKlane said, but it did not come out smoothly, and he regretted revealing that he even had a voice after he spoke.

"I could put some makeup on him," Holly said.

"Yes," Ahmed said. "Try to make him look like an American whore. But no lipstick."

He said this in Pashto, and his men laughed at McKlane. Holly laughed as well.

"Take him and tie him to the chair in the studio. Tie him tight. Malalai will paint him like a clown for the people of America," he said in English.

As Holly applied makeup to him, doing it as softly as possible, she spoke to him in a whisper heard only by the two of them. She wanted to know if he had any strength left.

"Not much," he said.

"I am trying to save you."

"I know."

"I thought I was the only person who could save you once my brother called."

"Others are trying to save me."

"They are not here."

"No, they're not."

"I am here," Holly said.

"Yes, you are," Mac McKlane said.

"I love you," she said.

"I know."

Ahmed moved closer to them, but he did not hear them. He did not see the tear running down Holly's cheek, hidden beneath her *hijab.* Holly stood up. Mac looked awful.

"I don't know," Ahmed said. "Maybe a little lipstick would help?" Holly looked at him, ready to paint him further if her brother so wished.

Ahmed laughed. "Just joking," he said. "Terrorist humor. You look like camel dung, McKlane."

He stepped back and looked at one of his men.

"Assemble the warriors of God," he said. "Come, Holly, you must help me see them off." To the man who remained in the studio, he said: "Watch him as if your life depended on it, which it does."

He and Holly went to the driveway, where Ahmed's men stood waiting. They all snapped to attention.

One of the men saluted.

There were 11 of them, all battle-tested veterans of combat in Syria, Iraq, and Afghanistan, and they had secretly slipped through America's border with Canada. They had all enjoyed safe passage to Virginia through the Wahhabist underground of a few extremist Mosques.

"Today," Ahmed told them, "we strike at the heart of America. Today we poison their well. They will not recover from your acts of bravery, as they have done with the Twin Towers in the corrupt city of New York, or the bombing in Boston, or the slaughter in Orlando. These great events will be celebrated forever in our Muslim history, but what you men do today will kill more Americans than all these heroic acts combined, ten times as many Americans."

The terrorists raised their weapons and shouted.

"Malalai will not lead you today," Ahmed said. "She must cut off the head of the serpent."

"Malalai," the men shouted.

Holly said: "But you go with my blessing."

She took a black *hijab* and draped it over the AK-47 of the group's leader, Muhammed Abdelrahman.

"This is the banner of Malalai."

"Malalai," the men shouted.

She let her *hijab* slip off her face, pointing to the scar on her cheek. The men did not look away.

"Avenge Malalai," she said. "Avenge the death of every Muslim warrior who has ever journeyed to Paradise."

She covered herself again with her white *hijab*. Ahmed seemed quite pleased with his twin sister's speech.

"Go," he said to the squad of ISIL warriors standing at attention in front of him. They were well-disciplined. "Kill the infidels. Poison their well."

The men shouted. Nine of them headed for The Cold Springs Trout Club two miles away.

Two of them returned to the ravine that led up to the cave. Neither man would not stop there.

They continued climbing to the lookout tower that they had discovered near the satellite dish at the top of the mountain overlooking Leatherwood Farm.

They moved slowly, weighed down by their weapons, which included ground-to-air missiles.

Ahmed Kahn had learned valuable lessons in the Kingdom of Lesotho in southern Africa.

⊹⟶⫴⟶⫴⟶⫴⟶⫴⟶⫴⟶⫴⟶⊹

Roberta McCumber would not rely on the ability, bravery, good intentions, or fate of a 17-year-old UPS truck driver in Virginia to save America. That would be ludicrous. She had to destroy the satellite dish with a certainty that required professionalism at the highest military level.

Shadrach had told her that Charlton Tremwallis was on his way shortly after 6:00 a.m.

Knowing that the youngster might die as collateral damage, Roberta Macumber made the call.

A hangar door slowly rolled open in a dull green, domed building at the far end of the airport in Roanoke, Virginia. Restricted signs and 15-foot-high chain mail fences, strung along the top with circular barbed wire, surrounded the unmarked building.

Three MH-60L Velcro Hawk helicopters rolled onto the tarmac. They were variations of the original UH-60L Black Hawks, and their blades began to rotate.

One of the Velcro Hawks carried 11 combat troops and their equipment. The others had six-man crews and M102 howitzers. Three pilots and three navigators brought the total troop strength to 29 men and women.

All the helicopters had United States Army emblazoned on their sides.

The combat personnel served as Army Rangers with their faces painted for combat. The helicopters rose and banked towards Leatherwood Farms, just south of The Cold Springs Trout Club on the Jackson River.

At 150 miles an hour, it would be a reasonably short trip.

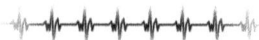

╌╬╌╬╌╬╌╬╌╬╌╬╌╬╌

Charlton Tremwallis slowed to a careful, quiet walk as he crossed the ravine at the top of Petersson's property. He rested, catching his breath, leaning against a tree with a red "Posted Land" sign on it.

He moved further back into the forest, lying flat on the ground when he heard the voices of men speaking a language he could not understand. They crossed less than 50 feet in front of him. In his camouflaged clothing, Charlton had become invisible. He had covered the wire cutters with leaves. The handles were bright red.

He watched as the men climbed a ladder into the treehouse built by Torbjorn Petersson. They had a lot of guns with them, and half a dozen rocket launchers. They went up and down the ladder on the tree several times.

Tremwallis had never shot another human being, but he did not think that killing these men would bother him. It would take two shots with his bolt action hunting rifle.

They would not have enough time to spot him before he chambered a second .204 caliber round to kill the last ISIL terrorist standing.

He carefully moved his Savage Arms Model Trophy Hunter Rifle into place.

In the prone position, he rested his eye behind its Nikon scope. He had done this often, hunting deer.

That's when he heard the chopping sound of approaching helicopters. He took his eye away from the scope, looking and listening. The sound multiplied, but he could not see them. He had to look for a safe hiding place.

But the terrorists in the treehouse did.

The ISIL warriors balanced their SAM rocket launchers on their shoulders and fired. They each did this twice, four ground-to-air missiles away within less than 30 seconds.

Charlton Tremwallis lay frozen in place as if he were watching a movie.

He did not shoot either man.

Ground-shaking explosions followed.

Chapter 22

The Battle of The Cold Springs Trout Club

Protecting a Beer Truck From a Single Bullet

The perimeter protecting The Cold Springs Trout Club changed from an encirclement of the area into a line of defense 400 yards in front of it, between the club and Petersson's farm further down the Jackson River. Sergeant Squirrel asked for a volunteer point man, and Fishbait raised his hand. He was the best trout fisherman in the bunch, and he dressed for the part. He thought it was silly to wear rubber waders, which he never did when fishing, but he assumed the role and put them on.

Squirrel gave him an assault rifle, which fit into his loose waders nicely, and he changed his opinion about the large rubber boots immediately.

"Don't fish," Squirrel told him.

"Huh?" Fishbait said.

"Do not put a line in the water, Fishbait."

"Then what the hell did you dress me up like this for?"

"You are the eyes and ears of all of us. You are our early warning system. Watch for terrorists, Fishbait. Do not fish."

It was like asking Fishbait to cut off his right arm. He had fished Bath County since he was old enough to walk, and he spent most of his spare time doing it. He had started as a child with a sapling, some fishing line, a cork floater, a hook, and worms that he found under rocks along the banks of the rivers in Bath County.

When Fishbait was 12, he started to act as a gofer for wealthy people who came to the Homestead to fly fish at the Cascades, a limestone creek that fell 350 feet over a four-mile run. Crystal clear water tumbled through 13 waterfalls into deep pools well-stocked with starving Rainbow trout.

Fishbait always knew where the biggest trout hid, and the fishermen he assisted and ran errands for as a gofer always appreciated his uncanny angling wisdom.

One year, a United States senator fly fished the Cascades, and when he asked some people at the Homestead Resort who the best fishing guide might be, everyone suggested Fishbait.

Fishbait didn't realize the importance of a title like "fishing guide," but people started paying him good money to do it. The United States senator was impressed by the lessons he received in "how to think like a fish" from his then 16-year-old guide. The senator gave him a gift when he left the Homestead. It was a book, a beautiful leatherbound edition of *The Compleat Angler,* written by Izaak Walton in 1653, with the subtitle of: "Or, The Contemplative Man's Recreation."

Fishbait had stopped going to school when he was 12 years old because his Daddy needed extra money to support a severe drinking habit. His father worked as a hired hand on a farm owned by a local family on the outskirts of Hot Springs. That's how he met "Tadpole" Carruthers, whose family owned the cattle farm. Tadpole and Fishbait were the same age, and they became best friends, separated only by wealth. They joined the Marine Corps Reserves together.

The book given to Fishbait by the Senator presented a bit of a problem because Fishbait could not read very well. Tadpole helped him through it, teaching him the difference between prose and verse, although Fishbait never could understand why anyone would misspell the title of a book on purpose like that.

The Compleat Angler became almost as important as the Bible to Fishbait. He openly credited the book, and his best friend, Tadpole, with helping him to get his GED. Without a General Equivalency Diploma qualifying him as a high school graduate, he would never have been allowed into the United States Marine Corps.

Now, at the age of 34, Fishbait was about to take his most fateful fishing trip.

"Do not put a line in the water, Fishbait," Sergeant Squirrel said once again.

"No fishing, pal," his friend Tadpole said.

Sergeant Squirrel handed him Jonathan Wainwright's, $325 Orvis Clearwater Fly Rod and Reel.

"Jesus Christ," Fishbait said. If someone had given him a bag of gold, it would have meant less.

He whipped the tip of the rod in the air, felt it meld into the nerve fibers of his right arm.

"No fishing," Squirrel said for the third time. Tadpole gave Fishbait a stern look.

"Yeah, right, I got this," Fishbait said, wiggling off the veranda in his waders, with an assault rifle stuffed in the left legging. He headed downstream, walking a little stiffly because of the burden of his weaponry, swishing the Orvis rod back and forth in the air.

Fishbait took up a position around a bend in the river about 200 yards in front of the line of defense, pretending to be a rich man staying at The Cold Springs Trout Club.

The Orvis rod worked like a feather in his hands, the best rod he had ever held.

He caught and released several Rainbows that were keepers within minutes of taking up his position. Hunting terrorists, he decided, might become his full-time job. He laughed at his cleverness. He spotted a rock in the river, and he pictured the monster living in its shadow.

He could feel the fish flicking its fins, waiting for food to drift into the eddies of the boulder.

He laid the line out perfectly. The hand-tied fly slipped into the water in front of the boulder; then it disappeared into the dark water. Almost immediately, he hooked a huge fish which had him wading out into the stream, as any good fisherman would surely do.

That's when he saw a man dressed in black, carrying an AK-47, staring at him from the far bank. Fishbait dropped the beautiful fishing rod into the water and reached for his cell phone, changing his mind and trying to pull out his assault rifle instead. It got hooked inside his rubber waders. Everything became slow motion.

Fishbait tugged at the assault rifle, feeling the waders rip.

He watched a line of bullets dance towards him in the water. He knew you couldn't move very fast if you were wearing stupid rubber boots.

"No fishing, Pal," Tadpole had said. His best friend was always right.

Fishbait's final thought was about the big fish he had hooked. He figured it must have been a Brownie because it hadn't jumped.

He wished he could have seen it.

‑‑‑‑‑‑‑‑‑‑‑‑‑‑‑‑‑‑

The dead fisherman instilled confidence in all nine of the terrorists. They assumed their attack came as a surprise. Fishbait never had a chance to pull out his assault rifle into view, so all of the terrorists thought he was just an early riser, an Infidel trying to get a head start on a day of fishing.

They had a picture in their minds, thanks to Google Earth, of the layout of The Cold Springs Trout Club.

They would attack the main building first, slaughtering all the infidels eating their breakfast, and then they would move to each log cabin and kill anyone they found, men, women, children, it did not matter.

They would send photographs and videos of their accomplishments back to Ahmed Kahn using their cell phones if they could pick up a strong enough signal. Then Ahmed would edit the terror they wrought into the beheading of George McKlane, a Lieutenant Colonel in the United States Marine Corps and a Director at Homeland Security.

After the slaughter of everyone at The Cold Springs Trout Club, the Pakistani drivers who drove the beer truck from New Jersey to Virginia, who were now among the warriors, would unlock the side panels, revealing the remaining 22 barrels.

The ISIL troops would then roll these 50-gallon barrels into the Jackson River, where they would be ripped apart by gunfire. That was how they would poison the well of America, killing tens of thousands of people downstream.

Lake Moomaw's shoreline would turn white with the skeletons of every animal that drank its water.

The fish kill would overpower any sulfur smell drifting up the valley from the paper mill in Covington.

Lake Moomaw would be a dead and dangerous swamp for many years.

After killing the fisherman, the terrorists picked up their pace. Even if no one had expected them, the gunfire that killed the fisherman would alert the infidels enjoying their breakfast at The Cold Springs Trout Club. It was essential to get to the main building as quickly as possible and start slaughtering the American Devils.

Some of the people they killed would be carrying guns. Everyone in America had guns. Their government was insane.

The terrorist attack fell apart 550 yards downstream from The Cold Springs Trout Club. All nine of the terrorists moved out of the thick forest undergrowth and onto the banks of the river. It was much quicker and easier to walk that way. They were also a lot easier to shoot.

"Don't kill them all," a staff sergeant of the Ranger Unit told Sergeant Squirrel. "They might have some information to share with our interrogators."

Two terrorists survived the firefight, although both ISIL warriors were wounded and in fairly bad shape.

Tadpole, who had come around in a flanking move, shouted that they had killed Fishbait, his best friend.

It was their only loss. Fishbait had never had a single enemy in his entire life. His name always produced a smile.

Sergeant Squirrel looked at his Ranger counterpart, who shrugged his shoulders and looked at the wounded ISIL prisoners on the ground surrounded by angry soldiers.

"They probably don't know that much," he said, walking off. None of the terrorists survived the Battle of The Cold Springs Trout Club.

The MH-60L Velcro Hawk Helicopters raced from Roanoke to Leatherwood Farms in less than 25 minutes. The pilots knew the insurgents had surface-to-air missiles, but if they flew low enough and fast enough, they could blow up the satellite dish and swoop into the farm without getting blown out of the sky.

It was a tactic that had worked well in Iraq and Afghanistan, although heavy fire from insurgents on the ground often brought down the American helicopters.

The Velcro Hawk helicopters carried countermeasures, including showering the sky with phosphorous fireworks, but that often didn't work with the more modern SAM missiles. The best answers were surprise and speed and then "go slow and low" as the helicopters approached the target.

It seemed highly unlikely that any ISIL ground troops would appear in the mountains of Virginia. So the Velcro Hawk pilots were comfortable racing towards their target, just 250 feet above the forest floor.

Visibility was perfect on this beautiful, sunny morning in late autumn, with a hint of color remaining in the trees.

When the pilots saw the ridge beyond which the Petersson farm lay, they started to put their helicopters into a "go slow and low" approach, dropping down to within 100 feet of the forest.

Roberta Macumber and her team stood in the Comm room at Homeland Security headquarters. They anxiously watched the lead pilot's view as the MH-60L Velcro Hawks approached the ridge.

"Make sure we get the name of that boy they sent to cut the cable," Roberta said to an assistant.

The assistant looked at a piece of paper and said: "Charlton Tremwallis. His name was Charlton Tremwallis."

The assistant suddenly realized he had used the boy's name in the past tense, collateral damage, and he tried to mumble an apology.

Nobody took notice. No one bothered to correct the mistake. "We'll send his parents a medal. Brave kid," Roberta Macumber said.

The boy was a hero, but a small price to pay for saving thousands and protecting millions from ISIL's terror.

They all crowded around the monitors that showed the approaching ridge in real-time.

~⩗⩗⩗⩗⩗⩗⩗⩗~

The ISIL warriors in the treehouse saw the helicopters when they were more than two miles away. The visibility was perfect. Ahmed Kahn had said they would fly to their death.

As the helicopters closed, the terrorists fired their rockets. They picked up two more SAMs, shouldered them, and fired again.

In Washington, everyone saw the rockets fired from the top of the ridge, trailing smoke out of the trees.

In the helicopters, alarms went off everywhere. They flared, but whatever the pilot said never got through.

The screens at Homeland Security went black.

"Godammit," Roberta said. "Did they get any of their missiles away? Did the helicopters SHOOT anything for Christ's sake?"

People were on the phone, dialing Roanoke, trying to get information, and hopefully confirmation.

There was none, only confusion.

───┤╟┤╟┤╟┤╟┤╟┤╟├───

Two of the Velcro Hawks exploded in balls of fire, twirling down into the side of the mountain and crashing into the forest. The third Velcro Hawk tried to climb higher, flaring all of its phosphorous sparks as if it were a display at a 4th of July fireworks display.

It banked hard to the left.

The third SAM narrowly missed it.

The fourth did not.

It blew off the tail rotor of the Velcro Hawk.

The terrorists could see men jumping out of the third helicopter as it floated, starting to spin, briefly suspended in midair before it began its death spiral.

None of the jumpers would survive. It was a 200-foot drop. They had parachutes, and some of them opened, but they had no canopy control.

Several men were holding onto ropes thrown out the hatch as the helicopter plummeted into the forest. A massive explosion enveloped the few men who managed to get their chutes partially open.

The terrorists shouted, celebrating in the treehouse.

They picked up two more SAMs, which exhausted their supply. They fired the surface to air missiles into the burning forest a quarter of a mile away, laughing at the ground-shaking explosions that followed.

They hugged one another.

Suddenly one of the men sagged in the other man's arms. The side of his head did not bleed where the bullet entered, but the opposite side broke away and bled severely.

Were these infidels superhuman? Could they survive a 200-foot jump and start shooting? How was this possible?

The ISIL warrior picked up his AK-47 and emptied it in the direction of the burning helicopters. He put a new clip into the assault rifle and started to squeeze the trigger, leaning slightly out of the treehouse. The weapon never fired. The terrorist toppled out, falling to the floor of the forest with a thud, another perfect headshot.

Charlton Tremwallis stood up, moving quickly to the satellite dish. He cut the cable. Then he climbed into the treehouse for a better view, taking his Trophy Hunter rifle with him. He lifted the dead terrorist and pushed him off of Torbjorn Petersson's observation platform.

As the body fell to the forest floor, Charlton Tremwallis said: "This here is Mister Petersson's posted land, and he don't truck no trespassing."

Chapter 23

Good Morning, America, Greetings from ISIL.

Can a Kid in a Treehouse Finish Homeland's Job?

Ahmed Kahn took the knife from the left hand of Holly Smolkes. Then he showed her how he wanted it drawn across the neck of the Director of Homeland Security. Blood glistened on the knife as he did so. "You must do this very slowly," Ahmed told his twin sister. "If you cut the infidel's throat too quickly, he will not be able to scream."

It was one of Ahmed Kahn's pet peeves.

"The beheadings performed by our fellow holy warriors have always been too quick to appreciate properly," he said. "None of them understand the power of slowness."

"I understand," Holly said.

As Ahmed handed back her knife, she felt the stickiness of Mac McKlane's blood on its blade.

"You must feel the infidel's blood, Malalai," Ahmed Kahn said. "Feel it."

"Yes," she said, wiping the blood and her hands on her loose, black clothing. If Ahmed had only handed it to her by the handle, she might have had a chance to sink it into her brother's chest. She was running out of options.

If she could kill Ahmed, that would leave only the computer operator to worry about, and he was nowhere near his AK-47, which he had leaned against the wall of the computer studio.

Holly could kill him before he got out of his seat.

But Holly found herself holding the blade, and not the handle, and she knew her brother would step back and shoot her with his assault rifle if he suspected anything.

Ahmed Kahn trusted no one, and this was the reason he was still alive.

Holly looked at Mac's throat. He was not bleeding badly.

Suddenly the sound of a firefight drifted down the valley. They heard an enormous amount of shooting.

"All of the infidels are dying at The Cold Springs Trout Club," Ahmed said. "It is like that movie. I love to hear the sound of dying infidels in the morning."

"Go to hell," Mac said.

"Exactly, Lieutenant Colonel McKlane of Homeland Security, 2028586. But it's your trip, not mine."

"2028658," Mac corrected him.

"Of course," Ahmed said. "I am getting older. You, on the other hand, will not be getting any older, Director of Homeland Security, Mac McKlane."

He turned to the operator and asked him if everything was ready. The ISIL warrior said: "Ready when you are, CB."

"Jesus Christ," Mac said.

These people knew more about America than they deserved. It was an old joke about the great filmmaker Cecil B. DeMille, who staged an extraordinary car explosion down the side of a cliff. CB shouted through his bullhorn: "Did you get all that?" The camera operator on a hill had then shouted back: "Ready when you are, CB."

The joke was no longer funny.

Ahmed said: "I think you should come out and enjoy the show before you become a television star."

He stepped behind the chair and sliced the bonds of McKlane with his own, razor-sharp knife.

He cut McKlane's hands badly in the process, but not so much that he would bleed to death.

He tied a rope around McKlane, making him spin four times before tying a knot.

"To the driveway," Ahmed said.

Holly helped McKlane out of the studio, through the cabin, out the door, and into the drive.

He was very weak, severely beaten, unable to defend himself, or help her do so.

As they stepped into the driveway, explosions thundered down from the ridge behind the cabin.

"Ah," Ahmed said, grinning. "This is not quite like Lesotho anymore, Director McKlane. That will be my Holy Warriors blowing your helicopters out of the sky." More loud explosions thundered down the mountainside.

They continued shooting up on the ridge, although two of the shots sounded a bit different than the others.

They stood in the drive and watched as smoke began to rise behind the mountain.

"I want you to enjoy this, McKlane," Ahmed said. "The last thing you will ever remember will be your complete failure, your Devil Nation's defeat, and the annihilation of America by the Warriors of God."

Ahmed stood there, a proud organizer of the Jihad, an absolute future leader destined to hold an honored seat at the table of the Caliph.

Perhaps one day, he would even become the leader of the jihadist militant organization known as ISIL.

Caliph Ahmed Kahn of Nuristan, although the Caliph, of course, had no home.

Perhaps Ahmed Kahn al-Afghani.

That sounded nice. It had a ring to it.

In the treehouse built by Torbjorn Petersson, Tremwallis watched the fires burning in the distance. The wind was blowing south, and the flames would move away from his position, so Charlton remained in the treehouse. He turned his attention to the log cabin far below him.

Through his powerful Nikon scope, he saw a terrorist and a woman wearing a *hijab* lead a severely wounded man into the gravel driveway.

The injured man, he assumed, would be the Director of Homeland Security that everyone had been talking about back at The Cold Springs Trout Club.

The other two were the Terror Twins about whom Squirrel and Shadrach had spoken. These were the people he would have to kill. That would make four people in one day.

Charlton Tremwallis rested his eye comfortably behind the Nikon scope. He would kill the man first simply because he had never killed a woman, although he would kill this one.

It would be Holly's only chance. She pulled out her knife and took a swipe at her twin brother, missing him by inches as he took a quick step back. It was a foolish act of desperation.

"What are you doing?" Ahmed said. "You are Malalai. You are my sister, my twin, my blood. You are Malalai!"

Holly Smolkes stood there, tears in her eyes, looking at Mac McKlane and then back at her brother. She saw Ahmed Kahn start to raise his AK-47.

"I am Holly Smolkes," she said, "and I am an American." She said it loud and proud, knowing that it would be her final words. She tried to reach for Mac McKlane; perhaps they could die together.

"Then you are an American whore and I — "

He never finished the sentence.

It was a perfect headshot, with very little blood. Ahmed dropped in the driveway, dead before his face hit the gravel. Then there was a lot of blood.

His AK-47 remained silent.

In the treehouse, the boy who could shoot the whiskers off a Fairy Diddle running across a split rail fence ejected the shell of his first shot, reached in his pocket, got a new round, chambered it, and brought his eye comfortably back behind the scope. Finish off the Terror Twins.

He took a deep breath.

He put his finger softly on the trigger.

He had never killed a woman.

Why was she stroking his hair and kissing his face all over?

He released the pressure on his finger.

Suddenly another terrorist burst through the door of the cabin. Although Charlton Tremwallis could not hear what he said, the jihadist had shouted: "The network is down!"

The new terrorist had an assault rifle in his hand. He saw the body of Ahmed Kahn. He started to raise his AK-47 in the direction of the man and woman kneeling in the driveway, holding one another.

Charlton Tremwallis shot the terrorist before he could pull the trigger on his AK-47. It, too, was a perfect shot, but through the heart, not the head.

The End

Epilog

The fires raged in the mountains of Virginia for almost a week before they came under control. The cause of the inferno was an unfortunate collision of helicopters during a military training exercise.

The entire nation mourned the loss of 29 men and women, members of the elite Army Rangers.

A Congressional committee quickly formed to discuss all the safety issues with the MH-60L Velcro Hawk Helicopters, and also all the dozen or so iterations of the old UH-60A Black Hawks.

The committee disbanded before it ever officially met.

Tadpole's family buried Fishbait in their family cemetery. It included a 21-gun salute from his fellow Marine Reservists. Posthumously, he received a Purple Heart and a Bronze Star. They put an Orvis Clearwater Fly Rod and Reel in his casket.

Charlton Tremwallis' complexion started clearing up in a matter of months, not long after he finally delivered a severely overdue package to that cute girl that lived nearby. When she introduced him to her friends, she said: "This is my hero." Sworn to secrecy, she never explained its true meaning.

Charlton Tremwallis visited Homeland Security in Washington, D.C. He met with Roberta Macumber, who suggested a new career path for him that did not include driving a UPS truck. Shadrack and Sookie Ringer, who knew and liked Charlton, took him to visit Mac McKlane in the hospital. "You saved his life," they said. "You can save many more people."

Charlton said he'd think about it.

Captain George McKlane arranged the burial of Torbjorn Petersson next to his grandmother, Ernestine. The ashes that they buried included some from a black bear, which seemed fitting since his first name derived from the same beast in Sweden.

Not many people attended Torbjorn's burial, but a very frail Captain George, Sharonda, Samuel, and General McKlane and his wife Martha stood at his gravesite with respect and quite a few questions that would never have proper answers.

Leatherwood Farms became part of the George Washington National Forest on the understanding that they would care for Torbjorn's cabin and the Petersson Cemetery in perpetuity. When the Springtime floods came, they filled Lake Moomaw. Only a few acres of the farm ever went underwater. Torbjorn kept his promise to Gammy.

No lake will ever touch your grave.

The Cold Springs Trout Club went bankrupt. Its owner, Jonathan Wainwright, ended up in state and federal court on numerous fraud and conspiracy charges, which would eventually lead to his incarceration in a reasonably comfortable prison.

His lawyer, Sally Leigh Newbart, lost her license to practice law and faced similar charges with him.

When Wainwright asked Jason Raleigh Newbart for help, Newbart declined, saying that it would be a definite conflict of interest.

Holly Smolkes spent many days with Mac at the Walter Reed National Military Medical Center in Washington, D.C. He would eventually enjoy a full recovery.

At first, Holly felt that Homeland Security guarded her as carefully as the man she loved, but for different reasons. After Roberta Macumber and others debriefed Mac McKlane, things changed. Homeland asked her to visit the unit, where she received a standing ovation.

"Welcome to Homeland Security," Roberta Macumber said. "We've been looking for a few good women like you."

Holly teared up. She vowed that she would work well with others. Joining the unit made her untouchable by Rossellini's associates.

The FBI shut down the unit assigned to find Anthony Silberg, the criminal who stole escrowed funds from Accelerated Realty Sales. The radio waves of a ground-penetrating radar system discovered bones 22 inches below the ground floor slab of Rossellini Towers in Miami. They did not bother digging them up. They closed the case, and mysterious sightings of Silberg stopped.

Accelerated Realty Sales reopened under new management, but they acquired more lawsuits than listings. They quickly closed.

Martha Krumble eventually had a baby, an 8 lb 6 oz girl. True to her word, she named her, "George."

Brigadier General George McKlane asked Sharonda and Samuel Nelson what they would do when Captain George died. He had barely made it to Torbjorn's burial in Virginia.

"Well," Sharonda said, "I guess we can do whatever we want. We're thinking of joining the Peace Corps and going to Tanzania. That's where both Samuel's and my roots lie. In the Southern Highlands of Tanzania."

But that's another story: The author will publish *African Heartbeats* next year.

About the Author

Temple Emmet Williams

His first book was an award-winning memoir called **Warrior Patient:** *How to Beat Deadly Diseases With Laughter, Good Doctors, Love, and Guts.* It received a **B.R.A.G. Medallion** from the Book Reader's Appreciation Group. It also won a **2015 Gold Medal at the Reader's Favorite Book Award**s in Miami, Florida. It won an **International Red Ribbon** in The Wishing Shelf Awards in 2016. It has been a best-seller on Amazon.

Temple grew up in Ohio. He went to Hotchkiss and Yale University. As a journalist, he was nominated two times for the Pulitzer Prize as a reporter for the *World-Telegram & Sun* in New York City for a seven-day, front-page series called "I Was A Subway Cop." He worked as an Editor at *The Reader's Digest* and was the editor-in-chief of an international news magazine in Africa. He was a copywriter and creative director at leading advertising agencies around the world, including Leo Burnett and Ogilvy Mather.

He lived in Africa for six years and in Europe for almost as long. He and his wife, Kerstin, who is also his content editor, currently live in Boca Raton, Florida. *African Heartbeats* is their third novel in the Heartbeats Series. *Poison Heartbeats* was the second, and *Wrinkled Heartbeats* was the first

Acknowledgments

Thanks to the first professional writer who took me under his wing and dared me to make a difference with words, fifty-one years ago: Hayes Jacobs at the New School for Social Research. He wrote in *The New Yorker*.

Thanks also to all the great newspaper and magazine people who turned me into a journalist. Richard D. Peters became my first editor at the *New York World-Telegram & Sun*, and Otto Krause at *News/Check* magazine in South Africa became the last.

Neither the publications nor the people exist any longer, except through the fingertips of the hundreds of men and women that each of them so selflessly influenced.

Thanks also to the extraordinary people who turned me into an editor many years later: Ed Thompson and Mary Lou Allin at *The Reader's Digest*.

Their lessons, their wisdom still influences both how and why I write.

Thanks also to the great copywriters and art directors who taught me the power of words and pictures combined, especially Steve Trygg, Thomas Roth, David Ogilvy, Leo Burnett, and Rudy Perz (who invented the Pillsbury Doughboy). I can no longer write without a camera clicking in my mind.

Thanks to all the people who make a book possible, especially the readers who use their time and their intelligence to put a stamp of approval or even disapproval of what a writer has to say. I refer not just to the people who buy a book, although they remain the most vital part of the process.

Thanks to 19 people who took a critical look at *Poison Heartbeats* during its journey to publication: proofreaders, editorial readers, fellow authors whom I respect, over a dozen professionals who let me invade their lives for advice.

My principal proofreader has the eye of an eagle and a forgiving heart.

I can review my book a half a dozen times, assure myself that it is "clean," and ***Judy Greenman*** will swoop down on it, discovering dozens of mistakes. To me, this borders on magic, and I thank her for her time and her extraordinary effort.

A fellow editor from my time at *Reader's Digest*, **Phil Dion**, spent four days at our home in Boca Raton. He has been a magazine editor for a prestigious think tank, an economics reporter in Washington, D.C., a document manager for a U.S. government agency, and an editorial consultant in the United States and abroad. He is one of the world's best professional line editors, in my opinion, and he did a masterful job on *Poison Heartbeats*. Contact him at *phdion2008@gmail.com*.

Cheri L. Florance, Ph.D., is an international brain scientist, trained at the National Institutes Of Health. She has completed many missions for the United States government as well as numerous foreign countries in Europe and the Middle East.

She is the daughter of a Navy Commander fighter pilot, and the mother of a U.S. Army Officer deployed to Afghanistan in the Corp of Engineers. An award-winning expert on brain health, she has been interviewed by Oprah, honored by the White House and is the author of *The Maverick Mind* and *A Boy Beyond Reach*, stories of hope for children and adults with symptoms of autism. Visit *http://www.ebrainlabs.com.*

Cheri Florance may have a greater understanding of *Poison Heartbeats* than I do, even though I wrote it. For me, it was a natural, well-researched process. For Cheri, it was, well, I'll let her speak for herself:

Poison Heartbeats is a mental jewel box of twists and turns. As an internationally known brain doctor, I review a book to determine the value of entertainment and brain exuberance.

Poison Heartbeats: A Critical Read

Poison Heartbeats is so captivating and timely that I could not put it down- reading till the wee hours and then again at dawn. We live inside the minds of the Director of Homeland Security, twin terrorists separated in war-torn Afghanistan, tycoons who are corrupt killers, down-home country folk, and an extended military family unit. Temple Williams' ability to move from voice to voice gives us insight into our complex world of aggression and defense. He weaves such a fascinating story of the players' relationships that we devour the pages one after another.

Poison Heartbeats: A Brain Builder

What an opportunity to enjoy an obstacle course for exercising your mental zeal. As brain scientists, we have learned recently, that our brains can experience growth called exuberance or death called pruning at any age. One of the best ways to stimulate brain exuberance is to activate your mind's anticipation machine. The brain craves "**nexting,**" and in Mr. William's Poison Heartbeats, we are compelled to discover what will motivate each complex character's **next** act. We push our memories to tie strategies from past chapters to those unfolding. We excite our brain processors to analyze and evaluate the intertwining of plots, places, and people. I recommend Poison Heartbeats not only as a great literary creation to enjoy but as a complex mental smorgasbord to gobble hungrily. *– Cheri Florence, PhD*

Cheri Florence's review explains why I have become an Indie author. I read it with humility.

Sybil Rosen is an extraordinary playwright and author with whom I had the honor of sharing an awards platform in Miami in 2015. Her books include *Living in the Woods in a Tree: Remembering Blaze Foley* and *Riding the Dog*. Readers fall in love with Sybil because she exudes deep, gentle wisdom and the loving touch of an author who cares about every word that she writes. She treated my work with kindness. After a dozen people went through *Poison Heartbeats* looking for errors before final proofing, Sybil still discovered 14 typos. She is a fantastic person.

Charles Freedom Long is an author whom I respect and admire. He was an organizational psychologist who has lived and worked in the health and social welfare systems of the U.S., Canada, England, and Africa.

He was kind enough to take a look at *Poison Heartbeats* before its publication. He spotted some problems that escaped me, and I thank him for it. He is the award-winning author of *Dancing with the Dead*.

Robert Eggleton has written the best Sci-Fi satire I ever read, with one of the most important messages that families need to understand. His novel is called *Rarity from the Hollow*. The book is a gem, and his generosity inspires me (he contributes part of his royalties to the cause he champions).

Robert is a spirit lifter, a man who has spent a lifetime smoothing out wrinkles in other people's lives.

Please read his book.

Josef Peeters is an Australian author, woodcarver, and caravan park owner. He did a masterful job of improving and correcting *Poison Heartbeats*.

His editorial heart is in the right place and trustworthy. If you're ever in Australia, look him up. Of course, you can always visit him in cyberspace at

http://lakesidecaravanpark.wixsite.com/josef.

Irene Schyberger, born in Sweden, broke through the glass ceiling before people knew it existed. In the corporate world, she managed mega stores for IKEA in Malmö, Stockholm, and Washington, D.C.

She was a Vice President at Spode & Royal Worcester, Orrefors/Kosta Boda, and Crystal Clear. She's a true professional, and she can spot a mistake on a page of one of my books after I have reviewed it a dozen times. It remains an unexplained secret.

Ronald A. Feldman is the author of *IF TRUTH BE TOLD, little secrets, BIG LIES,* and *The Crossover Mystery.* He is an exceptional writer who helps me by example as well as in person. He has shown me what putting your heart on a page looks like and means.

Lisa Kearns has been one of Amazon's leading book critics for many years. She has published reviews of over 2,000 products during the past 13 years with integrity and honesty. Lisa puts her heart into them. I have read many of her literary assessments, and she inspires me to purchase books because of her guidance. Her opinions of *Warrior Patient, Wrinkled Heartbeats,* and, now, *Poison Heartbeats,* continue to surprise me with their clarity, leadership, and insight.

Shari Risoff is the author of *Released: A True Story of Escape from an Abusive Marriage* and *Accidental Sabbatical.* She began to write full time during her accidental sabbatical. She edits books for other authors. She does not usually read this genre, but she helped me with it and suggested she'd probably buy the first novel in the series. Writers in need of an editor can get in touch with Shari at *projectmavens@risoff.com.*

Arnold Granet offered several excellent suggestions as he read through the book in its preliminary form. His ideas made the novel better, more of a stand-alone work, and for his guidance and raw brainpower, I thank him. Arnold Granet is a rock-solid critic.

Anne-Marie Reynolds is an English woman currently living in Bulgaria. She reads two or three books a week and is an author herself, and she is a professional editorial reviewer at Readers' Favorites.

Christian Sia says that a book he read on a flight to India in 2014 turned him into an avid reader for life. "I love the smell of books, and I love the exciting and entertaining stories within them."

He is a professional copy-editor and a freelance editor for several writers.

Michael Marnier got hooked on writing because of Mark Twain and his short story, "The Celebrated Jumping Frog of Calaveras County." The frog was named Dan'l Webster, and its owner lost a $40 bet when a con man poured buckshot down the frog's throat before a jumping contest. Dan'l couldn't hop an inch. Michael Marnier's work does not bother with buckshot or frogs. No, sir. It's white sharks with attitude and a Navy SEAL who's larger than life and every bit as exciting as the tall tales he tells. Mix in some tequila and great supporting characters, and you have an author who's in his comfort zone writing thrillers based on life experiences. Michael also pays attention to details, like some of the errors he discovered in my book. Thanks.

Divine Zape is a stay-at-home mom with an avid thirst for reading and a degree in political science from the Far Eastern University.

Ruffina Oserio graduated from the Far Eastern University of the Philippines with a Degree in English. She was a teacher for over four decades before retiring. She loves edge-of-the-seat thrillers.

Katelyn Hensel opened her book review website, *Unabridged Andra*, two years ago. She says: "I have reviewed over 300 books in my two years as a blogger and love it."

She is a freelance editor, copy editor, developmental editor, and a proofreader for novelists, non-fiction writers, and journalists.

All of these people have contributed their time and energy to the publication of **Poison Heartbeats**. I have learned over many decades of writing that it takes an army of people to make a good book *before* it ever goes on sale.

But there is one person without whom this book would never exist in its present form.

"Thank you," to my primary editor, a content critic with whom I can comfortably argue and, sometimes, bicker. Almost without fail, I eventually realize that her editorial comments and judgment are correct and that her heart and brain are genuine and in the right place.

I bow to you, **Kerstin "Kickan" Williams**. You have been my soul mate and partner for 47 years, and you improve everything I do and everything I am.

Warrior Patient

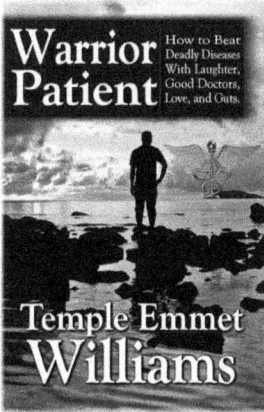

"This book may have saved my life!" That's how Robert Eggleton, the author of *Rarity in the Hollow* (an extraordinary science fiction satire), began his five-star review of this award-winning, best-selling memoir.

Enjoy the stunning, surprisingly funny, and timeless story of someone who recovers entirely from a relentless series of medical problems, many resulting from the system designed to prevent them.

Wrinkled Heartbeats

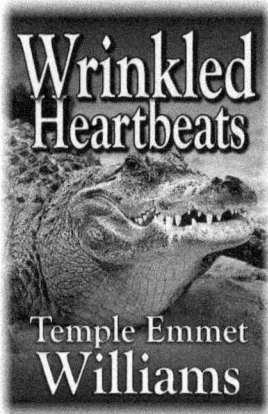

Wrinkled Heartbeats is the author's first "Heartbeats" novel, which the 2016 *Next Generation Indie Book Awards* recently chose as one of six finalists in the category of "Best First Novels under 80,000 words." It won the coveted *Awesome Indies Approval Badge*. It also won a *Silver Medal* in the crowded Action Fiction category at the *Reader's Favorite Book Awards* in Miami, Florida.

Please, write a review on Amazon

You have to be a member of Amazon to write a review.

(1) Browse to https://www.amazon.com/dp/B01MG1F1WV
(2) Next to the book's profile picture on the top left, you'll see a "reviews" notice. Tap or click on it.
(3) You'll go to a page that has a box that says: "Write a Customer Review." Tap it.
(4) Write or copy your review into the review box, go through their rating questions, rate it up to five stars, and save it.

Thank you for spreading the word.